ASPECTS OF TOURISM 13
Series Editors: Chris Cooper (*University of Queensland, Australia*),
Michael Hall (*University of Otago, New Zealand*)
and Dallen Timothy (*Arizona State University, USA*)

Sport Tourism Development

Thomas Hinch and James Higham

CHANNEL VIEW PUBLICATIONS
Clevedon • Buffalo • Toronto • Sydney

This book is dedicated to:
Lorraine, Lindsay and Gillian
&
Linda, Alexandra and Kate

And to the memory of
Robert O. Hinch

Library of Congress Cataloging in Publication Data
Hinch, Thomas.
Sport Tourism Development/Thomas Hinch and James Higham.
Aspects of Tourism: 13
Includes bibliographical references
1. Sports and tourism. I. Higham, James E.S. II. Title. III. Series.
G155.A1H56 2003
338.4'791–dc22   2003017656

British Library Cataloguing in Publication Data
A catalogue entry for this book is available from the British Library.

ISBN 1-873150-63-6 (hbk)
ISBN 1-873150-62-8 (pbk)

Channel View Publications
An imprint of Multilingual Matters Ltd

UK: Frankfurt Lodge, Clevedon Hall, Victoria Road, Clevedon BS21 7SJ.
USA: 2250 Military Road, Tonawanda, NY 14150, USA.
Canada: 5201 Dufferin Street, North York, Ontario, Canada M3H 5T8.
Australia: Footprint Books, PO Box 418, Church Point, NSW 2103, Australia.

Typeset by Florence Production Ltd.
Printed and bound in Great Britain by the Cromwell Press.

Contents

List of Illustrations viii
Acknowledgements xi
List of Case Study Contributors xiii

Part 1: Introduction
1   Sport Tourism in Times of Change. 3
      Introduction. 3
      Sport tourism in times of change. 4
      The foundations of sport tourism development 5
      Sport tourism development and space 8
      Sport tourism development and time 9
      Management principles for sport tourism development 10
      Further reading 12

Part 2: Foundations for Sport Tourism Development
2   The Study of Sport Tourism 15
      Introduction. 15
      Conceptual foundations. 15
      Scholarship in sport tourism 20
      Conceptualising sport as a tourist attraction 24
      Management implications and opportunities 27
      Conclusion 28
      Further reading 29
3   Sport Tourism Markets 33
      Introduction. 33
      Conceptualising demand for sport tourism. 34
      Active sport tourism markets. 39
      Event sport tourism markets 44
      Nostalgia sport tourism 48
      Management implications and opportunities 49
      Conclusion 50
      Further reading 51

4   Development Processes and Issues 55
     Introduction 55
     The concept of development 55
     Sustainable development.............................. 57
     Planning... 59
     Development issues................................... 60
     Management implications and opportunities 69
     Conclusion... 72
     Further reading 73

Part 3: Sport Tourism Development and Space
5   Space: Location and Travel Flows...................... 79
     Introduction 79
     Sport, tourism and space 79
     The spatial analysis of sport tourism in central
     locations.. 84
     The spatial analysis of sport tourism in peripheral
     locations.. 89
     The spatial analysis of active sport tourism in
     peripheral areas 92
     Management implications and opportunities 93
     Conclusion... 94
     Further reading 95
6   Place, Sport and Culture 99
     Introduction 99
     Place.. 99
     Culture, place and identity.......................... 102
     Marketing place through sport........................ 109
     Management implications and opportunities 111
     Conclusion... 113
     Further reading 113
7   Environment: Landscape, Resources and Impacts 118
     Introduction 118
     Sport tourism landscapes, environments and resources 119
     The landscapes of sport 119
     Environmental impacts of sport tourism 126
     Sport tourism in the built environment 126
     Sport tourism in the natural landscape 130
     The impacts of event sport tourism: A paradigmatic shift ... 133
     Management implications and opportunities............. 134
     Conclusion 135
     Further reading 135

Part 4: Sport Tourism Development and Time
8   Sport and the Tourist Experience 141
      Introduction 141
      The anticipation phase 141
      Sport and the study of tourist motivations 144
      Sport tourism visitor experiences..................... 147
      Travel and tourist experiences....................... 147
      Sport and competition experiences 151
      Sport and tourism systems........................... 154
      Sport tourism and visitor behaviour 155
      Recollection and visitor satisfaction................. 157
      Management implications and opportunities 158
      Conclusion 159
      Further reading 159
9   Seasonality, Sport and Tourism....................... 163
      Introduction 163
      Seasonal patterns and issues in tourism 163
      Seasonal patterns and issues in sport 166
      Strategic responses.................................. 173
      Management implications and opportunities 178
      Conclusion 179
      Further reading 179
10 Evolutionary Trends in Sport Tourism 184
      Introduction 184
      Cyclical relationships in sport and tourism 184
      Nostalgia sport tourism 189
      Major trends affecting sport tourism 191
      Management implications and opportunities 198
      Conclusion 199
      Further reading 200

Part 5: Conclusions
11 Management Principles for Sport Tourism Development 207
      Introduction 207
      Foundations for sport tourism development 207
      Sport tourism development and space.................. 208
      Sport tourism development and time 210
      Principles of sport tourism development............... 211
      Concluding statement................................. 214

Bibliography 216
Index 242

Illustrations

Figures

2.1 The confluence of sport and tourism 18
2.2 Sport tourism and related contextual domains 22
3.1 Conceptualisation of the relative engagement of
    spectators and participants in elite and non-elite sport
    contests. 45
4.1 Sustainable sport tourism. 59
8.1 Factors influencing the sport tourism visitor experience 148
9.1 The expansion of the New Zealand representative rugby
    season (1975–2002) 168
9.2 Sport influences on patterns of tourist seasonality. 171
9.3 Hierarchical model of seasonal sport tourism constraints 177
10.1 Innovation in sport. 189

Tables

2.1 Selected definitions relating to the study of sport tourism 19
2.2 The value of sport tourism and activity holidays in the UK 21
3.1 Sport tourism demand groups and requisite visitor
    facilities 35
3.2 Sport tourism types and visitor profiles. 36
3.3 Conceptualisation of sport tourists based on sport and
    travel motivations 37
3.4 Sport tourism activities classification. 38
4.1 Numbers of tourist brochures according to their theme 75
5.1 Theory of sports locations 82
5.2 Spatial dynamics of sport tourism in peripheral areas 90
5.3 Top ten destinations visited by sport-orientated and less
    sport-orientated tourists: German, Dutch and French
    nationals. 92
5.4 Skiing worldwide. 96

7.1 Interpretations of sport landscapes 120
7.2 Resource base for sport tourism development 123
8.1 Sport tourist typologies 142
8.2 Sport motivation profiles of sport tourists who play golf 145
8.3 Average visitor expenditures at state college football
     games 150
9.1 Seasonal travel patterns of outbound sport tourists with
     both strong and casual sport focus from Germany, the
     Netherlands and France (1999) 172
10.1 Key trends in sport 192
10.2 A comparison of modern and postmodern sport 196

Case Studies

2.1 Sport tourism education
     Sean Gammon, University of Luton 30
3.1 Olympic teams as market segments
     Laurence Chalip, University of Texas 52
4.1 Sport tourism and regional development in France
     Charles Pigeassou, Université de Montpellier 74
5.1 Travel flows and spatial distribution in the ski industry
     Simon Hudson, University of Calgary 95
6.1 Spaces of identity and places of representation:
     Kuala Lumpur 98
     Michael Silk, University of Memphis 114
7.1 The impact of America's Cup 2000 on the city of
     Auckland, New Zealand
     Mark Orams, Massey University 136
8.1 US college football: The sport tourism experience
     Heather Gibson, University of Florida 160
9.1 The Otago Highlanders and seasonal patterns of travel
     James Higham, University of Otago, and Thomas Hinch,
     University of Alberta 180
10.1 The Mecca of golf: St Andrews, Scotland
     Richard Butler, University of Surrey 200

Focus Points

1.1 Participation youth football in Scandinavia 6
1.2 Sport, heritage and culture 7
1.3 The British Tourist Authority 8
1.4 Lillehammer 1994 and the Olympic Environmental
     Charter 9
1.5 Sport and tourism seasonality 11

2.1 The development of one-day cricket as a tourist attraction 27
3.1 Non-elite event sport tourism in New Zealand 47
4.1 The Barmy Army 65
4.2 Canadian Sport Tourism Alliance strategic plan 70
5.1 The Melbourne Sports and Aquatic Centre 83
6.1 The Arctic Winter Games 105
6.2 Stadium design in Korea 112
7.1 Wanaka Snowfest: Bringing extreme nature-based sports
     into the urban environment 125
7.2 Sport tourism in environments that are designed for other
     purposes 129
8.1 Celebration of France's FIFA World Cup victory: Paris,
     12 July 1998 153
8.2 Team sports and visitor behaviour 156
9.1 The Vuokatti Ski Tunnel (Finland) 169
10.1 Marine sport and the evolution of 'cold water' resorts 186
10.2 Snowboarding: From non-competitive sport to high
     entertainment drama 188

Acknowledgements

Our research interests in sport tourism, and the work leading to the publication of this book, have brought us various debts of favour. Mike Grover (Channel View Publications) and Aspects of Tourism series editors, Chris Cooper (University of Queensland), Michael Hall (University of Otago) and Dallen Timothy (Arizona State University) provided valuable assistance from the outset of this project. The planning and production of the original book proposal was made possible by a grant from the University of Alberta, which allowed the authors to work together in Edmonton, Canada, in June and July 2001. The writing of the book took place during periods of sabbatical leave in 2002, granted by the University of Alberta and the University of Otago, for which the support of Mike Mahon (Faculty of Physical Education and Recreation, University of Alberta) and David Buisson, Kathy Rabel and Michael Hall (School of Business, University of Otago) was critical. Reidar Mykletun (Dean), Lone Litlehamar and colleagues at the Norwegian School of Hotel Management (Stavanger, Norway), where James Higham spent four months during the latter part of this project, provided a stimulating writing environment. The research assistance provided by Nichola Costley (University of Otago) during the initial preparation for this book was of great value, as was the contribution of Aggie Weighill (University of Alberta) during the later stages of this project.

We are particularly appreciative of the Case study contributions of Dick Butler, Laurence Chalip, Sean Gammon, Heather Gibson, Simon Hudson, Mark Orams, Charles Pigeassou and Michael Silk, whose insights have stimulated our work in the field of sport tourism. Our deliberations on this subject have also been influenced by the contributions of several other researchers, many of whom are cited thoughout the text. In the early stages of our collaboration the Sports Management Association of Australia and New Zealand and the Leisure Studies Association (United Kingdom) hosted conferences that were valuable in developing our thoughts on sport tourism.

Those who have supported our primary research in sport tourism, particularly the Otago Rugby Football Union (New Zealand) and the Arctic Winter Games (Canada), have contributed to the production of this book. The technical and administrative support of Carol McNeil, Hui Shin Ngiam (University of Alberta), Frances Cadogan, Mel Elliot, Rosie Ferris, Michael Hamblyn (University of Otago) and John Reynolds (Cambridge University Library) has been invaluable. We are also indebted to all of our colleagues with the Faculty of Physical Education and Recreation at the Univeristy of Alberta and the Department of Tourism at the University of Otago. Thank you for providing a stimulating and enjoyable academic environment.

This book has been written during extended periods away from home, during which time the authors have received the great support of family and friends too numerous to mention but certainly appreciated. Finally, the support of our immediate families, Lorraine, Lindsay and Gillian, and Linda, Alexandra and Kate, has been critical to the completion of this book. We are thankful for their help and understanding.

Thomas Hinch
Edmonton, Alberta
James Higham
Dunedin, New Zealand

Case Study Contributors

Richard Butler, University of Surrey (UK)

Richard Butler is Professor of Tourism in the School of Management at the University of Surrey, having returned to England after 30 years in Canada at the University of Western Ontario. He trained as a geographer, with degrees from Nottingham (BA Hons) and Glasgow (Ph.D.) Universities, and has served as President of the International Academy for the Study of Tourism, and of the Canadian Association for Leisure Studies. He has research interests in destination development, sustainability and tourism, tourism in small islands and remote locations, and the relationships between the media, popular culture and tourism. He is currently editing two volumes on the Tourism Area Life Cycle Model and is the co-editor of the *Journal of Tourism and Hospitality Research*.

Laurence Chalip, University of Texas (USA)

Laurence Chalip is Professor and Coordinator of the Sport Management Program at the University of Texas at Austin. He has published three books and over 50 articles and book chapters. He is a Research Fellow of the North American Society for Sport Management and has won two service awards from the Sport Management Association of Australia and New Zealand. In 2000, Dr Chalip was appointed to the International Chair of Olympism.

Sean Gammon, University of Luton (UK)

Sean Gammon is the coordinator of the BA (Hons) in Sport Tourism at the University of Luton and he was instrumental in the initial development of this programme. His research interests focus upon the development of sport tourism typologies and exploring the relationship between nostalgia, pilgrimage and the sport tourism experience.

Heather Gibson, University of Florida (USA)

Heather Gibson is an Assistant Professor in the Department of Recreation, Parks and Tourism at the University of Florida. She teaches and researches in the sociology of leisure, tourism and sport. Some of her recent research projects include the tourism associated with college sport in the USA, the role of leisure in the lives of retirement-aged women, and the meaning of sport for athletes with disabilities. Her background in sport and tourism led to her interest in sport tourism and she has been researching in this area since the early 1990s.

James Higham, University of Otago (New Zealand)

James Higham is a Senior Lecturer in the Department of Tourism, School of Business, University of Otago. He studied Anthropology and Geography and completed a Ph.D. (University of Otago) in 1996, which examined the wilderness perceptions of international visitors to New Zealand. His empirical research and publication interests in sport tourism date to 1994. They focus on the strategic development of sports events, sport tourism development, seasonality in sport and tourism, and the spatial travel flows associated with regional and provincial sports teams. His interests in sport include squash, tennis, rugby union, cricket and football.

Thomas Hinch, University of Alberta (Canada)

Thomas Hinch is an Associate Professor with the Faculty of Physical Education and Recreation at the University of Alberta. His research interests focus on the relationship between travellers and the places that they visit. He has examined this relationship in the context of sport tourism, tourism and indigenous people, and tourism seasonality. Tom's interest in sport tourism has evolved from his experience as a competitive athlete in his youth, his experience as a recreational athlete at present, and his long-standing fascination with travel and with tourism destinations.

Simon Hudson, University of Calgary (Canada)

Simon Hudson is an Associate Professor in the Tourism Management Group at the University of Calgary. He has an MBA from California and a Ph.D. from the University of Surrey in England. Prior to working in academia, he spent several years working for UK ski operators in Europe, and he now consults for the ski areas in Banff National Park, Canada. The ski industry is the focus of his research, and Continuum published his first book in 2000 called *Snow Business: A Study of the International Ski Industry*. He has a new book on *Sports and Adventure Tourism* with the Haworth Press and is now working on his third book about the marketing of tourism in Canada. He is the marketing editor for the *International*

Journal of Tourism Research, and is on the editorial board for the *Journal of Teaching in Travel and Tourism* and the *Journal of Travel Research*.

Mark Orams, Massey University (New Zealand)

Mark Orams is the Director of the Coastal Marine Research Group. His research interests primarily lie in marine tourism, where he has a specific focus on marine mammal tourism. He is also, however, a competitive yachtsman and was a member of the crew of 'Steinlager 2' – the winning entrant in the 1989/90 Whitbread Round the World Yacht Race. He was a member of Team New Zealand for its successful defence of the America's Cup in 2000 and continues to be part of the team attempting to repeat that success during the thirty-first defence of the Cup in 2003.

Charles Pigeassou, Université de Montpellier (France)

Charles Piggeasou is a Senior Lecturer with the Faculté des Sciences du Sport et de l'Éducation Physique at the Université de Montpellier 1. He completed the undergraduate programme in psychology and sociology at the Sorbonne; then a graduate programme in sociology at the Université de Paris VII. Charles obtained a position as lecturer at the Université de Montpellier 1 in 1981. He is currently in charge of a Masters programme in sports management and sports tourism, in which he teaches sports management, strategy and the delivery process to undergraduate and graduate students. His main research and publication interests focus on sport services and sport tourism processes.

Michael Silk, The University of Memphis (USA)

Michael Silk is an Assistant Professor in the Department of Human Movement Sciences at The University of Memphis. His research revolves around the role of cultural intermediaries in the corporate reimagining of national cultures, the practices of televised sport professionals and the place of sport within the political, economic and cultural shifts and realignments of late capitalism. He has recently published in *Media, Culture and Society*, the *Journal of Sport and Social Issues*, *Sociology of Sport Journal*, *International Review for the Sociology of Sport*, the *Journal of Sport Management* and *Culture, Sport and Society*. In addition to these articles, Michael has published a number of book chapters and is the editor (with David L. Andrews and C. L. Cole) of *Corporate nationalism(s): Sport, cultural identity and transnational marketing* (Berg, 2003).

Part 1: Introduction

Chapter 1

Sport Tourism in Times of Change

In terms of popular participation, and in some aspects of practice, (sport and tourism)
are inextricably linked . . . and there are sound reasons for those links to strengthen.
(Glyptis, 1989: 165)

Introduction

The World Tourism Organization and International Olympic
Committee hosted a major international conference on sport and tourism
in February 2001 (Barcelona, Spain). This conference represented a defining moment in the recognition of the relationship between sport and
tourism by the leading international organisations for sport and tourism.
It built upon the reality of tourist demand for sport experiences, the
expanding industry response to this demand, and the increasing body
of academic research and publication in the field of sport tourism.
Sports, particularly large-scale sporting events dating back to the ancient
Olympic Games, have long influenced travel (Keller, 2001). However,
the high numbers of travellers currently seeking active and passive
involvement in sports is a more recent development (Delpy, 1998). It is
increasingly clear that the scale, complexity and potential of sport
tourism, as well as the expanding mutual interests of the sport and
tourism industries that have developed as a consequence, demand that
academic and industry expertise be directed toward this field. This book
is about sport tourism and its manifestations in space and time. It seeks
to articulate the defining qualities of sport that explain its unique contribution to tourism. It then applies tourism development concepts and
themes to the study of sport tourism. Three key questions emerge in the
context of sport tourism development: 'What makes sport unique as a
tourist attraction or activity?', 'How is sport tourism manifest in space?',
and 'How do these manifestations change over time?'

The book is organised into five parts. Part 1 (Chapter 1) introduces the
purpose, structure and goals of the book. It describes the development
and growth of sport tourism, and then raises questions that are intended

3

to demonstrate the relevance and challenge the assumptions that the reader may have on this subject. Part 2 (Chapters 2–4) is titled *Foundations for sport tourism development*. This section is intended to provide the reader with fundamentals in the study of sport tourism, sport tourism markets and development processes and issues relating to sport tourism. Much progress has been made in the study of sport tourism in recent years (Glyptis, 1991; Redmond, 1991; Gammon & Robinson, 1997; Weed & Bull, 1997a; Green & Chalip, 1998; Gibson, 1998a; Delpy, 1998; Standeven & De Knop, 1999; Turco *et al.*, 2002). Chapters 2–4 provide an opportunity to review current insights into sport tourism as a basis for the discussions that follow.

Part 3 (Chapters 5–7) focuses on the spatial elements of sport tourism development. These chapters examine sport tourism development in relation to space, place and the environment. Each of these topics represents important aspects and manifestations of development. Part 4 (Chapters 8–10) examines sport tourism development in relation to time. The short-term, medium-term and long-term time horizons provide a temporal framework that allows the authors to consider the immediate sport tourism experience, sport tourism and seasonality, and the dynamic interrelationship between sport and tourism within evolutionary frameworks. Part 5 (Chapter 11) concludes with a consideration of the management principles that, based on the preceding discussions, may serve to guide sport tourism development in the future. This structure provides a framework that allows the authors to raise questions relating to sport tourism development and to address these questions through the application of tourism development theory.

Sport Tourism in Times of Change

Democratisation, the process of opening access to previously restricted opportunities, is a term that applies to the development of sport and tourism in the latter half of the twentieth century (Standeven & De Knop, 1999). Participation in some sports remains defined by factors such as social class. 'Irrespective of culture or historical period, people use sport to distinguish themselves and to reflect their status and prestige' (Booth & Loy, 1999: 1). The existence of post-class egalitarian consumer cultures in sport is refuted by Booth and Loy (1999) who state that similar status groups generally share lifestyle and consumption patterns. The links that exist between socio-demographic status, lifestyle and consumption patterns in sport and tourism heighten the value and utility of defining sport tourism markets in practice.

That said, the forces of globalisation (Bernstein, 2000) and democratisation (Standeven & De Knop, 1999) have had significant implications for the consumption of sport and development processes in sport tourism

(Chapter 4). The modern development of sport tourism, then, stands at the cross-section of contemporary trends that include:

(1) the expanding demographic profile of participants in sports (Glyptis, 1989);
(2) heightened interests in health and fitness in western societies since the 1970s (Collins, 1991);
(3) increasing demand for active engagement in recreational pursuits while on holiday since the 1980s (Priestley, 1995); and
(4) growing interest in the prominent roles played by sports and sports events in urban renewal and urban imagery, and the potential to leverage tourism opportunities associated with sports events (Getz, 1998).

These processes have been driven by economic and political forces (Cooper *et al.*, 1993; Gibson, 1998a; Collins, 1991; Nauright, 1996), and by changing social attitudes and values (Redmond, 1991; S. J. Jackson *et al.*, 2001; Kurtzman & Zauhar, 1995). They have also been facilitated by technological advances, such as satellite television broadcasting (Halberstam, 1999), that have influenced the 'sportification of society' (Standeven & De Knop, 1999).

Faulkner *et al.* (1998: 3) note that 'as a consequence of these developments, the geographical extent and volume of sports related travel has grown exponentially'. Glyptis (1989) provides an early demonstration of these trends. She notes in a study of western European countries that all had experienced strong growth in interest in recreational sport during the 1980s. Furthermore, participation was increasing in all social strata, most sports were receiving participants from an expanding social spectrum, and all had recorded significant increases in youth holidays, short breaks and second holidays. The two decades that have followed have served to strengthen these trends (Hall, 1992a; IOC & WTO, 2001).

The Foundations of Sport Tourism Development

The growth of sport tourism justifies critical consideration of relevant development issues. This task requires that sport tourism is defined and conceptualised in ways that highlight rather than obscure the diversity of interests in sport and tourism. A number of definitions exist in this field and afford the opportunity to study sport tourism from a variety of perspectives. For the purposes of this book sport tourism is conceptualised by considering sport as a tourist attraction, and by highlighting the defining qualities of sport that collectively constitute a unique contribution to tourism (Chapter 2). This approach is intended to give prominence to the dynamic and complex nature of sport and tourism, thereby helping to clarify the parameters and scope of this book.

The diversity of the sport tourism market is explored in Chapter 3, which highlights the rich diversity of motivations, and therefore the varied approaches to market segmentation that exist in sport tourism. Bale (1989: 9) notes that 'work-play, freedom-constraint, competition-recreation, and process-product are only some of the continua on which sports can be located'. Thus the experiences of sport tourists are likely to vary considerably with the motivations that travellers hold towards their chosen sports. The motivations associated with sport tourism niche markets raise intriguing questions for sports event organisers and promoters, sports associations, managers of sporting venues, destination managers and tourism marketers. To what extent, for example, are highly competitive professional athletes interested in tourist experiences at a sport destination, and how may the potential of this market be fully achieved? The promotional opportunities that derive from the association of high-profile athletes with specific tourist destinations are part of this potential. How does tourism based on professional sport differ from the tourism development opportunities associated with recreational sport (Focus point 1.1)? Tourist experiences relating to sport vary within and between niche market segments, which raises questions as to how these markets can be better understood by sport and tourism managers who seek to meet changing sport and travel preferences.

Focus point 1.1

Participation Youth Football in Scandinavia

The largest football tournament in the world, as measured in terms of participation, is the Gothia Cup (Göteborg, Sweden). In 2002 it attracted 25,100 participants (average age 15.5 years), representing 1246 teams from 118 countries, who took part in a tournament that included 3420 games played on 72 fields. The opening ceremony was attended by 40,200 people and the finals by 26,700 spectators. The tourist corollary of this event is significant. Direct tourist income of SEK 18 million was spent in the city of Göteborg, generating significant tax income. The Gothia Heden Centre received 295,000 visits in five days during the event. Television broadcasts of the Gothia Cup were carried in nine countries and Swedish newspapers published 1152 articles on the event. International media coverage was provided by 102 accredited journalists from 28 countries (Tourist Authorities of Göteborg, 2002). Similarly, the Norway Cup, which was founded in 1972, is contested annually by over 1200 teams from around the world. It involves youth teams with players aged 13–19 years in eleven- and seven-aside competitions. The tourism implications of the competition are substantial. It attracts over 20,000 participants and, due to their age, it also attracts large entourages of team personnel and family support. In a deliberate attempt to encourage secondary trips and leisure activities, all participants are entitled to free travel with the Oslo Transportation System and are entitled to gratis entrance into museums and outdoor swimming pools in Oslo. Participants also receive a multi-language guide to touring in Norway. The fact that 573 journalists representing print, radio and television outlets from the USA, Mexico, Brazil, Jamaica, Angola, Nigeria, South Africa, China, Thailand and the UK were accredited in 2001 demonstrates the international significance of this event (Leisure Time, 2002).

The logical extension of this market analysis is consideration of development processes, sustainability and planning interventions. Development issues that are of particular interest to sport and tourism practitioners include those related to commodification/authenticity, globalisation and industry fragmentation. Hitherto, little consideration has been given to the modification of sports competitions (e.g. through rule changes, length and timing of the competition season and the televising of live sport) and the implications for perceptions of place and destination imagery associated with sports (Focus point 1.2). The relevance of these processes and issues are introduced to the reader and explored in Chapter 4, thereby providing an important part of the foundation upon which the subsequent chapters are based.

Focus point 1.2

Sport, Heritage and Culture

Heritage and culture contribute to making tourism destinations unique. Sport and sports venues often represent a unique expression of the culture of the destination. Sports venues such as Lords (cricket), Wimbledon (lawn tennis), Twickenham (rugby union), St Andrews (golf), Wembley (football) and Royal Ascot (horse racing) are recognised as the spiritual homes of their sports. Sport's most prestigious tournaments are contested at these venues. With time, each has developed its own aura of tradition. Each represents a significant expression of the heritage and culture of Britain (BTA, 2000). Other sports that represent distinctive cultural elements of a destination include baseball (USA), Gaelic football and hurling (Ireland), Australian Rules football (Australia), thakraw (South-east Asia) and Asian martial arts such as sumo wrestling (Japan), tae kwon do (Korea) and Thai boxing (Thailand). These sports may form an important and unique part of the visitor experience at a destination.

Sport Tourism Development and Space

Chapters 5 to 8 consider how sport tourism is manifest in space and how these manifestations may be influenced. Chapter 5 explores the inter-relationships linking sport tourism-generating areas and destinations with the travel patterns associated with sport tourism markets. The basic concepts and themes for this chapter have their roots in economic geography. These concepts are drawn from the study of sports geography and the spatial analysis of sports (Bale, 1989, 1993a). Relevant management implications relate, for example, to the allocation of franchise areas within a league or decisions on where to build, develop or enhance sport facilities and areas. The ways in which sports may influence the spatial travel patterns and itineraries of visitors travelling within a destination, whether sport functions as a primary, secondary or tertiary attraction, are also discussed.

The sports played in an area influence the meanings that are attached to this space (Focus point 1.3). Concepts of place, culture and place promotion are explored in Chapter 6. In many ways, sport infuses tourism spaces with one of the most authentic types of attractions. The link between culture and sport takes many forms: sport and culture, sport as

Focus point 1.3

The British Tourist Authority

The British Tourist Authority (BTA) identifies four pillars of tourism in Britain: heritage, countryside, cities and sport. Sport, in all its diversity, has been recognised in the BTA marketing strategy as one of the main attractions for overseas visitors coming to Britain. The British sport tourism market alone is estimated to be worth over £1.5 billion annually, and empirical research shows that sports featured prominently in 25–30% of all tourism in Britain in 2001. Britain is regularly the focus of international tourist and media attention as it hosts many prestigious sporting events. This exposure has consolidated Britain as the 'birthplace' of many of the world's most famous sports. The BTA established the Sports Tourism Department in January 2000 to promote Britain as *the* country to visit for the sporting enthusiast and to encourage more overseas visitors to watch, play and experience sport in Britain. Since that time, the BTA has developed a sport tourism marketing plan and strategy, a range of printed and electronic promotional items and a range of merchandise to assist in marketing the sport tourism product in Britain. The BTA uses sports stars such as David Beckham (football) and Ian Botham (cricket) to promote tourism in the regional destinations where they have made their names as sportspeople (Manchester and Yorkshire respectively in these cases) (BTA, 2000).

culture and sport subcultures. All of these variations contribute to the meaning attached to sport tourism places. Strategies that incorporate these cultural variations can be used to promote place to a variety of markets. There are, however, significant challenges associated with the commodification of culture.

The environment is the subject of the third spatial dimension (Chapter 7). This chapter considers the common resource base for sport and tourism facilities and infrastructure. Quite different issues are associated with natural resources and built facilities in sport tourism. Outdoor sports, such as downhill skiing, for example, tend to be dependent on specific types of landscape, with the potential for irreversible environmental impacts (Focus point 1.4). Other types of sport are more transportable and feature standard facilities that can be built in locations designed to maximise market access. The environmental, social and cultural impacts of relevance to each are, once again, quite different. This requires recognition of the distinct management requirements of those sports that are resource-dependent versus those that are relatively resource-independent.

Focus point 1.4

Lillehammer 1994 and the Olympic Environmental Charter

In planning the Lillehammer (Norway) Winter Olympics all building projects were required to conform with rigorous design objectives and regulations so that developments would complement existing landscape and architecture. Design objectives differed between permanent and temporary constructions. A range of energy-saving devices and techniques, including heat pumps using surplus energy from the process of ice making, were introduced for this event. These innovations brought numerous benefits. Mutual interests in sport and environmentalism were fostered. So, too, was the protection of environmental features that attract both active and event sport tourists, levels of visitor satisfaction, the reputation of the sports event and the reputation of the destination as clean and attractive. In 1995, the year following the Lillehammer Winter Olympics, the International Olympic Committee added the environment, alongside sport and culture, as a new dimension of the Olympic Movement (Chernushenko, 1996).

Sport Tourism Development and Time

Part 4 (Chapters 8–10) considers the manifestations of sport tourism in time. Chapter 8 explores the short-term temporal horizon of sport

tourism. The visitor experience is concerned with the timing and duration of visits, engagement in sports, touristic and leisure activities at the
destination and visitor expenditures. It is also associated with recollec-
tions of the tourist experience and, therefore, visitor satisfaction and
repeat visitation. Different forms of sport tourism manifest themselves in
contrasting tourist experiences. Chapter 8 explores manifestations of sport
tourist experience employing the framework developed by Clawson and
Knetsch (1966), which has been applied widely in the study of the tourist
experience. It also examines the relevance of the sport and tourism
systems that mediate the sport tourist experience at a destination. This
approach is intended to provide informed insights into strategies that
may influence and enhance sport tourism visitor experiences.

The medium term or seasonal dimension of sport tourism is the subject
of Chapter 9. Few tourism destinations are unaffected by systematic seasonal fluctuations in the tourism phenomenon. Strategies designed to
extend shoulder seasons or create all-season destinations are commonplace. Therefore, the manner in which sports moderate, or may be engi-
neered to alter, seasonal patterns of visitation is worthy of discussion. The
reverse also applies, whereby tourism may influence patterns of seasonal
participation in sport. It is not enough to know that there are seasonal patterns of sport and tourism; it is also important to understand the reasons
for those patterns. Leisure constraints theory provides insights into such
patterns. Consideration can then be given to strategies, such as facility
design, pricing and promotions and event production, that may moderate
or alter patterns of seasonality in sport and tourism (Focus point 1.5).

Chapter 10 examines the interrelationship between sport and tourism
within an evolutionary or long-term context. Tourism development
processes, as conceptualised in the evolution in tourism destinations
through a life cycle (Butler, 1980), may be influenced by the powerful
dynamics of sport. For example, evolving spatial patterns of sport may
have a direct bearing on tourism development. The reverse is also true,
as tourism may impact upon the types of sports practised in destination
areas. Golf serves as a good illustration of this process, given its introduction into the 'new world' by Scottish migrants and diffusion into new
regions throughout the world in response to tourist demand. Nostalgia
sport tourism is a unique form of tourism in which tourists search for
sporting experiences associated with earlier periods. Current trends also
suggest that a dynamic future is likely for the sport tourism industry.

Management Principles for Sport Tourism Development

The capacity for sport and tourism managers to influence the nature
and pace of change, through carefully considered management strategies,

---

Focus point 1.5

Sport and Tourism Seasonality

The technology of modern stadia and arenas allows many sports to be performed without interference or interruption caused by the natural elements. The extent to which sports may become detached from the influences of the weather is, in many cases, so complete that sports managers may moderate the seasonal context of sports. The retractable stadium roof has significant implications for sport and tourism seasonality. Indeed, the first international rugby and cricket fixtures contested indoors took place out of season at the Millennium Stadium, Cardiff (Wales) in October 1999, and the Colonial Stadium, Melbourne (Australia) in July 2001 respectively. The former features a playing surface that rests on pallets which can be removed and replaced when necessary. Sapporo, situated in Hokkaido, Japan's northernmost island, features a futuristic Dome, where World Cup matches were played in 2002. The Sapporo Dome is an all-weather covered stadium designed with a view to the local climate conditions, particularly heavy snow in winter. This hi-tech facility, which combines indoor and outdoor arenas and an unprecedented hovering football stage, makes it possible to play at any time of year regardless of the weather. The natural grass playing surface can be moved in and out of the stadium, being kept outside the dome to allow the grass to grow when not in use and then moved inside when needed. The entire lower section of the field is rolled into the Dome on a cushion of air. At the same time, a rotating seat system moves aside before the pitch turns sideways on its axis and the seating areas automatically slide back into place. The entire manoeuvre takes two hours to complete. The air inside is moderated by an air-conditioning unit and a natural ventilation system in summer, while in winter spectators are kept comfortable by a heating system applied directly to the seats.

Source: http://fifaworldcup.yahoo.com/en/da/c/sapporo.html

---

is discussed in Part 5 (Chapter 11). This discussion necessitates the consideration of existing trends and innovative ways of influencing them. For example, the challenges associated with commodification, finding a balance between progress and tradition, and the accelerated nature of globalisation in sport need to be systematically explored. Where sport and tourism managers collaborate effectively in addressing these issues, sustainable outcomes are more likely to emerge.

These themes form the structure of the following chapters. The foundations of the book lie in the geographical principles of space, place and environment. However, the application of these principles to sport tourism presents the challenges of a multidisciplinary approach. This book draws from the fields of sport management, the sociology of sport, consumer behaviour, sports marketing, economic, urban and sports geography and tourism studies in discussing the manifestations of sport tourism development in space and time. To illustrate points of discussion, Chapters 2–10 include Case studies provided by leading scholars in the study of sport tourism and related disciplines. Industry-based 'Focus points' are also integrated into each of these chapters to illustrate the relevance of these discussions to the practice of sport tourism development. Consideration of the management implications and strategies of relevance are also presented in each of Chapters 2–10. The overarching goal of this book is to advance theoretical thinking on the subject of sport tourism development and to demonstrate the practical relevance of points of discussion raised in the chapters that follow. This book also seeks to challenge the thinking of students in the academic study of sport tourism as well as professionals who stand at the cutting edge of the sport and tourism industries.

Further Reading

The discourse on sport tourism has expanded considerably in recent years. Useful contributions that introduce the reader to the subject of sport tourism have emerged in various forms. Standeven and De Knop's (1999) book titled *Sport tourism* provides a comprehensive introduction to the subject of sport tourism. A second book by the same name has recently been published by Turco *et al.* (2002). It takes a more applied approach to the subject, with chapters on topics such as evaluation and finance. The *Journal of Sport Tourism* is also a logical starting point for reading on this subject and the special issue of the *Journal of Sport Management* (2003) on sport tourism is a valuable resource. Keller (2001) provides detailed and valuable insights into the expanding links that exist between the fields of sport and tourism.

Part 2: Foundations for Sport Tourism Development

Chapter 2
The Study of Sport Tourism

From the stand point of theory, it is necessary to understand what sport tourism shares with, and what distinguishes it from other touristic activities.

(Green & Chalip, 1998: 276)

Introduction

Chapter 1 demonstrated the significant and expanding areas of mutual interest in sport management and tourism development. The tourism and the sport industries are catering to travellers seeking sport experiences. This reality, in combination with solid academic rationale, justifies targeted scholarly attention paid to the sport tourism phenomenon. While it is not being suggested that the study of sport tourism should become the sole domain of specialists, new insights can be gained by an increased focus on the confluence of sport and tourism. Such an approach offers the opportunity to examine untested assumptions, improve professional practice and more effectively and efficiently transmit information between sport and tourism managers. A focused approach to sport tourism will capture synergies leading to new insights into this phenomenon that would not otherwise emerge. Chapter 2 is an articulation of this argument. It will be presented by examining the conceptual foundations of sport and tourism, arguing in support of focused scholarly attention in this area and considering sport within a tourist attraction framework. The development of a sport tourism degree at the University of Luton (UK) serves to illustrate the processes involved in developing academic programmes in this field (Case study 2.1; see pp. 30–32).

Conceptual Foundations

The logical starting point to understanding the confluence of sport and tourism is to articulate the essence of each of the parent disciplines. This is not a simple task, as multiple definitions exist for both concepts (Hinch & Higham, 2001). A range of definitions for sport and tourism can be justified in different contexts. While agreement on a single universal definition is unlikely and perhaps undesirable, some consensus concerning the defining parameters of both sport and tourism does emerge from the respective literatures in these fields of study.

Domain of sport

The popular perception of sport is best reflected by the adage that sport is what is written about on the sport pages of daily newspapers (Bale, 1989). However, a cursory comparison of the sport pages of newspapers from a variety of countries demonstrates that sporting activities vary substantially between places. While attractive in terms of its simplicity, this definitional approach fails to capture the essence of sport in terms of the commonalities found in diverse sporting activities.

Definitions arising from the study of sport sociology are particularly insightful when combined with the concept of tourism. One of the most influential definitions of sport to emerge within this area is Loy *et al.*'s (1978) game occurrence approach. They conceptualise sport as a subset of games, which in turn is a subset of play. Sport is described in terms of institutionalised games that require physical prowess. In a similar fashion, McPherson *et al.* (1989: 15) defined sport as 'a structured, goal-oriented, competitive, contest-based, ludic physical activity'.

Sport is structured in the sense that sports are governed by rules that relate to space and time. These rules may be manifest in a variety of ways, including the dimensions of the playing area and the duration and pacing of the game or contest. They also tend to be more specific in formal variations of a sport, especially as the level of competition increases. In informal variations of a sport these rules are often very general; for example, the unwritten etiquette of surfing (A. Law, 2001).

Sport is also defined as being goal-oriented, competitive and contest-based. All three characteristics are closely related. Sport is goal-oriented in the sense that sporting situations usually involve an objective for achievement in relation to ability, competence, effort, degree of difficulty, required skill set and mastery or performance. In most instances this goal orientation is extended to some degree of competition. At one extreme, competition is expressed in terms of winning or losing. Alternatively, competition can be interpreted much less rigidly in terms of competing against individual standards, inanimate objects or the forces of nature. In the context of sport tourism, the latter interpretation of competition offers a much more inclusive approach that covers recreational sports, such as those commonly associated with outdoor pursuits. It is also inclusive of the 'sport for all' concept of participation (e.g. Nogawa *et al.*, 1996). Competition is probably best conceptualised as a continuum that ranges from recreational to elite. Closely associated with competition is the contest-based nature of sport, in which outcomes are determined by a combination of physical prowess, game strategy and, to a greater or lesser degree, chance. Physical prowess consists of physical speed, stamina, strength, accuracy and coordination and, when viewed in these terms, across the whole competition continuum, it is one of the most consistent criteria used to define sport (Gibson, 1998a).

The final aspect of sport that is highlighted in the definition presented by McPherson *et al.* (1989) is its ludic (playful) nature, a term which is derived from the Latin word *ludus*. This component of the definition states that sport is rooted in, although not exclusive to, the concept of play. Those activities that are seen as pure work would not normally be considered sport, but the presence of some degree of work, in and of itself, does not rule out an activity as sport. Professional sport therefore fits this definition, as does recreational sport. The presence of play in sport is accompanied by uncertain outcome and sanctioned display. Uncertain outcome helps to maintain suspense throughout a sporting engagement. It also presents unique advantages in terms of tourism authenticity (Chapter 4). Sanctioned display tends to emphasise the exhibition of athletic skills and, as such, it broadens the scope of involvement to spectators as well as participating athletes.

Domain of tourism

Tourism definitions can be classified into those associated with the popular usage of the term (e.g. Simpson & Weiner, 1989), those used to facilitate statistical measurement (e.g. WTO, 1981) and those used to articulate its conceptual domain (e.g. Murphy, 1985). Definitions arising from all of these perspectives tend to share three key dimensions. The most prevalent of these is a spatial dimension (Dietvorst & Ashworth, 1995). Tourism involves the 'travel of non-residents' (Murphy, 1985: 9). To be considered a tourist, individuals must leave and then eventually return to their home. While the travel of an individual does not in itself constitute tourism, it is one of the necessary conditions. A variety of qualifiers have been placed on this dimension, including a range of minimum travel distances, but the fundamental concept of travel is universal.

A second common dimension involves the temporal characteristics associated with tourism. Tourist trips are characterised by a 'temporary stay away from home of at least one night' (Leiper, 1981: 74). Definitions developed for statistical purposes often distinguish between tourists and excursionists. The distinction between the two is that the former visit a destination for at least 24 hours, while the latter visit for less than 24 hours (WTO, 1981). Often in popular literature and the media, however, the term tourist is used to refer to both groups.

A third common dimension of tourism definitions concerns the purpose or the activities engaged in during travel and it is within this dimension that many sub-fields of tourism research find their genesis (e.g. eco-tourism, adventure tourism). Of the three dimensions, this is perhaps the one characterised by the broadest range of views. For example, dictionary interpretations of tourists tend to focus on pleasure as the primary travel activity (e.g. Simpson & Weiner, 1989), while definitions developed for statistical and academic purposes tend to include business activities (Murphy, 1985). Specific reference is made to sport in the tourism defin-ition of the World Tourism Organization (1981), which lists it as a subset of leisure activities.

Confluence of sport and tourism

These definitions clearly imply a significant convergence of interests in tourism, and sport (Figure 2.1). Sport is an important activity within tourism, and tourism and travel are fundamentally associated with many types of sport. The specific confluence of the two concepts varies according to the perspectives of stakeholders and their particular inter-ests in sport tourism. The diversity of interests in sport tourism gives rise to an important question that academics and industry practitioners must address. Is the study of sport tourism supported by a strong theoretical foundation and dedicated academic literature?

Defining sport tourism

Attempts to articulate the domain of sport tourism have resulted in a proliferation of definitions (Table 2.1). These definitions tend to parallel

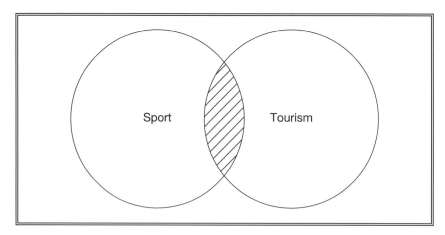

Figure 2.1 The confluence of sport and tourism

Table 2.1 Selected definitions relating to the study of sport tourism

Dimension	Definition and source
Sport tourism	Travel for non-commercial reasons to participate or observe sporting activities away from the home range (Hall, 1992a: 194)
	An expression of a pattern of behaviour of people during certain periods of leisure time – such as vacation time – which is done partly in specially attractive natural settings and partly in artificial sports and physical recreation facilities in the outdoors (Ruskin, 1987: 26)
	Holidays involving sporting activity either as a spectator or participant (Weed & Bull, 1997b: 5)
	Leisure-based travel that takes individuals temporarily outside of their home communities to participate in physical activities, to watch physical activities, or to venerate attractions associated with physical activity (Gibson, 1998a: 49)
	All forms of active and passive involvement in sporting activity, participated in casually or in an organised way for non-commercial or business/commercial reasons, that necessitate travel away from home and work locality (Standeven & De Knop, 1999: 12)
Sport tourist	A temporary visitor staying at least 24 hours in the event area and whose primary purpose is to participate in a sports event with the area being a secondary attraction (Nogawa *et al.*, 1996: 46)
	Individuals and/or groups of people who actively or passively participate in competitive or recreational sport, while travelling to and/or staying in places outside their usual environment (sport as the primary motivation of travel) (Gammon & Robinson, 1997: n.p.)
Tourism sport	Persons travelling to and/or staying in places outside their usual environment and participating in, actively or passively, a competitive or recreational sport as a secondary activity (Gammon & Robinson, 1997: n.p.)

the spatial, temporal and activity dimensions of key definitions for tourism (Gibson, 1998a). Sport is often positioned as the primary travel activity, although Gammon and Robinson (1997) make a distinction between sport tourists and tourism sports. The latter recognises sport as a secondary and sometimes even an incidental travel activity. These various levels of involvement in sport are assumed under the term sport tourism in this book. Most definitions include spectators as well as athletes and recreational as well as elite competitors (Hall, 1992b; Standeven & De Knop, 1999; Weed, 1999). They also tend to include explicit requirements for travel away from the home environment along with at least an implicit temporal dimension that suggests that the trip is temporary and that the traveller will return home within a designated time. Somewhat surprisingly, the major limitation of existing definitions is that the concept of sport is rather vague. This causes challenges in an international context, given differing cultural interpretations of sport. Such differences are problematic when discussing sport tourism development, as sport is the central focus of the development process.

For the purposes of this book, sport tourism is defined as sport-based travel away from the home environment for a limited time, where sport is characterised by unique rule sets, competition related to physical prowess and play (Hinch & Higham, 2001). Sport is recognised as a significant travel activity whether it is a primary or secondary feature of the trip. It is seen to be an important factor in many decisions to travel – one that may feature prominently in the travel experience – and is a significant consideration in the visitor's assessment of the travel experience. This definition enables the adoption of an attractions approach to the discussion of sport tourism development.

Scholarship in Sport Tourism

Sport studies and tourism studies share many of the same institutional characteristics. Both are relatively new areas of academia that have worked hard to be accepted as respected fields of scholarship. Both disciplines have recently developed systematic interests in sport tourism, which have manifested themselves in a growing body of literature (Glyptis, 1991; Gibson, 1998a; Standeven & De Knop, 1999).

Perhaps the most frequently used argument for focused study in the realm of sport tourism is the significance of the practice of sport tourism throughout the world. A survey of Canadian travellers found that 37% participated in sport or were spectators at a sporting event (Canadian Tourism Commission, 2002). It was also estimated that sport travel was valued at about $CAN1.3 billion annually within the Canadian economy. Even conservative estimates suggest that the overall value of sport tourism in the United Kingdom is approximately £2.61 billion annually (Table 2.2)

Table 2.2 The value of sport tourism and activity holidays in the United Kingdom

Item	Value (£ million)
Sport tourism	
1. Short and long domestic holidays (excluding incidental sport)	1640
2. Independent overseas tourists	142
3. Day visits	831
Total	2611

Source: reprinted with permission from Collins and Jackson (1999: 175)

(Collins & Jackson, 1999). Despite the methodological challenges of arriving at economic impact estimates (Crompton, 1995), it is clear that the level of expenditure associated with sport tourism is significant.

It has also been demonstrated that other benefits accrue as a result of sport tourism. Weed (1999) has highlighted a number of these, including the increased supply of urban-based sport facilities and developments that can be used for locally based sport. In recognising the mutual interests of sport and tourism, it is possible to capture the synergies of joint funding, research and strategic initiatives. Notwithstanding these benefits, there are also potentially negative aspects of the sport tourism link (Weed, 1999). For example, the introduction of 'nuisance activities' to the countryside, particularly mechanised sports such as trail biking, jet-skiing and skidooing, has the potential to cause significant social and environmental impacts. Adventure and extreme sports, such as BASE jumping which takes place in the Lysefjord and Trollveggen regions of Norway, are characterised by safety and liability issues (Mykletun & Vedø, 2002). In such cases the advantages of developing a better understanding of the dynamics of sport tourism are that these impacts can be recognised, understood and managed in the development process.

Scholarly justification

The study of tourism and the study of sport are both characterised by numerous hyphenated sub-fields. In an age of competitive funding in academic institutions, the danger of splintering existing fields of study is a real as well as a perceived threat. At the 2001 meeting of the Leisure Studies Association in the United Kingdom, critics of sport tourism argued that insight into this phenomenon is most likely to emerge from within the respective realms of tourism studies and sport studies. This implies that collaborative approaches can be adopted using interdisciplinary and multidisciplinary approaches on an *ad hoc* basis. Resistance to any fundamental shift towards a sub-field in this area is perhaps due to the relatively early stage of theoretical development for sport tourism. This position is strengthened by the fact that considerable insight into the relationship between sport and tourism has been gained through existing programmes of study. Particularly useful contributions have been made through the work of tourism researchers focusing on, for example, outdoor recreation and adventure sports.

Hall (1992a,b) not only identified sport as a major special interest of tourism, but also articulated three related tourism domains, including hallmark events, outdoor recreation (adventure tourism) and tourism associated with health and fitness (Figure 2.2). Of these three related domains, the area of hallmark events is probably the most direct link to sport, as epitomised by national championship competition finals, such as American football's Superbowl, and international sport mega-events like the Olympic Games. The profile and scale of these sport events attracts the attention of both tourists and tourism researchers. This attention is reflected in the prominence of sport-based articles published in journals such as *Event Management*, and increasingly published in journals such as *Current Issues in Tourism*, *Tourism Management* and the *Annals of Tourism*

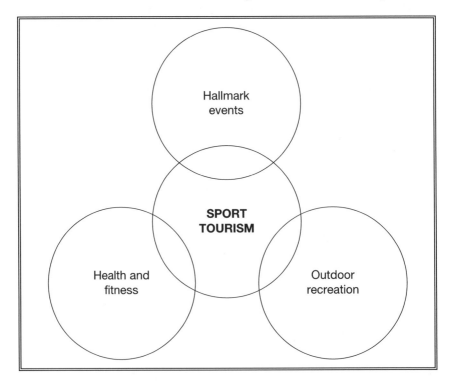

Figure 2.2 Sport tourism and related contextual domains

Research. However, Ritchie's (1984) classification of hallmark events identifies sport as just one of seven event categories, although others have argued that it is one of the most significant of these categories (Getz, 1997; Ryan *et al.*, 1996). While providing significant insight into sport tourism, these publications have not highlighted the distinguishing features of sporting events relative to other types of events. Even if they did, events only comprise one aspect, albeit a high profile one, of sport tourism.

Outdoor recreation represents a second related area that is inextricably linked to sport tourism. The essence of this contextual domain lies in recreational activities that occur within natural settings, many of which are commonly classified as sports, such as canoeing, skiing and surfing. One of the most dynamic components of outdoor recreation is adventure tourism. Hall (1992a) identifies adventure tourism as a rapidly growing segment of the special interest tourism market. Once again, there is a clear overlap between outdoor recreation and sport tourism both conceptually and in terms of research activity. However, these domains are not synonymous. A substantial amount of sport activity occurs outside the realm of the natural environment, while, conversely, many tourism activities that occur in natural settings are inconsistent with the definition of sport used in this book (e.g. camping, picnicking).

Health and fitness activities provide a third related domain of relevance to sport tourism. The essence of this domain is evident from both historical and contemporary perspectives. The former is most commonly illustrated by the tourist activity associated with the therapeutic spas of eastern and Mediterranean Europe in Roman times (Hall, 1992a). In a contemporary context, travel to partake in therapeutic spas continues, but a health focus is also found in resorts featuring activities such as tennis and golf (Redmond, 1991; Spivack, 1998). While the realm of health and fitness can be defined in ubiquitous terms, it has generally been treated much more narrowly in the literature.

Research in all three of these areas has contributed to the understanding of sport tourism, yet the essence of sport extends beyond the collective parameters of these related domains. The defining characteristics of sport and their relevance to tourism are not the central interest of research related to hallmark events, outdoor recreation or health tourism. Focused study on sport tourism can, therefore, provide new and challenging insights into this field of expanding academic and industry interest.

A growing body of literature

Just as the market place has responded to consumer demand for sport tourism products and services, the academic community has started to consciously respond to a gap in the literature related to sport tourism. Initially, this response was relatively isolated and *ad hoc* (Garmise, 1987), but over the past two decades a steady flow of scientific publications has contributed to a maturing body of literature.

Evidence of academic activity related to the study of sport tourism includes conferences focused on the subject, seminal articles in tourism and sport management journals (e.g. Gibson, 1998a; Green & Chalip, 1998), special themed issues of tourism and sport journals (e.g. *Journal of Vacation Marketing*, 1997; *Journal of Sport Management*, 2003), the establishment of a series titled the *Journal of Sport Tourism*, as well as a trade journal titled *Sports Travel*, the publication of authored (e.g. Standeven & De Knop, 1999; Turco *et al.*, 2002, Weed & Bull, 2003) and edited manuscripts on this topic (e.g. Gammon & Kurtzman, 2002) and the initiation ' of academic programmes specialising in undergraduate and graduate education in this area (e.g. University of Luton; see Case study 2.1 on pp. 30–32). Consequently, synergies that are inherent in a well-established body of literature are beginning to emerge as new sport tourism research initiatives are consciously positioned relative to earlier studies.

Gibson (1998a) has provided what is perhaps the most complete review of the sport tourism literature to date. It is structured around active, event and nostalgia sport tourism. Not only does Gibson provide a critical analysis of existing literature in this area, but she articulates the need for better coordination among agencies at a policy level, multidisciplinary research approaches and greater cooperation between tourism and sport-centred units in academic settings.

Conceptualising Sport as a Tourist Attraction

Green and Chalip (1998: 276) have noted that 'from the stand point of theory, it is necessary to understand what sport shares with, and what distinguishes it from other touristic activities'. Tourist attraction theory provides a useful framework for gaining insight into these unique aspects of sport tourism. While the idea of sport as a tourist attraction is not new (e.g. Rooney, 1988), the theoretical basis of tourist attractions has only recently been considered in detail (Hinch & Higham, 2001; Higham & Hinch, 2003). As a consequence, the management implications of consciously treating sport as a tourist attraction have not been fully explored. Leiper's (1990: 371) systems approach to tourist attractions provides a useful means for doing this. He defined a tourist attraction as 'a system comprising three elements: a tourist or human element, a nucleus or central element, and a marker or informative element. A tourist attraction comes into existence when the three elements are connected.'

The first component of Leiper's (1990) attraction system is the human element. The tourist or human element consists of persons who are travelling away from home to the extent that their behaviour is motivated by leisure-related factors. Leiper makes five assertions about the nature of this behaviour:

First, the essence of touristic behavior involves a search for satisfying leisure away from home. Second, touristic leisure means a search for suitable attractions or, to be more precise, a search for personal (*in situ*) experience of attraction systems' nuclear elements. Third, the process depends ultimately on each individual's mental and non-mental attributes such as needs and ability to travel. Fourth, the markers or informative elements have a key role in the links between each tourist and the nuclear elements being sought for personal experience. Fifth, the process is not automatically productive, because tourists' needs are not always satisfied (these systems may be functional or dysfunctional, to varying degrees). (Leiper, 1990: 371–372)

The second major element of Leiper's (1990) tourist attraction system is the nucleus, which refers to the site where the tourist experience is produced and consumed. More specifically, in the context of sporting attractions, it is the attributes of the sporting activity that make up the nucleus of the attraction (Lew, 1987). Leiper (1990) recognises that attractions may play a variety of roles in a tourist's experience, which he describes in terms of a nuclear mix and hierarchy. A nuclear mix refers to the combination of nuclei that a tourist wishes to experience, while the hierarchy suggests that some of these nuclei are more important in influencing visitor decisions than others. This aspect of the attraction system reflects established sport tourism typologies associated with multiple sport trips and categories of sport tourists' motivations (Standeven & De Knop, 1999; Gammon & Robinson, 1997).

Primary attractions are those that have the power to influence a visitor's decision to travel to a destination based solely on that attraction. Secondary attractions are known to a person prior to their visit, but are not critical in the decisions about their travel itinerary. Tertiary attractions are unknown to the traveller prior to their visit, but may serve as centres for entertainment or activity once the visitor is at the destination (Leiper, 1990). This hierarchy is evident in sport tourism, with many travellers primarily motivated by a particular sporting opportunity, others whose travel decisions depend on a combination of sporting and non-sporting attractions, and still others whose original travel decision may not have been driven by sporting opportunities in the destination, but whose destination activities include sport. The attraction system, therefore, recognises that sport may function as a tourist attraction in a variety of ways for a variety of people. Appreciating the place of sport within a destination's nuclear mix and hierarchy of attractions, as it relates to different tourist market segments, has significant sport and tourism management implications (e.g. attendance, participation, travel flows, visitor behaviour, timing of visit, etc.)

The third element of the attraction system consists of markers, which are items of information about any phenomenon that is a potential nucleus element in a tourist attraction (Leiper, 1990). They may be divided into markers that are detached or removed from the nucleus or those that are contiguous or on-site. In each case, the markers may be positioned consciously or unconsciously to function as part of the attraction system. Examples of conscious attraction markers featuring sport are common. Typically, they take the form of advertisements showing visitors involved in destination-specific sport activities and events. Unconscious detached markers are even more pervasive. At the forefront of these are televised broadcasts of elite sport competitions and advertisements featuring sports in recognisable destinations (Chapter 6). Broadcast listeners and viewers have the location marked for them as a tourist attraction, which may influence future travel decisions. As an example, Chalip *et al.*'s (1998) paper on sources of interest in travel to the Olympic Games fits nicely with this framework.

In response to Green and Chalip's (1998) call to develop an understanding of sport tourism relative to other types of touristic activities, a fundamental similarity is that sporting attractions share the same basic framework as other types of tourist attractions. One of the key reasons that sport tourism merits focused study, however, is that, within this basic framework, sport is unique. The human element of sport attractions is distinctive in its breadth, which includes forms as varied as event-based sports, team and individual sports, active involvement in competitive or recreational sports and spectatorship. Similarly, the significance of the popular media as sport tourism markers is arguably unmatched by few, if any, other types of touristic activity. While these two differences are important, the unique features of sport as the nucleus of the attraction present the strongest justification for focused study on sport tourism.

The definition of sport tourism used in this book highlights these components of the nucleus. First, each sport has its own set of rules that provide characteristic spatial and temporal structures, such as the dimensions of a playing surface or the duration of a match (Bale, 1989). Second, competition relating to physical prowess encompasses the goal orientation, competition and contest-based aspects of sport (McPherson *et al.*, 1989). Third, sport is characterised by its playful nature. This last element includes the notions of uncertainty of outcome and sanctioned display.

Rules, competition relating to physical prowess and the playfulness inherent in sport make it a unique type of tourism attraction. Specific types of sport, such as football, skiing or BASE jumping, possess their own distinctive traits as tourist attractions, given their differences in these three areas. By analysing sports in the context of these three components, insight can be gained into the way they function as tourist attractions. The impact of changes to the sport attraction can then be considered within the broader context of the spatial and temporal dimensions of tourism (Focus point 2.1).

Focus point 2.1

The development of one-day cricket as a tourist attraction

The innovation of modern one-day cricket owes its origin in the late 1970s to Australian businessman, Kerry Packer, who created the rebel World Series Cricket by contracting the leading international players from around the world to represent teams in the World Series. In doing so he pioneered a new form of cricket that revolutionised the delivery and presentation of the game and that dramatically expanded the live and broadcast audiences of the sport. One-day cricket was developed for this purpose as a shorter, more exciting version of the traditional five-day game. The rule structure for international cricket was modified to include one innings per team, with each innings restricted to 50 overs (300 deliveries), therefore guaranteeing a result. A number of specific rules were introduced to encourage the batsmen to score runs quickly and play powerful shots to the boundary, thereby transforming a slow-paced game into an intense and entertaining sport. For instance, the one-day international (ODI) 'wide ball' rule states that the bowler is not allowed to pitch the ball deep on the leg side of the wicket, where run-scoring opportunities are limited. Field placement restrictions require the fielding team to place only two fieldsmen in the outfield for the first 15 overs to encourage attacking shot-making in the early part of each innings. The traditional elements of cricket competition were also modified for the purposes of the World Series. White player uniforms were replaced by coloured team uniforms, day/night games were introduced with the second innings played under floodlights and a white ball replaced the red ball to improve visibility for spectators and television audiences. These innovations have considerably altered the entertainment value of the sport. One consequence has been a significant expansion of traditional cricket spectator markets that now includes casual sport spectators and tourists. ODI cricket remains the leading edge of innovation in the sport of cricket. Many of the innovations of one-day cricket, such as the video umpire and use of floodlights when poor light would otherwise require play to be suspended, have subsequently been applied to the five-day game to enhance its spectator appeal.

Management Implications and Opportunities

Although the pool of specialised sport tourism professionals is growing, the majority of people currently working in this area tend to be qualified primarily within the disciplines of either sport or tourism. Notwithstanding the tendency for professionals to identify primarily with one or the other of the parent disciplines, it is important for managers to consciously consider the perspective of the 'other' partner. By doing so, sport and tourism professionals will be in a better position to develop innovative strategies in the pursuit of the mutual benefits of sustainable sport tourism development. Recognising the links between sport and tourism helps to ensure that the context for decision-making will be more conducive for success in sport tourism ventures.

The growing body of literature associated with sport tourism represents a new resource for managers involved in this area. Publications that help conceptualise the field and that provide insights into sport tourists' travel patterns and experiences, are a valuable resource for sport tourism professionals. Increased understanding of sport tourism markets enables managers to be more productive in target marketing and product development. In the context of organisational structure and strategy, the work of Glyptis (1991) and Weed and Bull (1997a) provides managers with useful directions for action. For those managers of organisations charged with capturing the benefits of sport tourism, the study of this literature will provide rich and valuable insights. Finally, given the early stage of development of this body of literature, managers can play a significant role in setting and supporting research agendas. Through their active involvement in research, managers will reap the benefits of an increased understanding of the dynamic field of sport tourism.

Viewing sport as a tourist attraction in its own right represents a major shift for many managers of sport and tourism enterprises. The underlying structure of sport in terms of rules, competition related to physical prowess and playfulness distinguishes it from other types of tourist attractions. Tourism managers can use this perspective to achieve a competitive advantage. For example, the uncertainty associated with sport competition outcomes provides significant advantages in terms of authenticity relative to many other types of tourism experiences. Similarly, in viewing their products as tourism attractions, sport managers can consciously tap into markets beyond their traditional geographic catchment areas. Targeted promotions that correspond to primary, secondary and tertiary levels of the attraction hierarchy are likely to be significantly more successful than the traditional approach of treating non-local sport patrons as a single homogeneous group.

Conclusion

Sport and tourism are closely related in terms of practice. Tourists participate in sports while on their travels and spectators and athletes travel in search for competition or in pursuit of their sporting passions. Despite the obvious overlap between sport and tourism, little is known about the dynamics of this relationship. Systematic advances in this realm will be greatly aided by focused study in the area of sport tourism in place of the *ad hoc* treatment of the subject that has characterised past activity in the parent disciplines of sport and tourism. Justification for a more focused approach lies in the fact that sport is a unique type of tourist attraction. This is demonstrated through the application of Leiper's (1990) tourism attraction system to the study of sport. The definition of sport tourism adopted for this book is consistent with this attraction orientation. It allows for the unique aspects of sport to be articulated in terms of the human element, nucleus and markers of a tourist attraction. By using this attraction framework it is possible to demonstrate 'what sport tourism shares with, and what distinguishes it from other touristic activities' (Green & Chalip, 1998: 276), which is a primary aim of this book. The book does this by focusing on the process of sport tourism development, which should, in part, address calls for increased theoretical foundations in sport tourism research.

Further Reading

Given its status as an emerging area of study, much attention has been directed towards defining the concept of sport tourism and to justifying its relevance as a subject of dedicated research. Three key publications in this context include Kurtzman and Zauhar's (1997b) article advocating study in this area, Gibson's (1998a) critical review of the sport tourism literature and Hinch and Higham's (2001) discussion of sport tourism research frameworks. Alternative definitions are reviewed and articulated in all of these articles, with McPherson *et al.*'s (1989) sociologically based perspective of sport being particularly influential to the way sport tourism is addressed in this book. Academic justification for focused study in this area is based on sport's significance as a tourist attraction. Leiper's (1990) seminal article on tourist attraction systems provides the fundamental framework on which this argument is based. Finally, the work of Weed and Bull (1997a) is essential reading for students and practitioners who want to know the potential management implications of the study of sport tourism. These authors clearly articulate the need to align policy, practice and the study of sport tourism.

Case study 2.1

Sport Tourism Education

Sean Gammon, University of Luton, UK

There has been a proliferation of sport tourism courses and awards being initiated over the past few years in Australia, New Zealand, the USA, Canada, the UK and continental Europe. Modules and short programmes are easier to justify and defend than specialised degree programmes at undergraduate and postgraduate levels. Degree programmes require a more extensive and persuasive rationale. Institutions that plan to implement sport tourism awards must prepare carefully considered and detailed proposals. This Case study explains the development of a BA (Hons) Sport Tourism programme at the University of Luton (United Kingdom) in 1998 as well as the curricular developments since that time. The BA (Hons) Sport Tourism degree was developed within the Department of Tourism and Leisure, University of Luton, which offers undergraduate and graduate courses in sports and leisure management, international tourism management, sport and fitness studies, sport development, sport marketing and travel and tourism.

Demonstrated Research and Publication

As with any subject, the amount of experience the teaching and support team has in delivering related courses, together with their overall research experience, can not only aid in moulding the degree structure, but can also help in achieving a successful validation. External examiners critically consider the research profile of the academic staff and their publication records in sport tourism and related fields. However, it is just as important to resist disciplinary protectionism, while emphasising the collaborative strengths of an institution in terms of theoretical cross-fertilisation. One of the dominant features of sport tourism is its multidisciplinary nature (Gammon & Kurtzman, 2002; Gibson, 2002). The academic staff involved in the validation of the Luton programme in 1998 had backgrounds in leisure, tourism, sport, sociology, psychology, anthropology, philosophy, management and business. Such involvement subsequently led to numerous collaborative projects and the inclusion and interest in the subject from non-sport tourism students.

Decide on a Name

The name of the award should be indicative of its contents and reflect the school/faculty in which it is situated – though at present there appears to be a predominance of programmes with a management or business focus (Swart, 2000). What is less certain is whether to use the term *sport* or *sports* in the title. Today, the terms are often used interchangeably and, although this is not a problem in itself, it does suggest a lack of subject uniformity, cohesiveness and, perhaps, academic credibility. Sport tourism was used in the title of the Luton award first to set some form of precedence and second to denote the nature of the programme. It should be appreciated that, although quite similar on the surface, the two terms have different meanings:

> Sports Tourism focuses upon competitive sporting travel, whereas the term Sport Tourism is a far broader concept which embraces sport as being both recreational as well as competitive; both institutionalised and transitory (Gammon & Robinson, 1999: 2).

Clear Rationale

Given the strong vocational/professional character of sport tourism, it is advantageous to get support from as many sport tourism-related organisations in the private and public sectors as possible. In today's economic and political environments it is vital not only to highlight the academic nature of the subject, but also to identify a market for graduates of the programme in terms of related career opportunities.

The rationale behind the development of the award at the University of Luton was ostensibly driven as a reaction to, and recognition of, the growth in sport-related tourism, along with the dearth of a suitably qualified workforce in this field. However, it was also an opportunity to extend the educational and career options for those students already taking Leisure and Tourism diplomas (UK). Usually students completing these courses would have to make a decision to either specialise in a sport- or tourism-related degree programme. The Sport Tourism BA therefore not only met with the usual academic requirements for new programmes, but also filled an important gap in the market. It was seen as a way to pool resources and expertise from the two already successful, yet seemingly disparate, fields – a relationship that has since proved to be extremely fruitful.

Each specific field, school or faculty will have its own strengths and rationales built around more corporate aims and objectives. The following points, however, were critical to the successful validation of the Luton programme:

- Highlight the growth in the practice of sport tourism and emphasise that educational institutions have not kept pace with the needs of the industry. Trained graduates who understand both sport and tourism are required if the needs of sport tourists are to be met.
- Show industry support for course content and confirmation of career paths.

- Identify sport tourism as a growing area of research activity.
- Identify the relevant research publications of prospective staff.
- Where possible, indicate subject interest through currently taught free-standing related modules and courses.
- Show success in managing related subjects (e.g. recreation, leisure, sport, tourism, etc.)
- Identify other institutions which successfully offer similar programmes and, where possible, obtain their support.
- Resist the protection of specific disciplinary interests as the multidisciplinary nature of the teaching/research team is a major asset.
- Highlight the popularity of leisure and tourism diplomas. In the UK, students completing leisure and tourism awards at college have to make a choice as to which subject they want to specialise in at university.
- Finally, communicate that the philosophical concept of people being brought together through tourism and sport will lead to a greater understanding of cultures and societies. Such programmes can be used to advance institutional goals related to internationalisation.

Further reading

Gammon, S. and Robinson, T. (1999) The development and design of the sport tourism curricula with particular references to the BA (Hons) Sport Tourism degree at the University of Luton. *Journal of Sport Tourism* 5 (2), 17–26.

Chapter 3
Sport Tourism Markets

Research into who is a sport tourist, and why sport tourists engage in this sort of tourism may prove to be more complex than is first apparent.

(Gibson, 1998a: 57)

Introduction

Delpy (1997: 4) states that a 'travel market focused entirely on partici-pating or watching sport is a unique and exciting concept'. Sport tourism is widely viewed as a niche sector for the tourism industry (Common-wealth Department of Industry, Science and Resources, 2000) that may be targeted to broaden the suite of visitor markets that are attracted to a destination (Bull & Weed, 1999). Sport tourism is a market that may be approached generically, as demonstrated by the mass tourism promotion of major sporting events. The reality, however, is that sport tourism is comprised of a diverse range of niche markets (Maier & Weber, 1993; Collins & Jackson, 2001). Chalip (2001) observes that many Australian cities targeted specific market segments during the lead up to the 2000 Olympic Games (Case study 3.1; see pp. 52–54). Indeed, Bull and Weed (1999: 143) also explain that

> sport tourism is really a collection of separate niches but while tourism associated with mega-sporting events . . . in major urban loca-tions is clearly evident, the potential of sport as a tourism niche elsewhere is perhaps less well appreciated.

Understanding sport tourist markets is an important aspect of the foundation for sport tourism development. Important questions include 'Who are sport tourists?', 'What factors motivate sport tourists?', 'To what extent do motivations differ between distinct groups of sport tourists?' and 'What travel experiences do sport tourists seek in association with the sports that they pursue at a given destination?' Addressing these ques-tions will provide valuable insights into niche market segments, and the basis for making market segmentation decisions. Market analysis, then, is critical to the effective development of sport tourism within the context of regional, national or international tourism destinations. The first part of this chapter discusses conceptual approaches to the classification of sport tourist types. This is followed by an examination of sport tourism niche markets and the means by which these markets are effectively segmented.

Conceptualising Demand for Sport Tourism

Conceptualising sport tourism is a useful starting point in the study of sport tourism markets. The distinction between spectatorship and physical participation, for example, is a fundamental difference that merits consideration. Glyptis (1989, 1991) introduced the terms 'general dabbler' and 'specialist' to describe different levels of tourist engagement in participant and spectator sports. Hall (1992b) also identified two types of active sport tourists: 'activity participants', who regard their participation as a medium of self-expression, and 'players', who are competitive in their participation. The distinction between 'sport-orientated holidays' and 'less sport-orientated holidays' is the conceptual basis for the study of sports activities during the outbound holidays of German, Dutch and French conducted by the World Tourism Organization and International Olympic Committee (2001).

Tourists who engage in sports at a destination do so with varying degrees of commitment, competitiveness and active/passive engagement. The sport tourism market may be segmented on these grounds into niche markets or 'demand groups', which differ in many aspects of the visitor experience (Chapter 8). Maier and Weber (1993) identify four demand groups based on the intensity of the sports activities pursued at the destination (Table 3.1). They also describe the unique resource development requirements of each demand group. The resource requirements that top performance athletes seek at a tourism destination relate specifically to the enhancement of performance in sport (e.g. training, sports science, sports medicine facilities). Occasional sports (wo)men and passive sport tourists, stand in significant contrast, given the priority that they also place in the tourist experiences that a destination may offer.

Reeves (2000) identifies six 'types' of sport tourists and explains the distinctions between them in terms of decision-making, motivations, lifestyle and spending profiles (Table 3.2). The diversity that exists within the sport tourism market is, once again, highlighted. However, it should be noted that Reeves's (2000) typology is illustrative rather than definitive. It contains generalisations relating, for instance, to visitor expenditures that require the support of rigorous quantitative market research. Furthermore, autonomy in destination choice may exist for 'driven' athletes based on alternative training philosophies. Despite these

Table 3.1 Sport tourism demand groups and requisite visitor facilities

Demand groups	Visitor demands and required facilities
Top performance athletes	Efficiency is the main aim during holidays. Access to competition and suitable training conditions and facilities are priorities for these travellers. When meeting the priorities of this group, tour organisers and destination managers need to give consideration to specific accommodation and dining demands (e.g. dietary requirements), as well as access to physicians, injury rehabilitation facilities and other performance-related services.
Mass sports	Preserving health and maintaining fitness is the aim of this demand group. Performance targets are individually fixed. The accessibility of holiday regions and the quality of sports facilities are the key considerations for this market segment.
Occasional sports (wo)men	Compensation and prestige play greater roles than sporting ambition in the pursuit of occasional sports. This demand group gives preference to less demanding sports, such as recreational skiing and bowling. Sporting activities receive no greater priority over cultural sightseeing and other interests within this market group.
Passive sports tourists	No individual sports activities are pursued. The focus of this group lies with mega-sports events and distinguished sports sites. Includes coaches and attendants to high-performance athletes, as well as media reporters. Requires high-volume infrastructures to accommodate the needs of large numbers of event sport attendees.

Source: reprinted with permission from Maier and Weber (1993: 38)

limitations, the value of this typology lies in its clear conceptualisation of sport tourist types. It provides marketing professionals with important insights into a range of tourist types that are represented within the sport tourism market.

Gammon and Robinson (1997) advance the conceptualisation of sport tourists based on the motivations held by tourists vis-à-vis their involvement in sport (Table 3.3). Their contribution lies in the distinction between two forms of sport tourism. They use the term 'sport tourism' where sport is the primary travel motivation with other touristic

Table 3.2 Sport tourism types and visitor profiles

Type	Decision-making	Participation	Non-participation	Group profile	Lifestyle	Spending
Incidental	Unimportant	Out of duty	Not relaxing, holiday-like	Family	Sport is significant	Minimal
Sporadic	Relatively important	If convenient	Easily contained/put off	Friends and family	Non-essential	Minimal except for 'one-offs'
Occasional	Sometimes determining	Welcome addition to tourist experience	Other commitments	Often individual, especially business tourists	Conspicuous consumption	High on occasions
Regular	Important	Significant part of enjoyment	Money or time become prohibitive	Group or individual	Important	Considerable
Dedicated	Very important	Central to experience	Due to unforeseen barriers	Individuals and groups of the like-minded	Defining element	Extremely high and consistent
Driven	Very important, but little autonomy	Sole reason	Through injury or fear of it	Elite groups or solitary	The profession	Extremely high but funded by others

Source: after Reeves (2000)

Table 3.3 Conceptualisation of sport tourists based on sport and travel motivations

Sport tourism	Individuals and/or groups of people who actively or passively participate in competitive or recreational sport while travelling. Sport is the prime motivation to travel, although the touristic element may reinforce the overall experience.
Hard definition	Active or passive participation in a competitive sporting event. Sport is the prime motivational reason for travel (e.g. Olympic Games, Wimbledon, London Marathon).
Soft definition	Active recreational participation in a sporting/leisure interest (e.g. skiing, walking, hiking, kayaking).
Tourism sport	Active or passive participation in competitive or recreational sport as a secondary activity. The holiday or visit, rather than the sport, is the prime travel motivation.
Hard definition	Competitive or non-competitive sport as an important secondary motivation that enriches the travel experience (e.g. sports cruises, health and fitness clubs).
Soft definition	Competitive or non-competitive sport or leisure as a purely incidental element of the holiday experience (e.g. minigolf, indoor bowls, ice-skating, squash).

Source: reprinted with permission from Gammon and Robinson (1997: 10–11)

activities an important, but secondary, element of the tourist experience. In the case of 'tourism sport', sport is the secondary or incidental component of the tourist experience. This conceptualisation complements the discussion of the tourism attraction hierarchy presented in Chapter 2. Gammon and Robinson (1997) also distinguish between active and passive involvement in competitive and non-competitive sports. Therefore, both 'sport tourism' and 'tourism sport' may be defined in terms of hard and soft participation. The distinction between the two lies in the seriousness with which travellers engage in their chosen sports. This conceptual framework captures the diversity of the sport tourism travel market, which varies along scales of participation and competitiveness, and where sport may function as a primary, secondary or purely incidental travel motivation.

Gammon and Robinson (1997), therefore, identify three dimensions that highlight the variation that exists within the demand-side of sport tourism. They include the status of the sport activity in the motivation profile of the tourist (primary, secondary or incidental), the level of involvement in the sport activity (active or passive) and the competitive or non-competitive nature of the sport activity. In doing so, they contribute to a better understanding of sport tourism consumer markets, which provides insights into the distinct sport- and tourism-related services and experiences required by each.

It is the extent to which sporting activities are pursued by tourists that forms the basis of Standeven and De Knop's (1999) conceptual classification (Table 3.4). The sport activity holiday segment of Standeven and De Knop's classification illustrates the diversity of the sport tourism market. Single sport activity holidays comprise those who seek to engage in

Table 3.4 Sport tourism activities classification

Classification	*Examples*
Sport activity holidays: Single-sport activity holidays Multiple-sport activity holidays	skiing, cycling, trekking sports camps, holiday clubs (e.g. Club Méditerranée)
Holiday sport activities: Organised holiday sport activities Independent holiday sport activities	golf, rafting, cruise ship sport activities adventure activities (e.g. bungee jumping)
Passive sports on holidays: Connoisseur observer Casual observers	Olympic Games, Masters golf, Wimbledon tennis championship, Kentucky Derby, museums, halls of fame, stadium tours hurling (Ireland), Thai Boxing (Thailand), Bull Fighting (Spain)
Active sports during non-holiday time	training camps, recreational sport during business and conference travel
Passive sports during non-holiday time	dragon boat racing spectatorship while in Hong Kong on business

Source: based on Standeven and De Knop (1999)

specific sports, such as downhill skiing, cross-country skiing or snow-boarding. The wider touristic element of the destination may carry little sway in the travel decision process in these instances. This market stands in contrast to the multiple sport activity holidays market for whom opportunities to engage in sporting pursuits are more broad-ranging, casual and less likely to be the sole focus of visitor activity. These, and other segments within this classification, are associated with distinct market characteristics. The terms active and passive are used in this classification in reference to sport participation and non-participation respectively. This should not be confused with other forms of active involvement in sport tourism, such as team management and officiating. Furthermore, in some sports, spectators are encouraged to be active in the support of a competitor or team (e.g. the 'Mexican wave', banner competitions, inter-session contests) as a means of generating atmosphere at stadia and other sports venues.

Redmond's (1990) tripartite sport tourism classification includes sport vacations, multi-sport festivals and world championships, as well as sports halls of fame and museums. Gibson's (1998a) literature-based analysis of sport tourism adopts a similar approach in a general analysis of sport tourism markets. Her classification includes active, event and nostalgia sport tourism. This schema serves as the framework for the following discussion.

Active Sport Tourism Markets

The active sport tourism market is constituted of individuals who pursue physical involvement in competitive or non-competitive sports while travelling. A number of recently published articles examine the active sport tourism market (Green & Chalip, 1998; Yusof & Douvis, 2001; WTO & IOC, 2001). However, Gibson (1998a: 53) notes that active sport tourism market research is generally 'scarce, usually descriptive and typically atheoretical'. In 1992, Gibson and Yiannakis introduced the term 'sportlover' to describe the growing travel market represented by individuals who are physically active and prefer to remain so while on holiday (Gibson & Yiannakis, 1992). More recently, Delpy (1998) profiled the active sport tourist as physically active, college-educated, relatively affluent and 18–44 years old. Such a generalised approach fails to capture the diversity of the market segments that exist in active sport tourism. In fact, numerous approaches to segmenting the active sport tourism market are evident, but not clearly stated, in the empirical research literature. These studies may be organised under the approaches to market segmentation identified by Swarbrooke and Horner (1999) as geographic, socio-economic, demographic and psychographic.

Geographic market segmentation

Geographic segmentation of the active sport tourism market, based on visitor origins or market location, is an effective approach to the study of sport tourism. The geography of sport establishes the link between place of residence and opportunities to engage in certain sports in specified locations (Bale, 1989; Rooney & Pillsbury, 1992). Proximity to sports resources, be they natural (e.g. surf beaches), built (e.g. sports stadia), or a combination of the two (e.g. ski resorts), bears upon the propensity to consume certain sports as competitors, participants and/or spectators. The link between nationality and patterns of sport participation is also well established. For instance, considerable differences exist in the sport activities engaged in by outbound tourists from Germany, the Netherlands and France (WTO & IOC, 2001). Sport-related trips account for over 50% of all outbound travel undertaken by German and Dutch nationals, compared to 23% in the case of French outbound travellers. These markets also support segmentation on the basis of 'sport-orientated' and 'less sport-oriented' holiday preferences. The former is the general preference of Dutch travellers. The latter, which involves holidays where active involvement in sport is a secondary rather than the primary point of the holiday, is the preference of 85% of French travellers. Geographic segmentation is based on important differences in the preferred destinations, tourist activities, spending patterns and travel seasons of the study groups:

> Three types of sport-orientated holidays – summer sport holidays, winter sport holidays, mountain holidays – enjoyed similar popularity among French and Dutch travellers. Germans preferred mountain holidays (43%) to summer holidays (19%). Skiing and hiking/walking were most popular activities among winter sport holidaymakers and mountain sport travellers, respectively. In the case of summer sport holidays, French travellers favoured diving/snorkelling, whereas Dutch and German travellers were keen on walking/hiking. (WTO & IOC, 2001: 4)

Patterns of active sport tourism participation can also be generalised at a national level. The largest single segment of the New Zealand domestic travel market identified by Lawson *et al.* (1997) was labelled 'sports devotees'. This segment represents 21% of the New Zealand domestic travel market, and its members are generally motivated by participation in sports at the tourist destination. The value of studies like this is enhanced when positioned alongside the results of national sport and physical activity surveys (Walker, 2001), which report current patterns of participation and trends in the popularity of sports. Such exercises provide sport and tourism managers with rich veins of information relating to the increasing intersection between, and changing patterns of, sport participation and travel preferences.

Socio-economic market segmentation

Socio-economic market segmentation is based upon variables like occupation and income. Participation in inexpensive, team-based contact sports like street basketball and baseball are typical of lower socio-economic urban youth in North America and Cuba (Thomson, 2000). Expensive, individual and non-contact sports are favoured by the upper social classes (Yiannakis, 1975). Booth and Loy (1999: 10) argue that 'sports such as golf, tennis, sailing, show jumping and skiing . . . reflect the upper class's unique aesthetic and ethical dimensions, temporal/spatial orientations, material and symbolic status signs'. These consumers of sport are 'free to play sport at midday, mid-week or out of season (by travelling to the opposite hemisphere), and . . . have the resources to play in exclusive and secluded places: cloisters, country clubs and lodges, and private game reserves' (Booth & Loy, 1999: 11).

Demographic market segmentation

Swarbrooke and Horner (1999: 95) confirm that 'segmentation based on subdividing the population on the basis of demographic factors has proved particularly popular in tourism'. The demographic profiling of sport tourism markets in North America shows, for instance, that active participation in sports varies on the basis of age (Loverseed, 2001). The most popular participation sports in the USA in 2000 included recreational swimming (94%), recreational walking (83%) and bowling (74%). Activities such as fitness walking, treadmill exercises and stretching, and sports such as golf and fishing, are the preference of the seniors market (55 years and older), while basketball, soccer and baseball are favoured by the youth market (6–17 years).

Socio-demographic variables often serve as a second step in sport tourism market segmentation. Tokarski's (1993) study of holiday clubs in Caldetas and Fuerteventura (Spain) and Corfu (Greece) highlights significant differences within the German sport tourism market that exist on the basis of age. Young German travellers (15–21 years) identified good weather, relaxation and sports activities as important factors in a successful holiday. Water sports such as swimming, surfing, water-skiing and diving held strong appeal for the youth market. The married and family travel markets were less inclined to actively engage in sports while on vacation, but the German senior market demonstrates a propensity to rediscover their interests in actively engaging in sporting activities (Tokarski, 1993).

Gibson *et al.* (1998) provide one of the more detailed demographic analyses of the active sport tourism market from a lifespan perspective. They profile the active sport tourist market in the early adulthood (17–39 years), middle adulthood (40–59 years) and late adulthood (60–91) life stages. While active sport tourism proved to be pursued particularly by those in early adulthood, 'a sizeable number of both men and women choose sport orientated vacations in middle and late adulthood as well' (Gibson *et al.*, 1998: 52). They, like Tokarski (1993) and Harahousou (1999), identify physical activity among people in late adulthood as an increasingly apparent trend. The active sport tourism market is also influenced by changes in societal conventions regarding female participation in sports. Gibson *et al.* (1998: 54) state that 'the subject of gender and sport is full of examples showing how gender-typed social expectations affect women's participation in sport and physical activity'. This situation is emerging from historical male domination of sport participation, particularly professional sports, due to changing societal ideologies about the gender-appropriateness of many sports (Wiley *et al.*, 2000). Pitts (1997: 32) also contributes to the demographic study of sport tourists. She profiles the gay and lesbian sport tourism niche market, describing it as a 'recognised . . . viable, potentially lucrative, chic and high brand loyal market'.

Psychographic market segmentation

Psychographic studies are founded on the premise that 'the lifestyle, attitudes, opinions and personality of people determine their behaviour as consumers' (Swarbrooke & Horner, 1999: 96). For example, the psychographic profile of *sport-for-all* participants differs from those who pursue technical challenge or competition through active involvement in sports. The defining criteria of sport-for-all include the absence of entry qualifications, championship prizes and competition between participants (Nogawa *et al.*, 1996). Instead, 'sport-for-all . . . emphasises the joy of sport participation and health-related fitness while de-emphasising excessive competition. The concept of a sport-for-all event is that every participant is a winner' (Nogawa *et al.*, 1996: 47). The active sport tourism market can be effectively segmented based on the differences between sport-for-all participants and their more competitive counterparts.

Active participation in some sports may also be associated with distinctive subcultures that are an expression of identity (Green & Chalip, 1998). Wheaton (2000) examined one such subculture in her ethnographic study of windsurfing. She observed that the emergence of new and individualised leisure sports, such as windsurfing, snowboarding and mountain biking, represents 'much more than . . . intermittent recreation; participants are involved in a multi-layered leisure subculture' (Wheaton, 2000: 256). Subcultures such as these are expressed in various ways, including life choices such as career, work time, place of residence and tourist destination preferences. Similar conclusions have been made in the case of snowboarding (Heino, 2000). Both studies suggest that the values associated with individual sports can be instrumental in shaping the attitudes and personalities of participants (Chapter 6). Less organised and regulated sports, such as beach volleyball, street basketball, touch rugby and skateboarding 'emphasise values such as excitement, spontaneity, rebellion, non-conformity, sociability and creativity, and these are assuming considerable importance within the context of youth culture' (Thomson, 2000: 34).

The psychographic profile of sport tourists also evolves over time. Donnelly and Young (1988) identify career stages that characterise subcultural identities. Such studies 'highlight the utility of leveraging event consumers' identification with a sport's subculture when promoting sports events' (Green & Chalip, 1998: 288). Indeed Green and Chalip (1998) propose that active sport tourists may give priority to sharing and affirming their identities over the competitive element of their participation in sport. An understanding of the psychographic profile of these niche markets, then, is of great managerial as well as academic relevance.

Behaviouristic market segmentation

This avenue of segmentation classifies consumers according to their behavioural relationship with a product (Swarbrooke & Horner, 1999), with implications for the visitor experience (Chapter 8). Millington *et al.* (2001), for example, profile the growing number of participants in adventure tourism, dividing the market based on soft (e.g. cycling, canoeing, horse riding) and hard (e.g. rafting, kayaking, climbing, caving) adventure activities. These adventure sports can be further differentiated based on the behaviours of participants. Downhill mountain bike racing and white water kayaking are extreme versions of sport that appeal to segments of the sport tourism market. They can be segmented based on the motivations and behaviours of participants, and then profiled demographically (Millington *et al.*, 2001). The link between motivation and behaviour, which is well established in the sport and recreation literature (E. L. Jackson, 1989), is of high relevance to sport tourism. It is important for destination marketers to understand the motivational and behavioural profiles of sport tourism market segments. They determine the desired visitor experience and the secondary activity sets that are associated with members of specific tourism market segments (Nogawa *et al.*, 1996).

The sport of skiing provides an illustration of the varied motivations and behaviours that exist within the tourist market (Klenosky *et al.*, 1993). Richards (1996), for instance, analysed the extent to which British skiers are motivated by technical challenge and the enhancement of skiing ability. This research identified a market segment that pursued and was stimulated by challenging skiing experiences. The quality of ski conditions and varied terrain were found to be fundamental to the experiences sought by this market segment (Richards, 1996). By contrast, the decision-making process of less experienced skiers was influenced more by price and accommodation. Participants in scuba diving (Tabata, 1992) and sport fishing (Roehl *et al.*, 1993) give increasing priority to the quality of the sport over other aspects of the visitor experience as they become more proficient in their sports. These studies confirm that the motivational and behavioural profiles of the sport tourist may be of greater relevance to sport and tourism managers than other approaches to market analysis.

Event Sport Tourism Markets

Event sport tourism, in its most prominent guise, involves travel to experience sporting events, where the body of spectators usually outweighs a small number of typically elite competitors (Getz, 1998). The most widely researched examples of event sport tourism include the Olympic Games, the Soccer World Cup, the Rugby World Cup and the Formula One Grand Prix. However, sports competition may or may not be the primary attraction of a sports event. The Wimbledon lawn tennis championship may be attended for its heritage and traditional value, the America's Cup for reasons of fashion and exclusivity, and the Superbowl for commercial and business purposes. Large-scale spectator sports events may, then, attract tourists for whom the sporting competition is a coincidental or secondary factor in their attendance. This suggests that the approaches to market segmentation to which reference has been made (Swarbrooke & Horner, 1999) are also applicable to the event sport tourism market, an exercise that requires further empirical research than currently exists. Getz (1998: 8) correctly points out that a 'more comprehensive, systematic research effort is needed to answer key questions such as who is the sport-event tourist'.

Much research in this field focuses on large scale spectator events. However, this is only a partial picture of the relationship between spectators and participants in event sport tourism. Event sport tourism includes non-elite competitor events, where the number of competitors may be large and the number of spectators negligible or non-existent (Figure 3.1). Exceptions to this general rule do exist where non-elite events attract large numbers of family and friends as spectators (Carmichael & Murphy, 1996). In some instances elite and non-elite competitors are accommodated in a single event, which creates a broad catchment range of elite athletes, spectators and non-elite competitors. The London, New York and Boston marathons provide evidence of the success of such events. The relation-

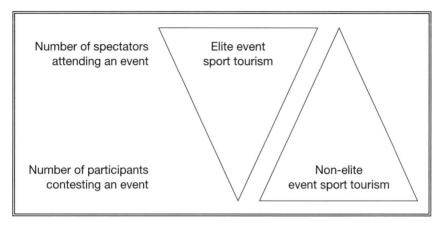

Figure 3.1 Conceptualisation of the relative engagement of spectators and participants in elite and non-elite sport contests

ship between participation and spectatorship in event sport tourism deserves more academic attention. These distinct forms of event sport tourism justify separate analysis as the markets, promotional possibilities, infrastructure requirements, tourist behaviours, travel patterns, and associated tourist experiences of each may stand in significant contrast.

Elite event sport tourism

Numerous avenues of tourism development may be associated with elite sport events. Faulkner *et al.* (1998: 1) emphasise the need for sport and tourism authorities to establish a set of conditions to ensure that this potential is captured. In a study of the 2000 Olympic Games they state:

> [I]n reality, there are both tourism opportunities that can be derived from hosting the games and offsetting negative effects, and the degree to which the former are accentuated and the latter ameliorated ultimately depends on the extent to which the leveraging strategies adopted by the industry and relevant public agencies are effectively integrated. (Faulker *et al.*, 1998: 1)

The build-up to the Sydney 2000 Olympic Games involved a coordinated leveraging programme to which both sport and tourism administrators actively contributed. The outcome was effective destination promotion, successful pre-Games training and acclimatisation camps, the stimulation of convention and incentive travel, the promotion of pre- and post-Games travel itineraries and the minimisation of diversion and aversion effects (Faulkner *et al.*, 1998). Leveraging elite sports events requires a clear understanding of the tourism development opportunities that exist beyond Games-induced travel. Indeed, recent Olympic Games have been studied to forecast and/or measure Games-induced travel (Pyo *et al.*, 1991; Kang & Perdue, 1991). Such studies have generally overestimated levels of visitation and, as Faulkner *et al.* (1998: 10) observe, 'once the normal level of travel to the host city is factored in to estimates the net effect of games induced travel is much reduced'.

It is important to acknowledge the diversion effects (real or perceived) which are often fostered by media attention paid to capacity constraints at the host destination (e.g. traffic congestion, over-demand for accommodation, inflated costs, security issues). Pyo *et al.* (1991) identify a range of factors that may discourage attendance at summer Olympic Games, including political boycotting, price gouging, crowding and congestion. Ticket distribution may also bear upon the propensity of sport tourists to attend events such as the Olympic Games (Thamnopoulos & Gargialianos, 2002). Chalip *et al.* (1998) present an analysis of sources of interest in travel to attend the Olympic Games. Such analyses provide valuable insights into the relative importance of the event itself, and of the destination hosting the event, in terms of the travel decision-making process. These studies offer information that is critical to the successful leveraging of sports events.

Sport tourism markets vary from one event to another. However, useful generalisations are possible. For example, Faulkner *et al.* (1998) employ the term 'sport junkies' to describe tourists who visit a destination specifically to attend a sporting event, but demonstrate little propensity to engage in pre- and post-event itineraries. This term describes a sport tourism market that is single-mindedly focused on the sport event itself. The Formula One Grand Prix racing championship is considered to generally attract this type of tourist. Not only are the tourists who come to this type of event likely to displace other types of tourists at a destination, they may be associated with specific negative impacts that are unique to this market segment (Faulkner *et al.*, 1998).

Alternatively, sport spectators may engage in a more casual relationship with the sports that they follow. In these cases 'general interest and match attendance can shift in response to wins and losses, the state of the venue, the appearance of star players and a change in the weather' (B. Stewart, 2001: 17). Casual consumers of sport present sport markets with unique challenges associated with accessing this element of sport tourism demand. The importance of studying and understanding the travel motivations and wider pre- and post-event itineraries of sport tourists emerges clearly from these studies. The leveraging of sport tourism events requires consideration of the sport and tourism product at the destination, supply and demand for sports facilities and services, and tourism experiences before, during and after the event (Faulkner *et al.*, 1998).

Non-elite event sport tourism

Bale (1989: 114) observes that 'even quite small sporting events can generate substantial amounts of revenue for the communities within which they are located' (Focus point 3.1). Destinations that are unable to host large-scale sporting events due to capacity constraints may compete to attract competitive but non-elite sport tourism events (Higham, 1999). Chogahara and Yamaguchi (1998), for example, report on the National Sports Festival for the Elderly (Japan). This study identifies that participants tend to engage in a wide range of tourist activities, particularly sightseeing and visiting hot spas both during and following the completion of the event. This study confirms that those who participate in less competitive sports events are more likely to take advantage of opportunities to engage in tourist activities at a destination. Little is known about

---

Focus point 3.1

Non-elite Event Sport Tourism in New Zealand

The 1995 Golden Oldies Rugby Festival hosted by Christchurch (New Zealand) attracted teams from 28 countries to a unique sporting celebration. The 'golden oldies' sport philosophy is one that promotes the fun, friendship and fraternity associated with recreational sports. It is one that provides opportunities for sports enthusiasts to travel with their families and team-mates, renew acquaintances, create new friendships and experience tourist destinations that they might otherwise not visit. In 1995, the two-week festival took place during the New Zealand tourist shoulder season, attracting 124 teams and 5000 participants. Similarly, in 1999 the New Zealand Masters Games, a biennial sports event, attracted 7000 high-yielding active sport tourists as competitors from around New Zealand to the city of Dunedin. This event has in recent years increasingly attracted competitors from overseas. Its seasonal scheduling contributes to the mitigation of a period of low domestic tourist activity in the host city. In 2002, the Masters Soccer World Cup was jointly hosted by several New Zealand cities. The scale of the event was appropriate to the secondary centres that hosted games. The active sport tourists who participated in this event were found to place little pressure on tourism infrastructure and required no development of sports facilities specifically to host the event. Their participation in the event took place in association with a wide range of other touristic activities. These examples confirm that non-elite sports events of moderate scale and extended duration may, in many cases, attract high-spending visitors during the tourist low season, and be combined effectively with secondary tourist activities in the destination region (Moore, 1995; McMurran, 1999).

the travel preferences of participants who form the less competitive element of the event sport tourism market. This niche market is characterised by travel motivations that are distinct from elite and competitive event participants. It is a market that presents unique opportunities to generate business opportunities for other tourist attractions and services within a destination.

The distinction between elite and non-elite event sport tourism is important (Figure 3.1). Carmichael and Murphy (1996) suggest that event sport tourists should be differentiated on the basis of spectatorship and participation, the latter including athletes, officials and coaches. Their study provides insights into visitor origin, length of stay, expenditure patterns, numbers of friends and relatives accompanying participants and their intentions to return to the town hosting the event. This points towards the tourist motivations that distinguish those who attend elite sports events, and those who travel to participate in non-elite sports competitions (Chapter 8).

Nostalgia Sport Tourism

Within Gibson's (1998a) classification framework, nostalgia sport tourism is the least researched and understood. This form of sport tourism includes tourist visitation to sport museums, halls of fame, themed bars and restaurants, heritage events and sports reunions. Nostalgia sport tourism is a rapidly developing sector of the sport tourism industry, but one that has hitherto been developed almost exclusively in North America. Stevens (2001: 68–69) notes that, in the UK, sports-based visitor attractions

> are limited to museums at Manchester United, Chelsea, Liverpool, Bolton, Aston Villa and Arsenal football clubs, the recently opened National Football Museum in Preston, the Wimbledon Tennis Museum, the Newmarket Horse Racing Museum and British Golf Museum that opened at St Andrews in 1990.

This short list pales alongside Redmond's (1990) extensive listing of sports museums in North America.

Gammon (2002) discusses the commercialisation of the past in tourism and relates this to sport tourism. He documents the growth of nostalgia sport tourism with reference to the mature sport nostalgia industry in North America (Redmond, 1990; Gibson, 2002). The resource base for nostalgia sport tourism focuses particularly on halls of fame and sport museums. While the former venerate the famous, the gifted or the exceptional, the latter contain collections of artefacts and memorabilia that celebrate a sport, rather than high-performing individuals or teams within a sport (Gammon, 2002). The growth in demand for nostalgia sport tourism is not yet reflected in a published body of research on this topic.

Nostalgia represents an avenue of sport tourism that demonstrates parallels with heritage tourism (Redmond, 1990). Bale (1989) notes that sport edifices may develop such a mystique that they become subjects of visitor attention in their own right. Examples of sports venues that are the subject of interest among nostalgia sport tourists include Wembley Stadium and the Wimbledon Lawn Tennis Club (London), the Athens (1896) and Berlin (1936) Olympic Stadia and the Holmenkollen ski jump (Oslo) (Bale, 1989). Numerous questions relating to the nostalgia sport tourism market currently remain unanswered. The need exists to understand why people engage in this form of tourism and how nostalgia relates to other forms of tourism and sport tourism at a destination. The focus of research in this field has hitherto examined resources for nostalgia sport tourism (Redmond, 1990), rather than the people who actually engage in this form of sport tourism (Gammon, 2002). How nostalgia sport tourism relates to demand for active and event sport tourism experience is also poorly understood. It is likely that this form of sport tourism has indistinct boundaries with active and event sport tourism. Travel packages that follow the tour matches of an international sports team, and which are often led by former star players, illustrate the overlap between event and nostalgia sport tourism. Similarly, cruise ship packages that offer passengers the opportunity to meet, or be coached by, sports personalities (Gibson, 1998a), hold elements of both active sport tourism and nostalgia.

Management Implications and Opportunities

The study of sport tourism markets raises important issues and opportunities in the fields of sport and tourism management. The active sport tourism market is comparatively well understood. Insights into changing patterns of participation in recreation and sports are achieved through the collection of census data and national sports surveys. So, too, are patterns of participation and inequities in access to sports, as they vary in terms of age, class, gender and race (Gibson, 1998c; Booth & Loy, 1999). This stands in contrast to the sporting preferences of visitors to a destination, which remain poorly understood. The collection of visitor data in surveys administered by national or regional tourism organisations rarely extends to the sporting interests of tourists. As a direct consequence, sports managers are generally unaware of the sports market potential of visitors to a destination. The same point applies equally to destination managers seeking to diversify the tourism product at a destination by tapping into growing demand for sport tourism experiences (Bull & Weed, 1999). A platform of market information is fundamental to the development of sport tourism at a destination. It is also a starting point from which an in-depth understanding of niche sport tourism markets may be developed.

Sports managers would also benefit from a more detailed under-standing of the diversity that exists within event sport tourism markets. Effectively leveraging the tourism potential of elite sports events, and developing event sport tourism markets, requires such an understanding. Changing the sport product to enhance the status of the sport as a tourist attraction (through rule changes, packaging and scheduling, for example) can generate new sport tourism markets, or expand existing markets (Higham & Hinch, 2003). The development or upgrading of sports facil-ities may be an effective strategy to access new markets for event sport tourism. These include the female, mature, family and corporate markets from local and non-local origins. Avenues of sport marketing that tradi-tionally centre on local and domestic sports markets can also be expanded or redirected to embrace international tourists visiting a destination as casual consumers of sport.

The profiling of sport tourists is an important step in segmenting the sport tourism market, thereby enabling niche markets to be identified and targeted. An understanding of the specific motivations and needs of niche markets is critical to the sport and tourism industries. Motivations to engage in sport tourism are complex, as Gibson (1998a: 57) notes: 'Research into who is a sport tourist, and why sport tourists engage in this sort of tourism may prove to be more complex than is first apparent'. The motivations, travel behaviours and tourist experiences differ markedly between sport tourism market segments based on partic-ipation and spectatorship (Hall, 1992b; Irwin & Sandler, 1998), levels of competence in a given sport (Richards, 1996) and the seriousness with which participants engage in sports (Green & Chalip, 1998).

Effective tourism management in the field of sport tourism requires an understanding of important points of differentiation within and between niche market segments, as this allows destination managers to match market needs (demand) to the sport tourism resource base at a destina-tion (supply). Furthermore, insights into the relevance of the destination in the travel and destination decision-making processes is important to destination marketers. These insights will improve the effectiveness of promotions that focus on the sporting and/or touristic elements of the visitor experiences to be achieved at a destination. They will also help sport managers to effectively develop products that meet the needs of a broad range of sport tourism niche markets.

Conclusion

This chapter confirms that sport tourism may be accurately conceptu-alised as a specialised market in itself, while also being characterised by numerous niche markets (Bull & Weed, 1999; Chalip, 2001). These niche markets can be differentiated through geographic, socio-economic, demographic, psychographic and behaviouristic segmentation techniques. The managerial relevance of sport tourism market research lies in the diversity of the constituent segments that collectively comprise the sport tourism market. The travel profiles (e.g. length of stay, modes of transport, accommodation preferences) and secondary tourism motivations (e.g. attractions, activities) that these travellers bring to the tourism destination are the subject of tourism market research. Sport and tourism market information pertaining to different niche markets is a prerequisite to the effective development of sport tourism at a destination.

More market research is needed in the realm of sport tourism. The travel motivations and preferences of distinct sport tourism markets, and the tourism development opportunities that they offer, have become subjects of a developing academic literature. Glyptis (1991: 181) observes that sport tourism development necessitates that 'sport and tourism authorities talk to one another and forge real working partnerships'. Detailed insights into sport tourism markets, and the development opportunities associated with these markets, will help to facilitate the establishment of such partnerships.

Further Reading

Varied insights into the diversity of sport tourism market niches are available in the *Journal of Vacation Marketing* (1997) special edition on sport tourism (volume 4, number 1). The various niches that exist within the sport tourism market are introduced by Glyptis (1991), Hall (1992b) and Maier and Weber (1993), and are explored conceptually in different ways by Gammon and Robinson (1997) and Standeven and De Knop (1999). Gibson's (1998a) review of sport tourism event, active and nostalgia market groups is a comprehensive and valuable resource. Examples of specific studies that address market segmentation in the field of sport tourism are provided by Yiannakis (1975), Gibson and Yiannakis (1992), Delpy (1997), Pitts (1997), Gibson *et al.* (1998) and Loverseed (2001).

The roles that sports play in creating and fostering identity is a subject of considerable interest to sport tourism practitioners. Booth and Loy (1999) offer intriguing insights into the historical role of sports in conferring status and inferring style. Green and Chalip (1998, 2001) offer essential readings on the important roles that subculture and identity play in sport tourism, particularly within the realm of participatory sports events. The implications for sport tourism destinations are explored in detail by Chalip (2001) and Bull and Weed (1999). Insights into the value of understanding specific market demands are also provided by Nogawa *et al.* (1996).

Case study 3.1

Olympic Teams as Market Segments

Laurence Chalip, University of Texas at Austin, USA

The Gold Coast is a single city, one hour's flight north of Sydney, Australia. It is a resort destination with an economy that relies on tourism. As the 2000 Olympic Games approached, tourism marketers on the Gold Coast worried that their city would not benefit from Sydney's hosting of the Games. In fact, early forecasts projected that the city would lose business as Olympic visitors and Olympic media would focus on Sydney. The challenge, then, was to identify a niche Olympic market that would fill room nights during the Games period, and that could generate media interest and positive word-of-mouth for the destination.

After examining the experience of past Olympic hosts, Gold Coast marketers decided that the best strategy would be to concentrate on a single market segment: the Olympic teams themselves. Teams from throughout the world would need a place to train in the build-up to the Games. Some might even be enticed to remain in their training camps during the Games themselves. If a team from a vital tourism source market could be attracted, the media associated with that team's training might be exploited to build the Gold Coast's brand.

In order to capture market share within the target segment, two actions were required. First, the Gold Coast would have to secure the interest of decision makers who would select the training locations for their teams. Second, in order to win the right to host them, the Gold Coast would have to enhance the products and services it could provide.

Securing the teams would only be the first step. In order to obtain the greatest tourism benefit, it would also be necessary to capitalise on their presence. Although having teams on the Gold Coast would fill room nights and generate associated tourist revenues, the media interest in Olympic teams could also be used to build future visitation. The Gold Coast would need to build the training into its advertising, promotions and public relations. It would also be necessary to generate positive media and word-of-mouth as a consequence of teams' presence.

Capturing Market Share

The destination's tourism marketing organisations had no experience if marketing to Olympic teams. Marketers first needed to determine what facilities and services teams would want. They had to match that against what the destination could realistically provide. Finally, they needed to bring their facilities and services to the attention of the right decision makers.

The first step was to conduct an audit of local facilities in order to develop a complete list of potential training venues. This included sports facilities, such as gymnasia, stadia, tracks, pools, velodromes and sailing and rowing venues. It also included support facilities and services, such as accommodation, transportation and sports medicine expertise. It was not sufficient to catalogue the facilities and services; it was also necessary to determine what the required Olympic standards were, and to identify facility improvements and new facilities that would be required.

The audit identified an array of potential training venues, but nearly all needed some improvement or augmentation to make them attractive to Olympic teams. It would cost the Gold Coast $AUS5.9 million to become competitive as an Olympic training destination. The city upgraded swimming pools, its hockey centre and its velodrome. It redeveloped its rowing course and built a new synthetic track. Coalitions of sports organisations, tourism providers, local universities and business people were brought together in order to plan and implement the work, and to market the Gold Coast to Olympic teams.

Marketing the Gold Coast began with the creation of an information kit that described the city, its services and its facilities. The kit was sent to every National Olympic Committee. In addition, local entrepreneurs and sports people who had contacts in the Olympic Movement networked through those contacts to reach decision makers. The city then produced a CD which could be tailored or updated as needed to provide information to Olympic teams enquiring about training on the Gold Coast.

Market Response

With the help of a local entrepreneur, the city attracted the entire British Olympic Team to the Gold Coast. The team established its headquarters at a local resort, and made arrangements to begin training six weeks before the start and to remain in camp until the end of the Olympic Games. This was a significant success for the Gold Coast because the UK is one of the destination's key source markets.

Although the British team would use much of the capacity that the Gold Coast offered, it would not exhaust the city's capacity. Consequently, deals were cut with teams from 15 additional countries for training camps in specific sports for which capacity remained.

Leveraging

In order to get the best tourism marketing advantage from teams that were training on the Gold Coast, destination marketers arranged to host international media that came to cover the training of their teams. The presence of the entire British team provided a particularly attractive media opportunity. Consequently, a special media centre was established for the duration of the British training camp. Although much of the media's interest would be on the training itself, Gold Coast marketers sought to provide media with familiarisation trips, interesting visuals of the destination and leads to stories about the locale. This generated stories and mentions about the Gold Coast.

Destination marketers also realised that the athletes would be interviewed extensively by their home media, so the marketers sought to generate positive word-of-mouth for the destination through the quality of hosting that was provided. In order to enhance their stay, teams were given information about local restaurants and points of interest. When it was desired, tours were arranged for coaches, officials, athletes or their families and friends to visit local theme parks, shopping centres, movie theatres, or nearby mountains and rain forest.

Finally, wherever possible, the Gold Coast sought joint promotions with the teams' sponsors. In the UK, the city's marketers jointly sponsored a contest with Kelloggs for which the prize was a trip to the Gold Coast, 'where the British Olympic team will train'. There was a similar promotion with Lloyds Bank. In addition, the Gold Coast was permitted to advertise itself on taxis in London using the BOA symbols as part of the campaign.

Impact

Hosting Olympic teams paid handsome dividends for the Gold Coast. The teams filled almost 40,000 bed nights, and injected $AUS15 million into the local economy. The city obtained new media contacts and was able to build a database of 302 journalists from around the world who could write stories about the city – a database that could be used in the future whenever the city hosted sports events. Advertising and media generated by hosting Olympic teams increased the destination's international appeal. Bookings from the UK increased over 20% immediately after the Olympics, and were up almost 15% from elsewhere in Europe. For the Gold Coast, Olympic teams had proven to be a valuable segment to target.

Further reading

Brown, G., Chalip, L., Jago, L. and Mules, T. (2002) The Sydney Olympics and Brand Australia. In N. Morgan, A. Pritchard and R. Pride (eds) *Destination Branding: Creating the Unique Destination Position* (pp. 163–185). Oxford: Butterworth-Heinemann.

Chalip, L., Green, B. C. and Vander Velden, L. (2000) Effects of polysemic structures on Olympic viewing. *International Journal of Sports Marketing and Sponsorship* 2, 39–57.

Chalip, L. and Leyns, A. (2002) Local business leveraging of a sport event: Managing an event for economic benefit. *Journal of Sport Management* 16, 133–159.

Faulkner, B., Chalip, L., Brown, G., Jago, L., March, R. and Woodside, A. (2000) Monitoring the impacts of the Sydney 2000 Olympics. *Event Management* 6, 231–246.

Chapter 4
Development Processes and Issues

Management of the process of renewal and the redesigning of products and services is a field where sport and tourism can exchange valuable experiences.

(de Villiers, 2001: 12)

Introduction

Change is one of the few constants in contemporary society. By understanding the nature and process of development, sport and tourism managers can better predict and influence the course of change. This chapter discusses the concept of development as it exists in relation to sport tourism. It is argued that, if sport tourism development is to comply with the dominant paradigm of sustainability, then planned and informed intervention into the development process is required. The latter part of this chapter highlights three key issues that need to be considered when planning for sport tourism development. These issues include commodification/authenticity, globalisation and partnership within the field of sport tourism. Failure to understand the challenges associated with these issues will compromise the development potential of sport tourism. The Case study that concludes this chapter demonstrates how sport tourism has been used as an agent for regional development in France (Case study 4.1; see pp. 74–76).

The Concept of Development

Development is an illusive term as its meaning differs with the context in which it is used. Members of a broad range of disciplines and professions interpret development in ways that make sense to themselves, perhaps more so than others. Even in the context of popular usage, fundamentally different meanings of the term exist. Common interpretations include development as philosophy, process, plan and product:

As a philosophy, development refers to broad perspectives concerning appropriate future states and means of achieving them. As a

55

process it emphasizes the methods, which might be employed to expand or bring about the potentials or capabilities of a phenomenon. A development plan sets out specific steps through which desirable future states are to be achieved and development as a product indicates the level of achievement of an individual or society, as in developing and underdeveloped countries. (Wall, 1997: 35)

Of these perspectives, the most common are development as a product and development as a process. In the case of the former, development is treated as a state. This approach is being used when reference is made to levels of development. Such levels are often assessed in terms of economic measures such as income and employment, but increasingly include non-economic measures such as the social conditions found in a region. In the latter case, development is seen as an evolutionary process. Freidmann (1986) described development as a process of change or as a complex of such processes. He suggests that these changes are predictable enough that intelligent statements could be made about them. Development, as used in the title of this book, refers to the process of development, and the issues and challenges associated with change in the way that sport tourism is manifested in space and time.

Sport tourism exists within social, cultural, political, economic and environmental contexts that are in constant flux. This is true of the factors that affect demand as well as those that affect supply. Change in sport tourism is, therefore, inevitable. Sport tourism managers, like those in other industry sectors, must deal with this change. Given its inevitability, sport tourism managers should be prepared to

welcome change and take up the opportunities that change offers. Change is a powerful and positive force which, when harnessed constructively, challenges individuals, groups and organizations to perform to their optimum capability. (Pigram & Wahab, 1997: 28)

Sport tourism managers seek change that is accompanied by positive impacts and implications. Growth in its various forms, including the number of sport-related visitors to a destination, the amount that these visitors spend and the physical development of sport tourism sites, may be the foremost objectives for sport and tourism managers. Nevertheless, it is inappropriate to simply equate growth with development, especially when a long-term perspective is taken that incorporates the various interests of all stakeholders (Atkisson, 2000; Binns, 1995). Development is not just change in terms of growth, but it is change that has a positive overall impact. It should, therefore, be assessed in the context of a full range of stakeholders and their often competing and sometimes contradictory goals.

While there is general agreement that development as a planned process should be aimed at positive change over time, there has been less agreement as to what should be used to measure change. Typically, economic measures have been used as indicators. This is consistent with the dominant political-economic system operating throughout the developed world '[in] which maintaining or increasing levels of economic growth has been a virtually unassailable policy goal' (Hall, 2000a: 6). Notwithstanding this entrenched perspective, definitions of development 'have tended to be broadened over time and development has gradually come to be viewed as a social as well as an economic process which involves the progressive improvement of conditions and the fulfilment of potential' (Wall, 1997: 34). Other indicators of development that have emerged over the past two decades include modernisation, distributive justice and spatial reorganisation (D. G. Pearce, 1989). The last of these – development as spatial reorganisation – is particularly relevant to this book. From this perspective, spatial form represents the physical manifestation of changing patterns of social relations. The appeal of this approach lies in its tangible expression in terms of space, place and physical impacts. While it is recognised that there are a variety of valid approaches to considering development, it is not possible to do them all justice in one book. The balance of this book focuses on development in its spatial and temporal dimensions.

Sustainable Development

Sustainable development is a contested concept. While few people would claim they do not support the principle of sustainable development, the meaning of the concept is not universally shared (Hall & Lew, 1998). Business advocates tend to emphasise 'development', while environmentalists tend to focus on 'sustainablity'. As a result, the phrase can sometimes seem like a contradiction in terms. Yet behind the rhetoric of the various stakeholders and scholars who debate its merits, it is a concept that holds widespread appeal. Tourism proponents have argued that 'conditions can be created (in tourism) so that real development, in terms of human betterment and enhanced life opportunities, is nurtured to be handed on to future generations for their growth and prosperity' (Pigram & Wahab, 1997: 3, 4).

The World Commission on Environment and Development (WCED) (1987: 4) definition of sustainable development is 'development that meets the needs of the present without compromising the ability of future generations to meet their own needs'. While there are many other definitions, most tend to focus on the sustainability of natural ecosystems. The WCED definition is, however, robust enough to include the sustainability of cultural resources. Mowforth and Munt (1998: 109) describe this type of sustainability as 'the ability of people or a people to retain or adapt elements of their culture which distinguish them from other people'. In the case of sport tourism, this aspect of the definition encompasses sport as an expression of culture (Chapter 6) as well as the impacts that sport tourism has on the physical environment in which it occurs (Chapter 7).

There is a difference between sustainable tourism and sustainable development (Wall, 1997). Sustainable tourism is 'tourism which is in a form which can maintain its viability in an area for an indefinite period or time' (Butler, 1993: 29). In contrast, tourism in the context of sustainable development is

> tourism which is developed and maintained in an area (community, environment) in such a manner and at such a scale that it remains viable over an indefinite period and does not degrade or alter the environment (human and physical) in which it exists to such a degree that it prohibits the successful development and well-being of other activities and processes. (Butler, 1993: 29)

Clearly, the latter goal is of a higher order. Maintaining sport tourism at the expense of the cultural and physical environments in which it exists contradicts the fundamental principles of sustainable development.

Accounting for this broader development context is challenging but necessary. The achievement of sustainable sport tourism requires a balance between social goals, economic goals and environment goals. While sustainable sport tourism is the focal point of Figure 4.1, the broader concept of tourism in the context of sustainable development is embodied in the spheres adjoining the centre. A healthy sport tourism economy should ideally support and enhance the social/cultural dimension of the community. It should also play a similar role in the context of the natural environment, which features prominently in many types of sport tourism activity. In addition, sport tourism social/cultural practices should serve as positive forces in relation to the natural environment. There is, however, no guarantee that the interaction between sport and tourism will necessarily be positive. To achieve positive outcomes, sport tourism managers must be conscious of the impacts of their decisions throughout the full range of these realms rather than just at the centre. This awareness must then be accompanied by a constructive integrated approach to development.

The sport and tourism industries have vested interests as well as a moral obligation to meet the goal of sustainability. At a micro level, sustainable development has a direct impact on the return on investment for sport tourism businesses. At a macro level, sustainable development has a direct bearing on the industry as a whole and the communities in which it functions. The natural tendency of sport tourism managers is to focus on economic goals, but, if environmental and social cultural resources are viewed as a form of capital, a strong business argument exists for sustainable practices (Hall, 2000a: 6).

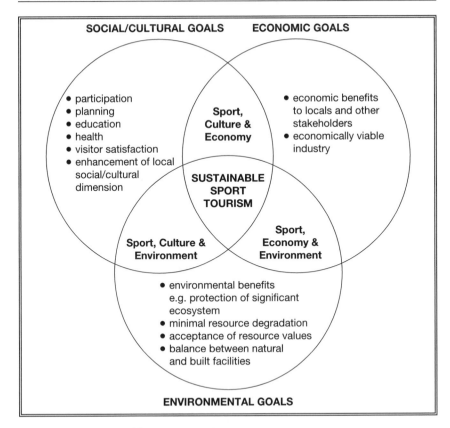

Figure 4.1 Sustainable sport tourism

Source: after Hall (1995)

Planning

Planning is a means of managing change. Given that sport tourism exists in a dynamic environment and given that these dynamics do not necessarily lead to sustainability, some sort of intervention into the development process is required to foster the type of change that helps stakeholders to achieve their objectives. Essentially, 'planning is a process of human thought and action based upon that thought' (Chadwick, 1971: 24). Planning in a sport tourism context, like planning in a general tourism context, is 'concerned with anticipating and regulating change in a system, to promote orderly development as to increase the social, economic, and environmental benefits of the development process' (Murphy, 1985: 156). It is based on the assumption that even a partial understanding of the dynamics of sport tourism and the world in which it operates provides the basis to influence change. By consciously initiating this type of process, managers of sport tourism will not only be acting in their best self-interests, but they will be making positive contributions to the sustainability of the social, cultural, economic and environmental systems in which they function.

The underlying process for planning is consistent across a broad range of fields and disciplines. It is based on an assessment of the current situation, likely changes that will occur in the environment in which the plan is being conducted, decisions on the desired end state, formulation of some sort of action plan and its implementation, followed by monitoring, assessment and adjustment as required (WTO, 1994; Inskeep, 1991). While the terminology and details of the planning process may change, it retains this basic framework (Case study 4.1; see pp. 74–76).

Development Issues

If planning interventions into the development process are to be successful, then informed consideration of the many issues that exist within the field of sport tourism is necessary. A number of specific issues are introduced and discussed in the chapters that follow, but three issues have particular significance in relationship to the dynamics that characterise sport tourism development. These issues, which are discussed sequentially in the remainder of this chapter, include commodification and authenticity, globalisation and strategic alliances and partnerships.

Commodification and authenticity

One of the most fundamental issues of sport tourism development is the process of commodification and its implications in terms of authenticity. The importance of this issue is predicated on the belief that the search for authenticity is one of the main driving forces for tourism (Urry, 1990; MacCannell, 1976). It also is predicated on the fact that sport represents a dynamic and increasingly prominent stage for the expression of culture. Plog's (1972: 4) warning that '[d]estination areas carry with them potential seeds of their own destruction', as they allow themselves to become more commercialized and lose their qualities which originally attracted tourists' needs to be carefully considered. Selling sport culture as a tourism product can have major impacts (both negative and positive) on sport within the destination community.

In a tourism context, Cohen (1988: 380) has defined commoditisation, a term synonymous with commodification, as

> a process by which things (and activities) come to be evaluated primarily in terms of their exchange value, in a context of trade, thereby becoming goods (and services); developed exchange systems

in which the exchange value of things (and activities) is stated in terms of prices for a market.

Similarly, in the context of sport, McKay and Kirk (1992: 10) defined commodification as

the process by which objects and people become organized as things to be exchanged in a market. Whereas cultural activities such as . . . sport once were based primarily on intrinsic worth, they are now increasingly constituted by market values.

These definitions feature the same fundamental characteristics; a process of commercialisation that superimposes economic values on things or activities that were not previously valued in this way. One important point of difference is that commodification is almost an axiom of tourism, given its commercial nature. Sport, on the other hand, has a rich non-commercial history, although there are certainly heightened levels of commercialisation associated with modern sport. Tourism is one agent of commercialisation as it 'packages' and 'sells' sport to travellers.

Tourism critics argue that the commercialisation of culture introduces economic relations into an area where they previously played no part. In the process of commercialisation, real authenticity is destroyed and a covert 'staged authenticity' emerges (MacCannell, 1973). As the fact that this staged authenticity is not real dawns on tourists, it thwarts their genuine search for authenticity. Cohen (1988: 383) has countered this argument:

Commoditization does not necessarily destroy the meaning of cultural products, neither for the locals nor for the tourists, although it may do so under certain conditions. Tourist-oriented products frequently acquire new meanings for the locals, as they become a diacritical mark of their ethnic or cultural identity, a vehicle of self-representation before an external public.

Critics of the commodification of sport suggest that the professionalisation of various competitions and the broader commercialisation of sport through the media and the interests of large manufacturing/retail corporations have had a detrimental effect. J. J. Stewart (1987: 172) articulates this position by arguing that

social hegemony of the commodity form is apparent as the practice of sport is shaped and dominated by the values and instrumentalities of a market . . . the idealized model of sport, along with its traditional ritualized meanings, metaphysical aura, and skill democracy, is destroyed as sport becomes just another item to be trafficked as a commodity.

A particularly good illustration of this line of argument is the commod-ification of the Olympic rings logo (Van Wynsberghe & Ritchie, 1998). The blatant commercialisation of this logo by way of licensing agreements presents a stark contrast to the altruistic tone of the Olympic Charter. Clearly, the commodification of sport is not always viewed as a problem. J. Williams (1994) points out that the commodification of sport has brought about several benefits, including new funds, better performances, improved stadia, professionalism in performance and staging, and some new sources of support and opportunities for grassroots development. He tempers this rosy picture, however, by noting that, in the process of capturing these benefits, the traditional power brokers of sport have abdicated significant influence to media, sponsors and corporate clients. For example, corporate interests in sport have influenced the reloca-tion of sporting events such as the Belgian Grand Prix (Formula One) to avoid locations where government legislation prevents tobacco company sponsorship.

Authenticity is closely related to commodification. It can be viewed in a number of ways. In a tourism context it has traditionally been viewed in relation to the authenticity of originals or the thing or activity that the tourists have come to see (Wang, 1999). This can be thought of as compa-rable to a museum curator's perspective, where experts in such matters test whether objects of art are what they appear to be or are claimed to be (Cohen, 1988). The sporting parallel is manifested in popular criticism of any break from tradition, especially in relation to rule changes. From this perspective, a thing or activity is judged to be authentic or not in a relatively objective manner. This approach has gradually given away over the past three decades to more flexible interpretations of authenticity, where it is appreciated that there is seldom an absolute authenticity, but that it is more often negotiated in some fashion. Wang (1999) has termed this 'constructive authenticity'. As part of the commodification process, the tourism industry has continued to present 'staged authenticity', albeit increasingly in a non-covert form. Rather than taking tourists to the back stage of a destination to experience real culture, tourism operators use the front stage where a destination's culture is presented in a controlled way via museums, heritage centres, cultural performances and other similar forums. A dedicated stage for tourism allows for greater influence over impacts and addresses the operational constraints associated with tourist activity, such as the restricted scheduling that typically charac-terises tourists. Cohen (1988) also discussed the concept of 'emergent authenticity', which reflects the gradual emergence of authenticity in the eyes of visitors. A classic example is Disneyland, which initially was viewed as being inauthentic, but which has 'emerged' as an authentic representation of American culture. Many of the new extreme sports would fit into this category.

Timothy and Boyd's (2002) review of the authenticity debate in the context of heritage tourism highlights several important issues that are especially relevant in relationship to nostalgia sport tourism. They suggest five types of common distortions of the past, including invented places or reconstructed pasts, relative authenticity that recognises the subjective nature of interpreting the past, ethnic intruders in the form of non-local interpreters, sanitised and idealised pasts and, finally, the unknown past in which it is recognised that interpretations of the past can only be partial. Sport tourism examples in these categories include fantasy sport camps, contradictory views of historic sporting matches, great geographic diversity reflected in the playing and coaching rosters, highly nostalgic interpretations of past sporting glory and hero worship and memories of the past built on selected statistical summaries associated with elite competition. All of these distortions compromise objective authenticity, but they do not necessarily detract from the experience of the visitor.

While many academics have criticised the tourism industry's failure to provide 'objective authenticity' (e.g. Boorstin, 1975; Greenwood, 1989), others have recognised that tourists sometimes seek contrived experiences as part of their desire to have fun (Moscardo, 2000; Urry, 1990). Butler (1996: 93) captures this notion in his view that

> most tourist destinations, and certainly those aimed at the mass market, are not intended, and never were intended to be examples of the real world. A holiday destination to most visitors is not the real world, it is generally an imaginary world, a wishful world, or a Shangri-La. . . . In the case of the present day tourists, it would appear that what most wish to take back home with them, most importantly, are themselves, intact, refreshed, happy, and with good feelings and memories.

Increasingly, it is acknowledged that tourists are searching for authentic experiences rather than authentic objects (McIntosh & Prentice, 1999). Wang (1999: 352) has articulated this 'rethinking' of authenticity, describing an activity-related authenticity which he refers to as existential authenticity:

> Existential authenticity refers to a potential existential state of Being that is to be activated by tourist activities. Correspondingly, authentic experiences in tourism are to achieve this activated existential state of Being within the liminal process of tourism. Existential authenticity can have nothing to do with the authenticity of toured objects.

This type of authenticity would seem to hold considerable relevance for sport tourism, with its focus on experience. It also represents an interesting dynamic in relation to the blurring of sport and entertainment. The

key seems to be engagement. If tourists are actively engaged as spectators or as active participants in a sport, they are likely to view their
experience as being authentic regardless of how others may assess the
situation. Sport is unique compared to other types of tourist attractions
in this regard. Its emphasis on performance, competition and uncertain
outcomes means that each event or active engagement in sport is
authentic. To a large extent, authenticity is what makes sport entertaining.

Wang (1999) expands on his interpretation of existential authenticity
by introducing four subcategories. The first of these is intrapersonal
authenticity as manifested in bodily feelings – a major dimension of active
sport tourism. Intrapersonal authenticity as manifested in self-identity is
the second subcategory. This category is described as 'self-making' and
is often found in sports like rock climbing, in which participants can reaf-
firm and develop their sense of identify. A third type is inter-personal
authenticity that enhances family ties. In a sporting context, family ties
are closely related to the concept of a team. Finally, interpersonal authenticity associated with touristic communities is paralleled in the fandoms
associated with various spectator sports (Focus point 4.1) as well as in the
emergence of subculture tribes, such as skateboarders or surfers. In many
instances the emergence of these new types of authenticity are closely tied
to changing external conditions, such as the process of globalisation.

Globalisation

The term 'globalisation' can bring forth a variety of reactions, as exem-
plified by the positive response to the concept of a 'global village' through
to the vocal protests decrying economic inequities and cultural imperialism that have become a predictable part of world economic summits.
Simply put, globalisation is the process that leads to an ever-tightening
network of connections that cut across national boundaries. It is characterised by the worldwide compression of time and space (Mowforth &
Munt, 1998).

In many ways, globalisation is a new way of looking at development and is manifested in a web of political, economic, cultural and social
interconnections (Harvey *et al.*, 1996). It is no longer possible for communities to function in isolation from other parts of the globe. Globalisation
is a complex process and a variety of interpretations and perspectives
have emerged (Silk & Jackson, 2000). The cultural imperialist interpretation sees local culture as being displaced by a foreign one, which causes
a homogenising trend and the creation of a common global culture.
This form of imperialism is often equated with Americanisation, as the
US economy and culture are viewed as the dominant forces in the global
system. A cultural hegemony interpretation sees globalisation as a two-
way process. Local communities receive global images, goods and

Focus point 4.1

The Barmy Army

The Barmy Army, which is synonymous with English cricket fans travelling overseas to support their national team, represents an emerging culture based around sport spectatorship. The term 'Barmy' was coined by the Australian media during the Ashes tour of 1994/95, because the English fans had travelled so far to support a team that lost on that tour to Australia, Australia A, Zimbabwe and the Australian Academy Side (youth team). This 'Army' of supporters grouped together at each match, singing and supporting their team, despite its hopeless performances. As the cricket results got worse, the intensity of the support increased and the Barmy Army rapidly became the focal point for both the media and the general public. Eventually, the passion and dedication of the Barmy Army was rewarded with an unlikely victory in the fourth test in Adelaide. The Barmy Army soon came to represent a unique style of fan support, with the use of songs, chants, irony and wit. During the last 10 days of the series, in excess of 8000 items of Barmy Army merchandise were sold. At the conclusion of that tour, the Barmy Army was registered as a trademark. The Barmy Army has travelled on all of England's subsequent tours to places such as South Africa, New Zealand, Sharjah and the Caribbean. Growing popularity and media attention have accompanied the Barmy Army on these tours. Giulianotti's (1991, 1995a) studies of the Scotland national football team and its 'Tartan Army' of supporters confirms that sports fans and the 'carnivalesque' is not unique to the sport of cricket.

Source: http://www.barmy-army.com/

services, but interpret them on their own terms. In this two-way relationship, local groups play key roles in the way global trends are manifested in their locale (Whitson & Macintosh, 1996). Finally, the figurational perspective advocates a view of globalisation as a process. This perspective emphasises a long-term historical approach that involves the examination of cases of domination and resistance over time. Maguire's (1999: 3) definition of globalisation fits this interpretation:

> Globalization processes are viewed here as being long-term processes that have occurred unevenly across all areas of the planet. These processes – involving an increasing intensification of global interconnectedness – appear to be gathering momentum and despite their 'unevenness', it is more difficult to understand local or national experiences without reference to these global flows. Every aspect of social reality – people's living conditions, beliefs, knowledge and actions – is intertwined with unfolding globalization processes. These

processes include the emergence of a global economy, a transnational cosmopolitan culture and a range of international social movements.

Media conglomerates and major sporting goods manufacturer/retailers like Nike have been identified as the most powerful forces influencing the globalisation of sport (Harvey *et al.*, 1996). While Maguire (1994) has argued that the influence of developments such as the Internet demonstrate that the globalisation process is not necessarily guided or planned, others like Goldman and Papson (1998) have demonstrated that major international corporations (e.g. Nike) have consciously developed promotional strategies aimed at global markets. The actions of these players in globalisation are driven by self-interest through the commodification of sport. Mowforth and Munt (1998) have suggested a similar dynamic in the case of tourism. There is a constant process of commodification driven by the tourism industry's relentless search for 'new destinations'. As these places are increasingly connected to tourism-generating regions, globalisation through tourism is manifested in a very tangible fashion. Tourism is, in fact, a significant force in the globalisation of sport. During his tenure as the Commissioner of the National Basketball League (NBA), David Stern noted the parallels between the way the tourism giant, Disney Corporation, operated its theme parks and the emerging business strategies of the NBA. He compared basketball stadia to Disney's theme parks, star players to star characters, basketball merchandise to Disney merchandise and game broadcasts to Disney movies (S. J. Jackson & Andrews, 1999). Given these self-professed parallels between sport, tourism and entertainment, it is somewhat surprising that tourism has received so little attention in the ongoing sport globalisation debates.

One of the most interesting aspects of these debates from a tourism perspective is whether globalisation is leading towards a homogenisation of sport culture or whether local resistance will retain or even foster greater differences between places. This is especially significant because, in a world where there is little difference between places, there really is little need to travel. Silk and Andrews' (2001) suggestion that electronic spaces or the 'space of flows' may supersede the 'space of places' has quite ominous implications for tourism. In the context of sport tourism, if sporting culture were to evolve into a homogeneous culture throughout the world, much of the existing incentive to travel for sport would be lost. This debate is, therefore, an important one for sport tourism development.

The essence of the homogenisation/heterogenisation debate in sport is nicely summarised in the words of Silk and Jackson (2000: 102):

> Homogenization heralds the advent of an era dominated by creeping global standardization. Heterogenization, however, rejects the influence of global technologies and products in favour of stressing the inherent uniqueness of localities. The former category suggests that

we are becoming more alike and heading towards a uniform global culture. The latter emphasizes cultural differences and the power of the particular.

Those who see the forces of globalisation leading to the homogenisation of sport have argued that there is ample evidence to suggest that sport culture is growing more similar throughout the world. For example, the emergence of homogeneous sportscapes as manifested in standardised stadia and sports fields (Bale, 1993b) is consistent with this view. Rowe and Lawrence (1996: 10) also suggest that cultural

> commentators find 'evidence' of this new phenomenon in international sports media spectacles (such as the Olympic Games and the soccer World Cup), geographically 'mobile' sports (such as basketball and golf), and US-originated advertising, promotion, marketing and 'packaging' practices (such as celebrity endorsements and the high-pressure sale of sports paraphernalia).

Yet, even commentators who show some level of support for this hypothesis recognise that there are other forces at work that seem to counter the processes of homogenisation:

> Globalization is accordingly best understood as a balance and blend between diminishing contrasts and increasing varieties, a commingling of cultures and attempts by more established groups to control and regulate access to global flows. Global sport development can be understood in the same terms: that is, in the late twentieth century we are witnessing the globalization of sports and the increasing diversification of sport cultures (Maguire, 1999: 213).

Many sport theorists share the view of coexistent forces for homogeneity and diversification (Merkel *et al.*, 1998; Washington & Karen, 2001; Harvey & Houle, 1994). At an empirical level, there is also support for the thesis that local resistance ensures that there is a significant degree of difference between local sport cultures. Despite global trends to export US sports like American football, regionally prominent sports like Australian Rules football and rugby league have prevailed in Australia (Rowe *et al.*, 1994). Similarly, it has been argued that New Zealanders have negotiated the introduction of basketball on their own terms (S. J. Jackson & Andrews, 1999). In the case of the World Cup of soccer held in the USA in 1994, analysts concluded that, while the motivations to hold the event in the USA were probably influenced by the desire to capitalise on forces of globalisation, the final outcome had little impact on the spread of soccer in the host country (Sugden & Tomlinson, 1996). In another context, Bernstein (2000) demonstrated through content analysis and interviews with journalists that, despite powerful forces of a global media, press coverage of the 1992 Olympics in Barcelona was characterised by local or national perspectives. Nationalistic interpretations of sporting events and performances still dominate media coverage.

Strategic alliances and partnerships

One of the underlying principles of sustainable development is the need for holistic planning; planning that encompasses the broad range of stakeholders associated with development. A prerequisite to holistic planning for sport tourism is not only recognition of the multiple players in the sport tourism industry, but a willingness and ability for these players to work together in pursuit of their common interests related to sustainable development. Until recently, however, effective partnerships in sport tourism have been found wanting. For example, a study of six European states in the early 1980s found a linkage between sport and tourism in the minds of participants, commercial providers and local authorities (Glyptis, 1991). However, despite this link, there was a lack of conscious integration by policy makers, planners and public providers at national level. More recently, Weed and Bull (1997a) noted that there are still very few joint sport tourism initiatives among the regional agencies responsible for sport (Sports Council Regional Offices) and tourism (Regional Tourist Boards) in England. Even in Australia, which is a leader in sport tourism partnerships, the primary rationale for the development of its recent policy on sport tourism was the lack of an identity and cohesiveness perceived in this area (Commonwealth Department of Industry, Science and Resources, 2000).

The need for partnerships and strategic alliances in tourism and in sport has been increasingly recognised over the past 10 years, especially as government resources that were traditionally directed toward these areas have been reduced (Jamal & Getz, 1994). While a broad range of models for partnership have emerged, they can generally be described as 'a voluntary pooling of resources (labour, money, information, etc.) between two or more parties to accomplish collaborative goals' (Selin & Chavez, 1995: 845). The environmental management outcomes of the Lillehammer Winter Olympic Games (1994), for example, were built upon effective partnerships and strategic alliances between central and local government, sport, tourism, environmental and community groups (Chapter 7).

Partnership is particularly important in a sport tourism context, given the many stakeholders involved. In his study of the restructuring of winter resorts in the French Alps, Tuppen (2000: 337) noted that development 'results from the actions of different organisations and interest groups in both the public and private sectors, often rendering management a complex task'. In addition to the sheer number and diversity of stakeholders who may be involved, the dynamic of power shifts among these stakeholders throughout the temporal course of development further complicates these partnerships.

There are various additional constraints to sport tourism partnerships. Competition between stakeholders, bureaucratic inertia and geographic as well as organisational fragmentation are typical (Selin & Chavez, 1995). In the specific context of sport tourism, the Commonwealth Department of Industry, Science and Resources (Australia) (2000) highlighted the lack of awareness of the mutual benefits of establishing alliances and difficulties in coordinating resources and information. Bull and Weed (1999: 151) added to this list of constraints the

> reduction of funding to the national and regional tourism agencies allocated to core functions, the adoption of increasingly narrow definitions of sport, and the cutting of the only statutory link between sport and tourism agencies in the abolition of the Regional Councils for Sport and Recreation as . . . policies that have limited the extent to which integration is likely to occur.

The bottom line is that successful partnerships need partners who recognise their mutual interest. Participating organisations must also be characterised by a domain focus that is goal-oriented rather than organisation-oriented. Promising initiatives in this area include the recent development of a background paper intended to lead towards a national sport tourism strategy in Australia (Commonwealth Department of Industry, Science and Resources, 2000) and the recent formation of the Canadian Sport Tourism Alliance (Traer, 2002) (Focus point 4.2).

Management Implications and Opportunities

The underlying premise of this book is that the sustainability of sport tourism can be encouraged by the active intervention of sport tourism managers into the processes of change. Managers can influence the development of sport tourism in its various event, active and nostalgic manifestations. Planning will not only help to optimise the redesign and development of sport tourism products and services, but will have both direct and indirect impacts on the milieu in which sport tourism functions.

Managers of sport tourism events need to be conscious of the challenges that they face in terms of commodification/authenticity, globalisation and fragmentation. They should, however, also be aware of the opportunities that accompany these issues. In terms of commodification and authenticity, managers need to protect the attraction, which is the essence of the sport. Care must be taken to keep the spirit of sport competition and entertainment spectacle in an appropriate balance. Media representations need to be rooted in place if sport tourism is to be encouraged

Focus point 4.2

Canadian Sport Tourism Alliance Strategic Plan

Over 200,000 sport events occur annually in Canada and more than nine and a half million Canadians regularly participate in sport, either as athlete, coach, official or volunteer. Sport travel is valued at $CAN1.3 billion, approximately 4% of total Canadian tourism spending. The Canadian Sport Tourism Alliance (CSTA) promotes a planned, coordinated and strategic approach to the hosting of national and international sport events.

Mission Statement

To increase Canadian capacity and competitiveness to attract and host sport events.

Objectives

To market Canada as a preferred sport tourism destination.
To facilitate networking, educational and communications opportunities.
To coordinate research, data collection, monitoring and reporting of activity within the sport tourism industry.
To build investment and involvement in the sport tourism industry from the public and private sectors.
To enhance the image and profile of the sport tourism industry.
To develop and facilitate access to national tools.

Action Plans

To achieve the CSTA's mission and objectives, this strategy assigns responsibility for action to six committees: Membership, Marketing and Communications, Training and Education, Research, Government Relations and Administration.

Source: Canadian Sport Tourism Alliance (2002)

(Chapter 6). The authenticity of the sport attraction should be retained without suppressing the dynamic evolution of a sport (Chapter 10). Relative to many other types of tourist attractions, sport has a major advantage in terms of the joys of performance and the unpredictable drama that sports embody. By maintaining the integrity of the game, spectators of sporting events will always have access to the 'back stage' of sporting destinations. This back stage is not controlled access to the 'locker room', but is epitomised by the throes of competition to which the spectator is privy, whether it is the glory of victory or the agony of defeat.

The implications of globalisation processes involve the global – local nexus. In many cases, the motivation for hosting major sporting events is to establish the host city as a major player in a global context. In order to meet this objective, the local context of the event needs to be emphasised. Strategies to foster a positive local identity and destination image must go beyond pre- and post-event cultural demonstrations and promotions. They should include significant local control and reflect a local as well as a global celebration. These strategies will tend to foster hospitality in the destination during the event and are likely to lead to a positive legacy. They also give the host city a chance to negotiate or resist aspects of global influence in the context of their own self-identity.

Like other types of sport tourism, sporting events have multiple stake-holders. If the event is to achieve its sport tourism potential, partnerships must be established and operationalised in a way that is mutually bene-ficial. The first step in such an exercise is to articulate the advantages and goals of cooperative partnerships. It is particularly important for the tourism industry to demonstrate the benefits of involvement for sport groups. Sporting interests must be convinced that their cooperation will result in increased gate receipts, facility development, new participants for their sport and similar types of benefits. It is not sufficient for the tourism industry to be a silent partner, and significant beneficiary, of sports events. Beyond the recognition of these benefits, specific strategies need to be developed to address the constraints to alliances and partner-ships that are discussed in this chapter. Unproductive competition between stakeholders needs to be avoided and initiatives that can over-come bureaucratic inertia are required. Communication linkages that reduce fragmentation between and within stakeholder groups are crucial.

In contrast to event sport tourism, active sport tourism involves the direct physical participation of the tourist. Because of this, it is especially well positioned to provide tourists with authentic experiences. Sport tourism managers should, however, be aware that there is a variety of levels of active participation, which need to be matched with different types of tourists (Chapter 3). Visitor characteristics, such as skill, comfort level with risk and competitiveness, need to be considered and appro-priate activity matches provided. The concept of experiential authenticity is particularly useful in developing sport tourism products that address bodily feeling, help individuals to define their sense of self, foster family or team dynamics and align individuals with emerging 'cultural tribes', such as those associated with extreme sports (Chapter 6).

The emergence of these 'cultural tribes' as a partial response to global-isation also offers interesting opportunities for active sport tourism. Destinations that have unique resources and facilities or that were the birthplaces of these emerging sports may have a significant competitive advantage. These niche markets can be substantial and may exhibit an enduring affinity for a destination. Traditional sports that have strong ties to a destination can also be fostered. In an increasingly connected world, spatially dispersed niche markets are becoming more accessible.

Active sport tourism would also benefit from strategies that overcome the barriers of organisational fragmentation. While the truly committed active sporting participants may be capable of overcoming constraints in pursuit of their sporting passions, the more casual participants may not. Cooperative efforts on the part of the broad range of tourism and sport operators that impact on these activities can provide substantial synergies in this area.

Finally, nostalgia sport tourism may also benefit from management action in response to commodification/authenticity, globalisation and organisational fragmentation. Of particular relevance in this realm are the implications of commodification and authenticity associated with the distortions of invented places, relative authenticity, ethnic intruders, sanitised and idealised pasts, and the unknown past. Tremendous opportunities for product development exist, but managers need to be conscious of the danger of distorting the past, whether the product is a sport museum or a fantasy training camp. In understanding these distortions, sport tourism managers can align their products with the appropriate market, thereby fostering satisfying tourism experiences.

The implications of globalisation for nostalgic forms of sport tourism are substantial. Although globalisation has not yet resulted in a uniform global sport culture, it has certainly changed the traditional role of sport in local communities. It has led to the early stages of an increased sense of alienation from place. Nostalgic sport tourism presents the opportunity to revisit periods where sport was attached more strongly to place. It provides sport tourists with the opportunity to connect to place in a way that seems to be increasingly difficult in the modern world.

Conclusion

Sport tourism development is about change and, if this course of change is to be sustainable, then sport and tourism managers must actively shape it. This can be accomplished through planned intervention into the change process. Successful planning is, however, dependent on a number of conditions, including a good understanding of the environment in which sport tourism functions. This chapter has focused on three issues that form important aspects of the sport tourism environment: commodification and authenticity, globalisation and the need to form strategic alliances and partnerships. While tourism is in itself a significant agent in the commodification of sport, the unique characteristics of sport as an attraction position it well in relation to the authenticity issue in tourism. Globalisation processes have been very active in sport, but, for the time being, they have not negated the importance of place in the sport tourism landscape. Finally, organisational fragmentation remains one of the major constraints to the continued development of sport tourism. There have, however, been encouraging initiatives in this area.

Further Reading

Development has been a popular topic in tourism for many years. Wall's (1997) work, along with that of Wahab and Pigram (1997) and D. G. Pearce (1989), provides a strong foundation in terms of tourism development. Higham and Hinch's articles (2002b, 2003) extend this discussion to a sport tourism context, as does the work of Hudson (2002). At the heart of tourism development is the concept of sustainability. Insights into the basic nature of this concept, as well as the issues associated with it, are clearly addressed in a volume edited by Hall and Lew (1998) on sustainable tourism from a geographic perspective. The seminal work of Cohen (1988) is essential reading on the topic of commoditisation and authenticity. Wang's (1999) more recent publication on authenticity in a tourism context provides a useful update on changing perspectives on this topic. A wealth of literature has emerged on the issues associated with globalisation. Two of the most useful sources in the context of globalisation related to sport tourism are Maguire's (1999) examination of these issues in the context of sport and Wahab and Cooper's (2001) edited volume on tourism and globalisation. Finally, the need to form strategic alliances in tourism has been particularly well articulated by Jamal and Getz (1994). More focused discussions in the realm of sport tourism are provided by Tuppen (2000) through a case study of the restructuring of sport resorts in the French Alps and by Bull and Weed (1999) in the context of sport tourism development in Malta.

Case study 4.1

Sport Tourism and Regional Development in France

Charles Pigeassou, Université de Montpellier, France

Tourism has long constituted a separate and autonomous branch of industry in France. The country receives more foreign visitors than any other (76.5 million in 2001) and has a very active domestic tourism industry, with over 40 million trips per annum by French citizens. Sport tourism accounts for approximately 7 million of the trips by foreign visitors as well as 10 million domestic tourist trips. This success as a tourist destination results from a rich and varied cultural inheritance, a privileged geographic situation and an attractive physical environment. It is also an outcome of an active tourist policy of the State, which helps to mobilise key resources and stakeholders.

For several decades the French State has actively pursued a tourism policy through active intervention into the tourism development process. Specific actions have included the creation of national tourism organisations for promotion and development, providing financial support through development contracts (e.g. support of 'Plan État-Régions') and cooperation with decentralised regional tourism organisations. On 3 January 1987, a national law was passed that created the obligation for each regional council (Conseil Régional) to set up a regional tourism organisation called the Regional Committee of Tourism (Comité Régional de Tourisme (CRT)). Each county council (Conseil Général) was also required to set up a local organisation called the Departmental Committee of Tourism. The Regional Committee of Tourism is charged with creating a regional plan for the development of tourism and leisure activities subject to the approval of the Regional Council. The Regional Council then assigns the implementation of the tourism policies to the Regional Committee of Tourism. Typically, these responsibilities include the conducting of further studies, economic planning, organisation, funding selected projects and the provision of technical support for marketing as well as for vocational training.

Given these responsibilities, an analysis of promotional activities within each of the CRT regions provides significant insights into the nature of sport tourism offerings, their relative importance and how they are used to position the region. Content analysis of tourism brochures distributed by the 22 CRTs (including web sites) was performed in order to gain insight into regional product offerings. This analysis was conducted during the last trimester of 2000.

An underlying assumption of this analysis is that the products promoted in the brochures are available throughout the region in sufficient quantity to meet demand. Sport tourism themes were identified on the basis of sport images tied to specific places. The thematic emphasis of the 92 brochures and web sites from 22 regions is shown in

Table 4.1. Sport tourism themes dominated 27 of the brochures making this the most frequent thematic category found across all the regions.

Table 4.1 Numbers of tourist brochures according to their theme

Theme of brochures published	Number of brochures
Map of the region	12
Brochure of general information	17
Guide or brochure for professionals and managers	5
Exploration of the region	13
Sports and leisure sports	27
Culture and heritage	10
Gastronomy	2
Period (weekend of Christmas) or season (summer, winter)	6

A closer examination of the tourism brochures highlighted sport tourism development in three main types of environments: marine, rural and mountain. Several of these regional environments featured specialised activities like golf or spa therapy, while the balance featured an integrative concept in which multiple sports were highlighted. The promotional messages developed by each CRT were designed to present a dynamic image of the region that was in keeping with the tourism products found in the area.

Three regional thematic configurations emerged from the analysis. The first configuration featured strong sport tourism offerings, which contained a diversified line-up of sport products. In these regions, sport tourism constituted a strategic priority for the development of the tourism. Brittany, Normandy or Côte d'Azure are regions that have adopted this strategy. The second configuration reflects less emphasis on sport tourism, but it remains an important component of the regional strategy for tourism development. Under this approach, sport tourism offerings form part of a diversified product strategy. Sport tourism is often presented as one component of a broader 'nature' or 'discovery' theme. The strategies of Lorraine and Limousin reflect this configuration. A third configuration was found in which sport tourism offerings were diffused and relatively insignificant. In this case, sport tourism products were not featured in specialised brochures, although they did appear sporadically in general tourism brochures. This type of region tended not to use sport tourism in a strategic fashion nor did sport tourism products appear to make a significant contribution to the tourism offerings in the region. Franche-Comté and Alsace adopted this type of strategy.

This characterisation of sporting tourism in terms of the way it is reflected in regional promotions demonstrates the varied sport tourism strategies that existed in France in 2000. The findings clearly indicate that sport tourism has become a useful tool for the strategic regional development of tourism in France.

Further reading

Pigeassou, C. (1997) Sport and tourism: The emergence of sport into the offer of tourism. Between passion and reason: An overview of the French situation and perspectives. *Journal of Sport Tourism* 4 (2), 20–38.
Pigeassou, C. (2002) Sport tourism as a growth sector: The French perspective. In S. Gammon and J. Kurtzman (eds) *Sport Tourism: Principles and Practice* (Vol. 76, pp. 129–140). Eastbourne: Leisure Studies Association.

Part 3: Sport Tourism Development and Space

Chapter 5

Space: Location and Travel Flows

Despite attempts to cast spatial and environmental relationships into a broader theoretical framework, there is still need to integrate such models into more comprehensive paradigms of land-use and tourist behaviour.

(Mitchell & Murphy, 1991: 65–66)

Introduction

Sport tourism development takes place within a complex milieu of spatial parameters. Different sports are reliant to differing degrees on natural and/or built resources. Some sports are rigidly anchored to specific and non-transportable natural resources. Others are relatively free of resource constraints and may be located where proximity to concentrations of population offers the greatest competitive advantage. Time/cost/distance thresholds also shape the spatial travel patterns of sport tourists. However, sport tourism market range and travel flows can be moderated by the strategic actions of sport and tourism managers. Successful strategies require that consideration be given to the relationships that exist between sport, tourism and space. This chapter discusses the locations where different forms of sport tourism take place and the 'movement of tourists from originating markets to leisure destinations of their choice' (Mitchell & Murphy, 1991: 57). It examines sport tourism resource requirements, destination hierarchies and travel flows. The locational requirements and travel flows associated with sports that take place in central and peripheral areas are then addressed, the latter illustrated in Case study 5.1 (see pp. 95–98), followed by consideration of spatial travel patterns associated with active sport tourism.

Sport, Tourism and Space

Space and place are concepts that are central to the geography of sport (Bale, 1989) and the geography of tourism (D. G. Pearce, 1987; Lew, 2001). Unlike recreation and play, sport requires defined spatial delineations, such as the length of a marathon course, or the spatial parameters for a football field or basketball court. The spatial boundaries that are applied to sports are written into rules and codes of regulations. These rules may be explicit in terms of player movement, as in the case of netball (where, for example, defenders must remain in the defensive half of the court), or implicit, where a defensive formation will be weakened or broken if a player moves out of position. 'In many cases sport involves the dominance of territory or the mastery of distance; spatial infractions are punished and spatial progress is often a major objective' (Bale, 1989: 12).

Tourism is also characterised by a spatial component. To be considered a tourist, individuals must leave and then eventually return to their homes (Chapter 2). Travel is one of the necessary conditions of tourism, and it is for this reason that the spatial implications of tourism are important. A variety of qualifiers have been placed on this dimension, including a range of minimum travel distances, but the fundamental concept of travel is universal.

The spatial element of sport tourism, as it is addressed in this chapter, centres on the locations and regions in which specific sports take place, travel flows associated with those sports and the ways that these flows may be moderated by sport and tourism managers. A variety of questions emerge from this discussion, associated with the resource base, location and management of sport attractions. For example, to what extent can sports resources be reproduced and transported? Similarly, what are the implications of changes within a sport in terms of the propensity of spectators to travel to attend a sporting event?

Spatial analysis of sport tourism

The spatial analysis of sport tourism involves the study of the locations in which sports occur and the movement of tourists to these locations. Such an analysis finds its theoretical foundation in the geography of sport (Bale, 1989, 1993a; Rooney, 1988), which introduces concepts such as central place theory, distance decay and location hierarchy for consideration in the study of sport tourism. This analysis also draws on the geography of tourism, which considers the 'spatial expression of tourism as a physical activity, focusing on both tourist-generating and tourist-receiving areas as well as the links between' (Boniface & Cooper, 1994). The spatial elements of sport tourism vary between sports that tend to be centrally located and those that take place in peripheral regions. Sport tourism in peripheral areas is generally based upon the presence of natural resources, which may be modified or complemented by built facilities. This distinction reflects Boniface and Cooper's (1994) tripartite classification of tourism resources as:

(1) User-orientated: centrally located, highly intensive developments providing proximity to markets and tourism infrastructure and based upon built or artificial facilities and attractions.
(2) Intermediate: located with a view to accessibility, based on resources that are built and/or natural. These areas tend to receive high levels of use.
(3) Resource-based: high resource quality and low intensity development. These areas are spatially removed from users and positioned on the basis of natural resource location.

The spatial concept of distance decay also applies to both sport and tourism. For example, in the case of sport, a discernible pattern exists in terms of the home or away status of a sports contest and the probability of winning. Not only is winning away less probable than at home, but 'the probability of winning forms a clear gradient according to distance from home' (Bale, 1989: 31). The further a team travels from its home venue, the less likely it is to win.

In the context of sport tourism, sports that take place in central locations are advantaged by proximity to markets. Residents of adjacent regions or from peripheral areas are less likely to travel to a sporting event or activity than those located nearby (D. G. Pearce, 1989). The gravity model of distance decay suggests that tourist flows decrease with distance from the origin (Boniface & Cooper, 1994). In theory, therefore, the power of attraction that a sport may exert upon the travel decision process diminishes as the distance away from the site or venue increases. The distance decay function that underlies the gravity model is influenced by increasing travel costs and declining knowledge of distant locations (Mitchell & Murphy, 1991). Therefore, in the case of event sport tourism, all other things being equal, the further a team travels to compete, the less likely it is that their home-based supporters will accompany them.

In reality, a linear distance decay function is moderated by a range of factors (Miossec, 1977), such as cultural and climatic characteristics, which may act as barriers or facilitators to travel (Cooper *et al.*, 1993; Mitchell & Murphy, 1991). Travel flows may be mediated by a number of interrelated variables (Boniface & Cooper, 1994). Zonal travel patterns can be 'modified by the hierarchy of resort destinations, the spatial advantages offered by major transport routes, and locations with outstanding (unique) reputations' (Mitchell & Murphy, 1991: 63). The distance decay function of sport tourism may also be mediated by such things as the quality of the opposition, the importance of the competition, the number of matches that will be played by a team and the travel distances between matches contested while on tour. Factors that may intervene to distort the distance decay function of the gravity model are not well understood and merit further attention.

Sport locations, location hierarchies and tourism

Modern sports exist in a continual state of change. The dynamics of change are often driven by economic processes that bear upon the structure of competitive sports (e.g. the development of new league competitions), the location of sport facilities and the rise and fall of sport attractions. Bale (1989: 77) refers to 'the growth and decline in importance of different sport locations', which parallels Butler's (1980) tourist area life cycle theory (Chapter 10). These dynamics have implications for the scale of the player and spectator catchment areas. Within the ranks of professional sports, the limitations associated with only drawing players from areas near the home team site are alleviated through external recruitment, player transfers and draft schemes. The spectator catchment, and the propensity for residents and non-residents in different regions to attend live sport, is a separate issue that is of particular relevance to sports marketing managers. Interests in this area may be significantly advanced in collaboration with tourism destination managers at sport locations.

Sports attractions, then, exist within a hierarchical organisational structure (Table 5.1) in a similar fashion to other tourist attractions (Leiper, 1990). This hierarchy reflects the fact that some sports centres primarily draw upon a local catchment, while others situated higher in the sports hierarchy draw upon district, regional, national or international catchments (Focus point 5.1). Bale (1989: 79) explains that sports facilities in central locations are situated 'as close to potential users as possible in order to maximise pleasure from the sport experience and to minimise

Table 5.1 Theory of sports locations

1. The main function of sports locations is to provide sports outlets for a surrounding hinterland. Sports facilities are therefore centrally located within their market areas.
2. The greater the number of sports provided, the higher the order of the sports location.
3. Low-order sports locations provide sporting facilities that are used by smaller catchment areas; the threshold population needed for the viability of a lower-order place is smaller.
4. Higher-order locations are fewer in number and are more widely spaced. They have large population thresholds.
5. A hierarchy of sports locations exists in order to make as efficient as possible the arrangement of sports opportunities for (a) consumers who wish to minimise their travel to obtain the sport they want and (b) producers of sports who must maintain a minimum threshold of customers to survive.

Source: reprinted with permission from Bale (1989: 78)

Focus point 5.1

The Melbourne Sports and Aquatic Centre

The Melbourne Sports and Aquatic Centre (MSAC) is a sports facility that caters for elite athletes and international events, while also fostering local and regional participation and 'sport for all' in a wide range of sports. The MSAC operates an event management staff and is designed with a view to hosting national and international sporting events in sports such as basketball, netball, swimming, badminton, gymnastics and squash:

> The primary purpose of the Centre is to host sports events and our challenge is to achieve this whilst minimising the interruption to regular activities and casual visitors. The design of the Centre facilitates this as activity in the Leisure Pool Area and Fitness Centre can continue uninterrupted even when events are taking place. (MSAC, 2002)

The facility is designed, managed and staffed to transcend the boundaries between local resident and tourist participation in both recreational and competitive sports. It provides a high number of sports and captures a broad and diverse sports market catchment. The Melbourne Sports and Aquatic Centre is a facility that is situated near the top of the hierarchy of sports locations.

travel, and hence cost'. This characteristic has been complicated in recent years, as new factors have emerged that influence the status of sports locations. These factors include facility sharing, changing access to infrastructure and travel nodes, proximity to tourism and service developments and associations with media markets (Stevens, 2001).

The notion that demand for sports decreases with distance from the location at which the sport is consumed applies to sport spectatorship, as well as participation. Bale (1989) introduces the term 'spheres of influence', which describes the power of attraction that sports teams exert upon spectators. As noted in references to the model of distance decay, the slope and range of the spatial demand curve for sport spectatorship is elastic. It may be influenced by factors that are, to some degree, beyond the immediate control of sports managers, such as the fortunes of the team (win/loss record), circumstances of the competition, league position and weather. A distinct range of factors influences the demand curve relating to sport participation. These factors include costs of access (White & Wilson, 1999), the standard of the sport resource and the uniqueness of the sport tourism experience. Additional touristic opportunities, such as visiting friends and relatives, or achieving other desired tourist experiences at a destination may also moderate the demand curve.

The Spatial Analysis of Sport Tourism in Central Locations

In practice, 'a vast number of physical, economic and social barriers will contribute to a distortion of the central place model' (Bale, 1989: 81). For example, the catchment population required to support a professional sports franchise will vary as determined by the propensity of residents within the catchment area to support the team. Small city teams, such as the Saskatchewan Roughriders (Canadian Football League) and Green Bay Packers (National Football League, USA), serve to illustrate that the level of support a team receives at its stadium may bear little resemblance to the population of the host city. The Roughriders, for instance, survive due to a strong team following from across the province of Saskatchewan. This example confirms that 'human and cultural factors can upset the rationally economic world predicted by central place models' (Bale, 1989: 82). These factors help to explain the higher than expected loyalty from within and beyond the local spectator catchment that some teams are able to generate.

Inter-urban travel is an increasingly common by-product of sport. Bale (1989: 112) notes that 'in an age of relatively easy inter-regional and international travel, sports events are able to generate substantial recurrent gatherings of peoples . . . and hence . . . [they contribute] . . . to the wealth and economic dominance of the big city'. The sports location hierarchy and the spatial demand curve, both of which are subject to change over time, influence the status of a sport tourism destination. In most cases, sports teams compete at a home venue to which spectators will travel from within the host region and, possibly, further afield (Higham & Hinch, 2000; Gibson, 2002). Traditionally competition leagues are characterised by a series of home and away games, which are attended by supporters of both teams in varying proportions. Home games tend to be dominated by hometown supporters, although sport and tourism managers may devise strategies to encourage visiting fans, casual spectators and tourists at a destination to attend a sports contest. It is also noteworthy that home team supporters are not necessarily hometown residents. As an example, since the return of Newcastle United Football Club to the English Premier League, an estimated 170,000 long-weekend trips to Newcastle have been undertaken by Norwegians who support this football club (Law, 2002).

Other models do exist in the spatial organisation of sport competitions. 'An alternative form of spatial organisation is for the sport to travel to the people in order to attract sufficient business to meet its threshold population' (Bale, 1989: 85). While some sports are rigidly anchored to specific and non-transportable natural resources, others are relatively free of resource constraints and may be transported (Chapter 7). A marathon course, for example, can be relocated to take advantage of concentrations of population, distinctive urban landmarks or unique scenic settings.

The 'periodic marketing' of sports involves a tour circuit incorporating a sequence of different venues where competition occurs. These are designed to improve spectator access to sports and are scheduled in cases such as golf (e.g. Professional Golf Association Tour) and tennis (e.g. Association of Tennis Professionals Tour) to take advantage of seasonal conditions at the destination (Chapter 9). Periodic marketing has two noteworthy implications for sport tourism. First, it transforms the athlete or contestant into a sports traveller as the tour circuit moves from one venue, city, country or continent to the next. Second, it creates the opportunity for sport tourism development associated with the regularly recurring visit of the sports tour. The International Rugby Board's (IRB) International Sevens circuit, most notably the annual tournament that is hosted in Hong Kong (China), has been developed and promoted as a sports festival, often in association with other urban tourist activities. Formula One, which currently involves 17 races in the annual Grand Prix circuit, is another example of an annual professional sport competition that has been developed on the principle of periodic marketing. So, too, have biennial and quadrennial sports events, such as the Fédération Internationale de Football Association (FIFA) soccer and International Cricket Council (ICC) cricket World Cups, International Amateur Athletics Federation (IAAF) World Championships and the Olympic Games. However, the cities that host these events alternate, as determined by a bidding process, which presents different challenges to sport tourism destination managers.

Sport tourism market range

The market range of a sports team varies according to a wide range of factors, many of which may be moderated or influenced by sports managers. These include style of play, team image, public promotion and the success of the team, which influence the status of a team as a tourist attraction (Hinch & Higham, 2001). All of these factors apply to the visiting team as well as the home team. A recent trend in North American professional sport leagues is to charge spectators a premium to watch the top-ranked visiting teams. 'Hallmark teams' are those that 'regularly attract large spectator crowds (and) have now become synonymous with tourism place promotion as well as short break leisure tourism packages' (Stevens, 2001: 61). Bale (1993a) notes that football clubs such as Liverpool, Arsenal and Manchester United receive high levels of media attention. This has helped to build a support base throughout England and, particularly in the case of Manchester United, all over the world. The implications for tourist market range are significant. Manchester United

Premier League games played at Old Trafford regularly attract between 4000 and 6000 international tourists to the Greater Manchester area (Stevens, 2001). Similarly, 46% of all spectators that attend Baltimore Orioles (USA) baseball matches at the Camden Yards stadium are sport excursionists and sport tourists, approximately 11,000 of whom remain in Baltimore for at least one night.

The spatial travel patterns associated with a sports team may be mapped using readily available secondary data, such as the places of residence of season ticket holders or fan club members. Extending the study of sport spectator travel flows to include 'casual' spectator markets requires the collection of primary data. These analyses may afford some idea of the range and specific regions from which sport tourism spectators originate. Extending market range beyond the geographical boundaries that a team actually represents may be achieved nationally or internationally through match attendance, as well as though merchandise sales or supporters club memberships. The continued success of a team influences its market range, but enduring success is very rare. This factor alone cannot explain the sustained and extended fan bases that some teams enjoy. Individual star players and the aura, glamour and heritage associated with teams and the venues at which they compete contribute to the enduring allure of some sports teams. The same factors influence the propensity of visitors to engage in nostalgia sport tourism. The atmosphere of the home stadium, colour and parochialism of the home fans and public presentation of prominent team players may also bear upon the supporter catchments that are generated by sports teams.

Sport, space and the visitor experience

The distances that sport tourists travel correlate with the sport tourist experiences that are pursued at the destination. The time/cost/distance thresholds of tourism are such that the increasing investment of discretionary time and income on travel will bear upon most aspects of the visitor experience (Chapter 8). For instance, the further sport tourists travel, the more likely it is that they will spend some time at the destination engaging in other types of touristic activities (Nogawa *et al.*, 1996). It is also noteworthy that the area that a sports team represents may in fact require 'home' supporters to travel considerable distances to support their team. A national team performing in international competition may attract 'home' supporters from throughout the country that it represents, many of whom travel as domestic tourists. Indeed, expatriates may also return to their country of origin to support or compete in sports teams. Thus, the spatial area that a sports team or club actually represents may vary considerably from the spatial extent of the team supporter and player catchments. This raises the prospect of spectators travelling as domestic or international tourists, without feeling that they are leaving 'home', but indeed feeling that they are *going* 'home', which may have interesting implications for the visitor experience.

Visitor expenditure patterns associated with the sport tourist experience are of particular interest to sport, tourism and service industries. Studies of the economic impacts of sport tourism are commonplace in North America (Schaffer & Davidson, 1985). Insights exist into 'both the costs and benefits to a community of attracting a professional sports outfit and the economic impact of an existing sports franchise on the city in which it is located' (Bale, 1993a: 77). The expenditures that may be associated with the location of a sports club or franchise in an urban area may include club expenditures, or those associated with the production of the sport, and expenditures generated by local and non-local spectators. Such expenditures will vary with the size of the urban area and the definition of its geographical parameters. Bale (1993a: 81) points out, in direct reference to English football, that 'as distance from the football club increases, the positive spill over effect on retailers is likely to decline until a particular point is reached at which the club has no direct economic impact at all'. It is noteworthy that the spending patterns of different sport spectator catchments may be quite unique, with variation between local and non-local visitor expenditure patterns particularly evident (Gibson *et al.*, 2002). However, relatively little research has been committed to this aspect of sport tourism (Chapter 8).

Sport tourism and the status of sport centres

Urban centres have been at the forefront of a new phase of entertainment consumption, which Belanger (2000) describes as the spectacularisation of space. This process is 'creating a new urban landscape filled with casinos, megaplex cinemas, themed restaurants, simulation theatres, stadia and sports complexes' (Belanger, 2000: 378). In many cases, this new urban landscape exists in nodal entertainment enclaves that function as 'tourist precincts' (Leiper, 1990). 'These group-specific combinations of spatially related attractions and facilities are called complexes' (Dietvorst, 1995: 165). The status of sports centres is enhanced when facility developments are planned in coordination with entertainment, tourism and service sector interests. The development of the modern stadium features prominently in advancing the status of sport centres that function as tourist destinations. The Astrodome (Houston) and Superdome (New Orleans) are examples of stadia that have been developed alongside hotel and convention centre complexes as part of urban regeneration and inner city tourist-based development programmes (Stevens, 2001). They have also stimulated development of the service industry, including travel agents specialising in sport tourism, to accommodate the needs of tourists.

These developments, in combination with ancillary tourism services, such as accommodation, transport, dining and entertainment, enhance the status of sports centres.

The concept of a sport centre gives rise to the concept of the sport tourism centre, sport tourism destination or sports resort. The attractiveness of sport tourism centres may draw upon the uniqueness of different sports regions that exist within a country (Rooney & Pillsbury, 1992). By definition, a sport tourism centre requires the presence of sports facilities and resources as well as tourism infrastructure and services (Standeven & De Knop, 1999). 'To the visitor the amenities appear to be related to each other; the whole is more attractive than each separate amenity' (Dietvorst, 1995: 165). Sport tourism centres have the capacity to accommodate significant inward travel flows at a destination. National and/or international transport nodes, an established accommodation sector, tourist attractions to complement the sport industry and a well-developed service sector, including tourism information services, contribute to its functionality. The development and management of sport tourism centres and regions in Upper Franconia/Bavaria (Germany), requiring the existence of both sport and tourism resources, is discussed by Maier and Weber (1993). They map the regional structure of the sport tourism industry, as measured in bed night availability, and the spatial distribution of resources relating to specific sports. In a similar exercise, Pigeassou (2002) documents the sport activities and distinct images associated with sport tourism centres and regions in France. He profiles the status of sport tourism in three regions, Brittany, Côte d'Azure and Limousin, in an analysis of printed and electronic tourism promotion materials. This study identifies the unique points of difference in a regional analysis of sport tourism, providing insights into appropriate development strategies in sport and tourism to enhance the status of sport tourism centres in these regions.

The evolution of sport tourism in central locations

Spatial change within the sports industry continually takes place within the urban milieu (Bale, 1989). This is particularly evident in the locational dynamics of team sports in Europe and North America. Sports stadia in Britain were originally located to take advantage of population concentrations and transport nodes. The strategy of minimum aggregate travel for sports spectators resulted in the development of sports stadia in inner city locations. Hub and spoke public transport networks brought the majority of supporters relatively short distances by train and bus to attend sports matches at central locations. However, these locational criteria have lost much of their relevance, given increasing stadium size and the demand for more parking facilities to match the growth in private car ownership. The situation of locational flux arrived relatively belatedly in British sports, although in recent times Manchester City, Liverpool and Everton football clubs have cemented the trend towards developing new stadia, often on new sites. By contrast, the situation in North America 'has been characterised since 1950 by a state of locational flux' (Bale, 1993a: 150). Over the past 50 years, many high-profile professional football, baseball and ice hockey franchises in North America have been relocated from one city, state or country to the next. The geographic delineations of sport competition have changed dramatically through this process. The expansion of professional ice hockey franchises to the warm weather climates of California and Florida aptly demonstrate this point.

The situation of locational flux has in many cases taken place in association with development of the tourism product, including tourist attractions that target the nostalgia sport tourist (Stevens, 2001). Nostalgia sport tourism has been actively developed in North America (Rooney, 1992). Sports halls of fame have often been positioned as tourist attractions, with traditional museum-style presentations being succeeded by new generation sport attractions, which feature cutting edge interpretive techniques, designs and technologies. This has not been possible in other parts of the world, given the static location of facilities. Stevens (2001: 69) notes, in reference to sport halls of fame in England, that their

> locations tend to be governed by non-market related criteria, such as location of administrative offices or the owners desire to convert a hobby into a public display. Most are located outside the major metropolitan areas, and when compared to the geography of major league franchises, and hence major stadium developments, it is apparent that the opportunity to physically link sports stadia with visitor attractions has largely been missed.

The Spatial Analysis of Sport Tourism in Peripheral Locations

Christaller (1963/1964: 95) states that tourism is 'a branch of the economy that avoids central places and the agglomerations of industry. Tourism is drawn to the periphery . . . (where) one may find, easier than anywhere, the chance of recreation and sport.' Sport tourism in peripheral locations (Chapter 7) is often based on the natural resources found there. Examples of these resources include mountains, lakes and rivers that form the resource base for sports such as mountain climbing, skiing, rafting, sailing, diving and angling (Orams, 1999; Hudson, 1999). Sport tourism in peripheral locations is typically resource-dependent and, therefore, determined by the physical nature of the landscape rather than proximity to market areas. Sport tourism market zones, travel patterns and tourist experiences in peripheral locations stand in contrast to those associated with sports that take place in central locations. The principles governing the spatial dynamics of sport tourism in peripheral areas are proposed in Table 5.2.

Sports space theory applied to peripheral areas suggests that the natural resource base, rather than market access, will determine the locations where sport tourism takes place. A ski resort, for example, is dependent on the requisite elevation, terrain and snow conditions, among other things, to allow participants to engage in their sport in favourable conditions. This is especially the case for niche sport tourism markets, where specific sport motivations requiring unique natural environmental attributes often apply. As Bourdeau *et al.* (2002: 23) observe, 'the location of sites and itineraries thus depends on diverse natural conditions which do not readily lend themselves to the satisfaction of geographic (accessibility), demographic or economic needs'. The resource requirements of

Table 5.2 Spatial dynamics of sport tourism in peripheral areas

1. The main challenge of the sports areas in the periphery is to facilitate visitor access and opportunities to engage in sports in natural areas. Sports areas are located in peripheral areas where natural resources and built infrastructures rather than centrality determine site location decisions.
2. Peripheral sports areas are reliant primarily on active sport tourists as participants rather than spectators.
3. The quality of the sport environment/resource, rather than the number of sports provided, determines the order of the peripheral area within a sports location hierarchy. Quality may be determined by uniqueness, naturalness/absence of impact, remoteness and features of the natural environment.
4. Peripheral sports locations exist in clusters of critical mass, allowing the development of a high standard and range of sports facilities that enhance the standing of the destination in the sports location hierarchy.
5. Higher-order locations are clustered in peripheral areas where natural features and developed infrastructure and services facilitate sport tourism.
6. Consumers of sport tourism in peripheral areas may be motivated by the desire to (a) engage intensively in their chosen sport and/or (b) maximise the tourism opportunities associated with the pursuit of their chosen sport.

sports may be moderated through, for example, snow-making technology in the case of alpine winter sports. Resources such as artificial ski slopes can be constructed at considerable expense in central locations, with immediate access provided for concentrations of population. Notwith-standing these points, the resource requirements of sport tourism in peripheral areas remain the fundamental characteristic of the locations in which they take place.

The inescapable circumstances of sport tourism in peripheral areas provide sport and tourism managers with unique challenges in terms of commercial development (Bourdeau *et al.*, 2002). Remoteness and terrain may limit access, while reliance on weather conditions and climatic uncertainty may compromise the viability of sports or render them impossible. The consequences include seasonal use variations, low-intensity use due to institutional factors, high mobility of visitors between sites and self-sufficiency on the part of many users in terms of service requirements (Bourdeau *et al.*, 2002). Where favourable natural resources and market access coexist, a competitive advantage also exists. The development of a critical mass of sport tourism activities and facilities in peripheral areas may stimulate further investment in transporta-tion and infrastructures, thereby improving access. The development of commercial operations in sport tourism, for example, will give momentum to the development of infrastructures required to facilitate participation.

This discussion suggests that, like central locations, a hierarchy of peripheral sport tourism destinations exists (Table 5.2). Higher-order destinations are generally located in peripheral areas where natural features and developed infrastructure and services are all present. 'Depending on the resources that they offer, and their reputation and use characteristics, sites generally become established in a very clear hier-archy, in which they are identified as being of local, regional or national interest' (Bourdeau *et al.*, 2002: 24). Their study of 2000 climbing sites in France identified a hierarchy in which 85% were considered to be of local, 13% of regional and 2% of national significance. However, the existence and the functioning of a peripheral sport tourism destination are deter-mined to a large extent by tourism infrastructure and services. Teigland (1999: 308) states, in reference to the 1994 Lillehammer Winter Olympics, that 'the influence zone of a particular Olympic Games will vary depending on the distribution of venues in different types of satellite areas ... [and] entry and departure points to the host country or region, especially areas close to airports receiving international visitors'. These principles of sport space assist sport tourism managers to understand the opportunities and potential, as well as the limitations that apply to active and event sport tourism development in peripheral areas (Case study 5.1; see pp. 95–98).

The Spatial Analysis of Active Sport Tourism in Peripheral Areas

The discussions offered in this chapter suggest that the majority of event sport tourism takes place in central locations, while active sport tourism tends to predominate in peripheral locations. Hudson's Case study (see pp. 95–98) focuses on the spatial analysis of active sport tourism, which has received comparatively little attention in the academic literature. One exception is an analysis of the destinations visited by active sport tourists of German, Dutch and French nationality (Table 5.3) (WTO & IOC, 2001). This study considers the destination preferences of 'sport-orientated' and 'less sport-orientated' travellers, which parallels Gammon and Robinson's (1997) distinction between sport tourism and tourism sport (Chapter 3). Study findings show distinct spatial travel patterns associated with active sport tourists of different nationality and motivational profiles (sport-orientated and less sport-orientated). Austria and France are the preferred destinations of Dutch nationals, just as Spain is the preferred destination of active sport tourists from France. Proximity plays an important part in destination choice (Cooper *et al.*, 1993); however, it is apparent that Austria and Switzerland are generally viewed as sport-orientated destinations, while Spain, for example, is the

Table 5.3 Top ten destinations visited by sport-orientated and less sport-orientated tourists: German, Dutch and French nationals (%)

Destination (top ten)	German		Dutch		French	
	Sport-orientated	*Less sport-orientated*	*Sport-orientated*	*Less sport-orientated*	*Sport-orientated*	*Less sport-orientated*
Austria	51	3	26	34	17	
Italy	19	14	5	5	13	4
Switzerland	9		8		19	
Spain	4	32	3		33	42
France	3	5	24	21		
Czech Republic	3					
Netherlands	2	7				
Denmark	1	3				
Great Britain	1		2	1		
Poland	1					
Other	6	36	32	39	18	54

Source: based on WTO and IOC (2001)

destination of choice for many less sports-orientated travellers from Germany and France.

A spatial analysis of golf highlights the variations that exist in the regional supply of sport tourism products (Priestley, 1995). Golf sport tourism associated with championship courses takes place mainly in Britain and the USA, where the Grand Slam Opens (British and US Opens and the Professional Golf Association) are played on a rotation basis. The spatial distribution of single integrated golf resorts stands in obvious contrast. 'Numerous resorts exist in the sunniest areas of the USA (Florida, Hawaii and California), on the southeast coast of Australia [and] similar resorts have appeared in the Caribbean, South Pacific and Indian Ocean islands' (Priestley, 1995: 210). Priestley (1995) also performs an analysis of demand for golf, which identifies the USA, Japan and the UK as prominent golf travel markets. The Japanese golf market is particularly important as the demand for golf in Japan has increased beyond the capacity of domestic golf courses. These findings confirm the importance of understanding established spatial travel patterns that exist in sport tourism, as they have implications for its continuing development.

Management Implications and Opportunities

This discussion highlights important differences between sport tourism development in central and peripheral locations, most notably in terms of resource requirements. Both exist within hierarchies that are influenced by quite different factors. The range and standard of sports facilities and the number of sports that a location serves influence the central sport location hierarchy. Higher-order sports locations may, for different sports, serve national or international market catchments. The planned development of sport tourism precincts can be used to enhance the status of the sport tourism location. Such actions should be planned and developed in association with transport nodes, places of accommodation and other elements of tourism infrastructure. The planning and development of peripheral sports locations, by contrast, offers the challenge of developing a critical mass of sport tourism resources and tourist infrastructure. This may require the linking of resources within coherent destination regions through, for example, the coordinated promotion of ski resorts or golf courses within a region. '[C]ooperation and coordination between singular municipalities concerning tourism seems to be advantageous' (Maier & Weber, 1993: 40). In both central and peripheral locations, sport tourism development interests are fostered when planned in a coordinated manner.

The factors influencing sport tourism market range are also different between central and peripheral locations. In event sport tourism, market range is influenced by factors such as performance, playing style and cultural factors relating to team loyalty. The status of a central sports location tends to be enhanced through the coordinated development of tourism infrastructure and services as well as sports facilities. Factors that determine market range for sport in peripheral areas centre on the quality and cost of the sport tourist experience. Market range may be moderated through strategic sport tourism development and marketing initiatives. Ease of accessibility is critical to the market range of sports that take place in central locations. Accessibility may be improved through innovative sports management, planned in association with tourism destination managers. Periodic marketing, for instance, is a means of taking sports to locations that offer, among other things, high market access. The challenge of sport tourism management in peripheral areas, by contrast, revolves around attracting sport tourists to peripheral locations, due to the impossibility of transporting many nature-based sports into central locations (Chapter 7). This requires the delivery and promotion of sport tourist experiences that are competitive in terms of quality, while recognising the constraints of time, cost, access and lifestyle that influence demand for peripheral sport tourism destinations. These constraints need to be considered in sport tourism development decisions.

Conclusion

This chapter highlights the factors that determine the locations of sport sites and the spatial dimensions of sport tourism travel flows. It extends the concept of the sport centre and the hierarchy of sport locations (Bale, 1993a) within the context of sport tourism. The prominence and status of sport tourism centres are determined by the range and quality of sports experiences, in combination with levels of service development and unique sport tourism products. Sports locations may command local, regional or national travel flows that can be actively influenced by sport and tourism organisations. However, the location of sport tourism activities in central or peripheral areas exerts a major influence of the market range, spatial travel flows and visitor patterns associated with the sport tourism phenomenon. An appreciation of travel flows that exist within the spatial dimension of sport tourism is fundamental for sport tourism development. Sports and tourism managers can enhance the status of sports locations, and thereby extend market range, through the implementation of development strategies. This goal is most effectively achieved when sport and tourism management initiatives are planned and implemented in a coordinated manner (Glyptis, 1991; Weed & Bull, 1997a).

Further Reading

The journal, *Tourism Geographies*, provides valuable insights into the study of the geographical principles of space, place and environment within the field of tourism. Lew's (2001) editorial in *Tourism Geographies* (Volume 3, Number 1) provides a concise review of the study of tourism and geography space. Hall and Page (1999) present insights into the geography of tourism and the study of geography space. Those with general interests in the geography of tourism are directed towards the writings of D. G. Pearce (1987, 1989), Mitchell and Murphy (1991) and Boniface and Cooper (1994). John Bale is the pioneer of studies in the geography of sport. His spatial analyses of sport, like those of Rooney (1988, 1992), are influential sources, which demonstrate considerable relevance to the study of sport tourism.

Specifically within the field of sport tourism, the study of geography space is significantly advanced by the work of Redmond (1990, 1991). A more recent example of work in this field is provided by Bourdeau *et al.* (2002). The regional analysis of sport and sport tourism is a subject of considerable relevance to the spatial analyses presented in this chapter. Rooney and Pillsbury (1992) offer a detailed regional analysis of sports resources and participation in sports in the USA. Similarly Maier and Weber (1993) present a regional analysis of sport and tourism resources, and consider the relevance of their discussions in terms of local and regional planning. Finally, Hall (2004) provides valuable insights into sport tourism in the built environment, with reference to the transportability of sports and its relevance to urban regeneration strategies.

Case study 5.1

Travel Flows and Spatial Distribution in the Ski Industry

Simon Hudson, University of Calgary, Canada

The current ski market is estimated at some 70 million worldwide. Of that number, 77% are alpine skiers, 16% are snowboarders, while the remainder prefer cross-country skiing. Europe accounts for approximately 30 million skiers, the USA and Canada between them generate an estimated 20 million skiers or boarders and Japan has 14 million. The majority of these participants are domestic. For example, fewer than one million Americans have ever been abroad for a skiing holiday. Approximately 6000 ski areas in 78 countries currently exist. Of the recorded ski areas, about 4000 are in Europe, fewer than a 1000 each are found in North America and in Asia, and about 100 are in the southern hemisphere, mostly in Argentina, Chile, Australia and New Zealand (Table 5.4).

Table 5.4 Skiing worldwide

Country	Resorts	Lifts	Skier visits (million)
Japan	460	3600	75
France	390	4143	56
USA	503	2269	57
Austria	604	3473	43
Italy	341	2854	37
Switzerland	288	1762	31
Canada	284	1375	17
Germany	491	1670	20
Sweden	415	950	12
Norway	207	405	8
Czech Republic	174	1500	4.8
Spain	33	294	4.3
Australia	18	139	2.6
Finland	117	505	2.0
Poland	71	110	2.0
South Korea	27	70	1.9
Andorra	5	115	1.5
New Zealand	26	64	1.1
Russia	104	32	0.9
Chile	14	84	0.8
Argentina	22	72	0.7
Bulgaria	4	50	0.6
Iran	20	45	0.5
Greece	17	40	0.4
Turkey	12	25	0.3
Lebanon	7	18	0.2
Slovakia	322	*	*
Slovenia	55	*	*
Serbia	19	*	*
China	100	*	*
Rest of the world	900 (approx.)	*	*
Total	6000	26,664	380.6

Note: * = unknown

Ski resorts can be divided generally into a tripartite location hierarchy based on the spatial extent of their market range:

(1) National resorts that attract people, generally from within a state, province or region within a country.
(2) Regional resorts that skiers will travel several hundred miles to reach. In Europe, these resorts will entice skiers across one or several countries. Examples are skiers travelling from the UK to Austria, or from New York to the Canadian Rockies.
(3) International destination resorts (300–400 in total) that attract skiers from all over the world, such as Whistler in Canada, Vail in Colorado and Zermatt in Switzerland.

In the first few decades of ski area development, most people did not ski beyond their own ski hills. The skiing market has matured rapidly in Europe and America, but is evolving faster in other areas of the world, such as eastern Europe, Korea and South-east Asia. The skier market has changed as people travel more and as ski companies become multinationals. Thousands of North American skiers visit the European Alps every year. Indeed, without European skiers, Canadian resorts would currently be showing negative growth.

In North America skiing in a mass tourism context emerged in the 1950s with increased private car ownership, the development of an interstate highway system and a marketing programme by the railroad companies, who originally created resorts to keep people using their trains during the winter months. The spatial distribution of ski areas in North America lies in the west and in the east. The north-east is the most densely populated area of the USA. For most Americans, travel time and cost are critical variables when deciding to ski. Sixty-seven percent of resort areas are within 74 miles or easy commuting distance of major metropolitan areas. Domestic skiers tend to confine their skiing to a couple of days on the weekends, but a small number of US skiers travel to Canada every year to ski (about 500,000). Thus, ski resorts can also be divided into weekend resorts, which require two or more hours of driving time, and vacation resorts, which are typically located in more remote locations where snow conditions are more consistent.

Because of the need for snow, appropriate terrain and the right climate, resort areas tend to be clustered in their spatial distribution, and therefore offer skiers several choices when they reach the mountains. This is the case in Canada, where most weekend ski area facilities are clustered around the eastern, most populated provinces, Ontario and Quebec, which are close to the American border, and the cities of New York, Boston and Philadelphia. However, the most popular resorts, particularly among overseas visitors, are in western Canada. The provinces of British Columbia and Alberta receive the greatest number of overseas skiers from the UK (about 80,000) and they account for around 40% of the revenues generated by foreign skiers. Mexico, Brazil and Argentina are proving to be a growing source of inbound skiers.

The significance of transport nodes and infrastructure in spatial tourism travel patterns is clearly evident in the European ski market. Vacation skiers from the northern countries, such as Germany, the Benelux countries, the UK and Scandinavia, represent half the skier market for the European Alpine countries. Austria receives 47% of the European winter sport tourism market, mainly from the UK and Germany. This compares with France (14%), Switzerland (11%) and Italy (11%). Accessibility to the latter two countries has improved with a new regional airport serving the Engadin region of Switzerland, with St Moritz at its heart, and the opening of the new international airport at Turin in Italy. However, British skiers are increasingly favouring France as a destination, using low-cost airlines and high-speed rail and road links via the channel tunnel. The policy of developing the world's biggest ski areas at snow-sure altitudes has paid dividends for the French, who boast over 56 million skier visits, and the country continues to invest in better road and rail links in the mountains. Andorra, located between France and Spain, is a beneficiary of easy access from Barcelona. With over 2.3 million skier visits, the main problem now is finding road space and lodging to accommodate growing demand.

Beyond Europe and North America, access remains an important consideration in ski area development. In China for example, where skiing is growing faster than anywhere else in the world, numerous studies have been conducted to determine the best locations within easy reach of the major populated cities. To date, the best option for the Chinese capital Beijing is Saibei, a rather basic resort created within 170 miles (272 km) of the capital.

Alongside Jilin province, Heilongjiang in the north-eastern corner of China appears to be the country's major boom area for resort development; especially around the city of Harbin, which has seen heavy investment in a modern airport and road network. The Provincial Government has announced plans to open up 250 new ski centres in that province alone in the next decade. It would join Austria's Tyrol and Canada's Quebec as one of the few 'regions' in the world to boast in excess of 100 ski centres.

Further reading

Hudson, S. (1998) There's no business like snow business! Marketing skiing into the 21st century. *Journal of Vacation Marketing* 4 (4), 393–407.
Hudson, S. (2000) *Snow Business: A Study of the International Ski Industry.* London: The Continuum International Publishing Group.
Thorne, P. (2000) 2001 – A global ski odyssey. *Ski Area Management* 40 (6), 47–49.

Chapter 6

Place, Sport and Culture

We have essentially treated sport and tourism as cultural experiences – sport as a cultural experience of physical activity; tourism as a cultural experience of place. It will come as no surprise, therefore, that the nature of sport tourism . . . is about an experience of physical activity tied to an experience of place.

(Standeven & De Knop, 1999: 58)

Introduction

Sport exerts a significant influence upon the meanings that people attach to space. These meanings are central to the experience of sport tourists, to the impacts felt by their hosts and to the strategies used by sport tourism managers. The validity of these claims will be demonstrated in this chapter by considering the unique nature of sport tourism places, by examining sport and culture in relation to place identity, and by considering sport as a strategy to sell tourism places. A Case study that explores the way that the 1998 Commonwealth Games in Kuala Lumpur (Malaysia) were used to influence the city's image highlights several important dimensions of these discussions (Case study 6.1; see pp. 114–117).

Place

Place is concerned with the meaning attached to space (Tuan, 1974). In postmodern terms, Crouch (2000: 64) expands on the difference between space and place by suggesting that

[s]pace can be a background, a context, a 'given' objective component of leisure and tourism. In that way it is seen as a location, a National Park or a site where particular leisure/tourism happens, a distance between things. Place can be a physical image that can be rendered metaphorical as the content of brochures, 'landscape' as a foil for what people might imagine they do. . . . In this way it may be that place is understood to be a cultural text that people read and recognize directed by the particular intentions of a producer or promoter.

While the geometric characteristics of space can be objectively measured, place is much more subjective in nature. Individuals and groups are constantly defining and refining the meanings that they attach to spaces. As other aspects of their lives change, so do the meanings that they attach to spaces. Place meanings are constantly being renegotiated. The negotiation of place helps individuals and groups to construct their identities and it provides tourism managers with the opportunity to promote and sell destinations.

Tourism places

In his seminal work, *Place and Placelessness*, Relph (1976) argued that the concept of sense of place was most applicable in the local environment, where individuals are in a position to develop deep attachments to place. He suggested that tourists were one of the least likely groups to develop a 'sense of place' in relation to the destinations that they visit because of the superficial nature of their experience and the tendency of the tourism industry to present 'disneyfied' landscapes devoid of deeper meaning. This view of tourism contrasts markedly from the position that tourism involves a serious pursuit of meaning and authenticity (MacCannell, 1973). More specifically, it has been persuasively argued by Cuthbertson *et al.* (1997) that many types of travellers are likely to form strong attachments to place, an example being those that nomadic people have to the places that they travel through.

Travelling for pleasure beyond the boundaries of one's life-space implies that there is some experience available at the destination, which cannot be found at home and which compensates for the costs of the trip (Cohen, 1996). Standeven and De Knop (1999: 57) build on this line of argument by suggesting that

> [the] nature of tourism is rooted in authentic cultural experience of places away from home that have different characteristics. Those characteristics are unique to each place, and the tourist views, feels, hears, smells, and touches them. Their differences (and their similarities) become a part of his or her conscious experience.

The destinations where authentic experience occurs become infused with meaning for those who visit them. Such logic suggests that the concept of place is very applicable to sport tourism. From the perspective of the tourism industry, the more meaningful that a destination is for visitors in a positive sense, the greater that destination's competitive advantage in the tourism market place (D. Williams *et al.*, 1992).

Sport places and tourism

The experiences of sport tourists '– staged or real – result from tourists' interactions with place' (Standeven & De Knop, 1999: 58). There are at least four possible sources of this meaning that have been highlighted in the literature. In the first instance, Bale (1993a) argues that there is a changing 'religious' allegiance of a substantial portion of the public. Rather than worshipping at Christ's altar, many people have substituted sport's altar. Tourism scholars have also adopted the metaphor of religion. MacCannell (1973) suggests that tourist travel is analogous to a pilgrimage. He argues that tourists are motivated by the search for the authentic. Cohen's (1996) existential mode of touristic experience also suggests that this type of tourism represents a pilgrimage for modern humans. Like pilgrims, tourists travel from the profane (origin) to the sacred (destination) and back to the profane (origin) (Graburn, 1989). In a tourism context, individuals define the sacred and the profane in a reflexive manner. Generally, however, tourism sites act as a refuge from modernity and the sacred forms a reality separate from the ordinary lives of travellers. The search for sacred sites may reflect a response to conditions of rootlessness that are increasingly characterising the postmodern world.

A second way that sport spaces become endowed with meaning is through the development of home-like ties to a site, even though that site may be far removed from one's residence. A particular sporting venue may become home as fans or active participants develop allegiances to the site (Chapter 5). This idea of 'home' contrasts with most technical definitions of the tourist, which provide an arbitrary distance threshold that, once surpassed, define a traveller as a tourist or excursionist. In doing so, interesting questions are raised about the meaning that these 'home' fans attach to the destination. For example, Nogawa *et al.* (1996) suggest that the distance travelled to a sport tourism destination is a significant factor in the type of behaviours demonstrated by the visitor, although the authors did not consider the psychological attachment of these visitors to the destination. In their study of visitors to university football games in Gainesville, Florida, Gibson *et al.* (2002) did, however, find that sport tourists who identified with the 'home team' tended to participate in few non-sport tourist activities while visiting the town. They speculated that sport tourists identifying with the 'visiting team' might behave more like 'typical tourists' in a destination.

A third way that sport spaces may become endowed with meaning is through aesthetics. In this case, place meaning is derived from a variety of sporting landscape elements that contribute to the aesthetics of a sport place (Bale, 1993a). The greater the variety within the ensemble, the greater the potential for gratification from the sport experience. Over time, a unique blend of elements may symbolise the sporting place in a way that was never imagined by the original designers of the sporting place.

Sporting heritage is the last element that Bale (1993a) highlights as influencing the way sport sites become endowed with meaning. The concepts of sport heritage places and sport heritage tourists fit well with the idea of nostalgia sport tourism (Gibson, 1998a; Gammon, 2002; Redmond, 1990). Support for this view is found in the prevalence of sport museums, tours of former Olympic sites and pilgrimages to the origins of various sports, such as golf at St Andrews in Scotland (Case study 10.1; see pp. 200–203).

While all of these factors infuse sport spaces with meaning to create sport tourism places, Bale (1989) notes the emergence of sportscapes as a counter trend. In fact, these sportscapes are an embodiment of 'placelessness' as described by Relph (1976):

> In the twentieth century sportscapes rather than landscapes have tended to characterize the sports environment. . . . New materials had changed the shape of the stadium and the texture of the surfaces; fields became carpets and parks became concrete bowls. Most sports require artificial settings, although the degree to which the natural environment needs to change varies between sports. (Bale, 1989: 145)

Sport is relatively unique in this regard. In few activities has there been so much pressure to make one place exactly the same as another (Bale, 1989). The rationale for this pressure is at least fourfold:

- an attempt to ensure spectator and participant comfort and safety;
- standardisation of the playing fields and sites, thereby providing an 'even playing field' and, in so doing, fostering fairer competition between places;
- a reflection of technological advances that have allowed for 'improved' performance; and
- an outcome of mass media broadcast requirements, both in terms of technological needs and in terms of market appeal.

This trend is closely associated with the broader process of globalisation as discussed in Chapter 4.

Culture, Place and Identity

Place is intimately tied to culture. The meanings that are attached to sport spaces are strongly influenced by the cultural context in which sport and tourism exist. Culture relates to sport in a number of ways, but three of the most tangible associations are: (1) cultural programmes run in association with sport events; (2) sport as a form of popular culture; and (3) subcultures in sport. Each of these cultural dimensions influences the meaning that is attached to sport spaces and, in so doing, they affect place identity and, potentially, place marketing for tourism.

Sport and culture

Sport and culture are often treated as separate but complementary activities. This treatment is particularly evident at major sporting events, which may have distinct cultural and sporting programmes. The opening and closing ceremonies of the Olympic Games provide a good example of the conscious mix of sport and culture, as do the separate Olympic cultural programmes organised by host cities.

There are three types of narrative approaches associated with the opening ceremonies of major sporting events. Moragas Spa *et al.* (1995: 105) have categorised them as history, party and show. In the first case, the ceremony is treated as a 'unique historic event taking place in that moment, although forming part of a historic chain'. The opening ceremonies of the 1995 Rugby World Cup in South Africa provided an example of the way that these events can be used to construct identity. This ceremony presented a vision of a harmonious 'rainbow' nation that was in keeping with a post-apartheid country trying to promote itself as a major tourist destination (Nauright, 1997a). In the second instance, the ceremony is treated as a celebration and pays particular attention to the event's cultural aspects. 'It is a peak experience; an explosion of culture, theatre and joy' (Moragas Spa *et al.*, 1995: 107). Performing arts that are indigenous to the hosting city are often showcased. Finally, the third type of ceremony is one of entertainment. This type of ceremony downplays the 'distraction' of the cultural and ritual structures of the event and tries to provide 'an entertaining introduction to the "real" excitement: the sports competition' (Moragas Spa *et al.*, 1995: 108). Each of these three approaches, but most particularly the second, may serve the explicit positioning of culture in relation to place.

The 'fine arts' programme held in conjunction with the sporting competitions of the Olympic Games is another example of the distinct but complementary association of sport and culture. The charter of the International Olympic Committee requires that a fine arts programme be held under the auspices of the local host committee. A variety of approaches have been taken with this arts agenda, but increasingly it has been used as a way to promote the host city and country. For the 2000 Summer Games in Sydney, a four-year plan was developed called the Sydney Cultural Olympiad. Its four main components were 'The Dreaming' in 1997, designed to showcase Aboriginal culture in Australia; 'A Sea Change' in 1998, which emphasised the eras of migration to Australia; 'Reaching the World' in 1999, featuring performance tours by elite Australian artists and performers; and, finally, 'Harbour of Life' in

2000, an on-site Sydney exhibition of the highest quality Australian and international artists. Stevenson (1997: 236) argued that the Sydney 2000 Cultural Olympiad was principally 'concerned with constructing and promoting images and representations of Australianness that will assist the symbolic and material sale of the Games'. This view is consistent with the statement of the Artistic Director for the Cultural Olympiad who stated that 'the four festivals of the Cultural Olympiad . . . are the greatest opportunity we have ever had to change national and international perceptions about Australia' (Voumard, 1995: 14a). Silk's Case study (see pp. 114–117) extends the idea that sport and culture can be used to construct place identity. He makes this point through an analysis of the 1998 Commonwealth Games in Kuala Lumpur. His analysis demonstrates the extent to which sport may be staged to construct a favourable place identity.

Sport as culture

Popular culture as manifested in sport is one of the main ways that humans develop personal and collective identities. It is through these personal and collective identities that place identity is developed. At its most basic, identity is the way that we perceive ourselves, as individuals and collectives, based on prevailing social and ideological values and practices (McConnell & Edwards, 2000). It is a social phenomenon developed through social and cultural processes as found in the press, television and other dominant cultural organisations. Identity is the way in which people make sense of the self through affiliation and bonds with other people and the cultures that define these affiliations (Dauncey & Hare, 2000).

National identity is typically thought of in the way that nations differ from each other in terms of stereotypes, symbols and practices, including those associated with sport (S. J. Jackson, 1994; McConnell & Edwards, 2000) (Focus point 6.1). McGuirk and Rowe (2001: 52, 53) have captured this idea more broadly:

> Places have come to be conceptualized as constructed through a dynamic articulation of their material and representational dimensions, and place identity is understood to be mutable, contingent and fluid. Cultural stocks of knowledge about places can, however, constitute a prevailing, often stubbornly persistent balance of forces that name, interpret and project place meanings. A place in this sense is a 'text', the meaning of which is continually being made, reproduced and re-made.

Place identity is influenced by many cultural attributes, but sport certainly appears to be one of the most dominant. Nauright (1996: 69)

Focus point 6.1

The Arctic Winter Games

The Arctic Winter Games (AWG) represent a unique sporting festival that combines athletic competition, cultural exhibition and social interchange between participants who reside in the northern latitudes of the northern hemisphere. These Games have been running on a biennial basis since 1970, with regular participating regions from all of Canada's territories and northern provinces, Alaska, Greenland and northern Russia. Recent competitions have attracted over 2000 athletes, coaches, mission staff, officials, cultural performers, spectators and media representatives in a celebration of sport and culture. Featured sports reflect the contemporary and traditional values of the indigenous cultures of the north. Along with modern winter sports, such as ice hockey, snowboarding and figure skating, there are a variety of traditional Inuit and Dene Indigenous sports, which are offered under the direction of native elders who share the cultural significance and provide coaching assistance to youthful athletes participating in these events. Examples include the knuckle hop, the Alaskan high kick and the sledge jump. Other northern sport activities include dog sled racing and a snowshoe biathlon. All of these sports are selected for their northern flavour, participant base and development potential. In addition to offering sport as culture, the AWG include a formal cultural programme, which is enhanced by a small cultural group of performing artists who accompany the athletic contingent from each participating region. Displays of visual arts and crafts are also shown portraying the north's varied and unique cultures. The host society weaves these elements into an impressive cultural programme, which culminates in a spectacular cultural gala. The Games are truly a celebration of sport and northern cultures. This mix of culture and sport provides a unique experience of place that cannot be duplicated in other types of tourism activities.

Source: http://www.awg.ca

suggests that not only is sport a factor in the process of constructing place identity, but

> [it] is one of the most significant shapers of collective or group identity in the contemporary world. In many cases, sporting events and people's reaction to them are the clearest public manifestations of culture and collective identities in a given society.

It is not just high-profile sporting competitions that influence and reflect place identity. Sports and leisure pursuits that occur on a daily basis in local communities are also important (Nauright, 1997b; Harahousou, 1999).

Place identity through sport is constructed in at least four ways that have particular relevance to tourism. These include (1) the association of particular sports to specific regions; (2) the unifying forces of competitive hierarchies found within sport; (3) identification with sporting success; and (4) the personification of place through sporting heroes and heroines.

Specific sports are commonly associated with particular nations. This connection may be based on a variety of factors, but one of the most powerful is the role that a given sport has played in a nation's heritage. An example of this type of association is that of rugby union in New Zealand. Fougere (1989: 111) has suggested that rugby

> served from the end of last century [1900] as a mirror to New Zealand society. It symbolized a pattern of social relationships that, in New Zealand eyes, made New Zealand both distinctive and admirable. As such it provided an important basis for the construction of a sense of national unity and individual identity.

The competitive hierarchy that exists in many sports is also an important factor in the promotion of place identity (McGuirk & Rowe, 2001). The principle reflected in the Bedouin saying, 'I against my brother, I and my brother against my cousin, I and my brother and my cousin against the world', reflects the aggregation of territorial interest that occurs within a competitive hierarchy (Fougere, 1989: 116). Place identity is fostered through a growing territory as successively higher levels of the competitive hierarchy are reached. In this process, many of the real differences and disparities that are found within these places are overshadowed or subsumed.

The relative success of a region in terms of its sport performance also influences the connection between sport and place identity. In addition to being in the 'news' more frequently, places with teams that consistently win major championships tend to be characterised as winners in their own right. Such success can provide a sense of common identity, even when there may be numerous other social and economic divisions that exist within the region (Bale, 1989, 1993a; McGuirk & Rowe, 2001). One has only to look at the national celebrations associated with World Cup football to see evidence of this dynamic (Dauncey & Hare, 2000).

Finally, sport heroes and heroines can have a strong impact on the way that we identify with place (Nauright, 1996; Dauncey & Hare, 2000). Canadians, for example, take tremendous pride in their ice hockey hero, Wayne Gretzky. Beardsley (1987: 109, 111) describes the reason for this sentiment:

> Because hockey so clearly defines the Canadian experience, Wayne Gretzky is the latest in a long line of hockey heroes who personify the hopes, wishes, and dreams of the Canadian people . . . by finding greatness in him, we find it in ourselves.

Sport subcultures

Sport subcultures represent a third cultural dimension of sport that is relevant to place identity in a tourism context. These subcultures are generally characterised by commitment to a particular sport, distinguishing symbols or cultural capital, and various career stages in terms of subculture membership. Sport subcultures also tend to have unique associations with place.

For example, the subculture of windsurfing has been described as a culture of 'conspicuous commitment' (Wheaton, 2000). This commitment is expressed in a number of ways, but at its core is the prowess, dedication and skill that members demonstrate in relation to their sport. Identifiable communities form around sports like windsurfing and these communities tend to share characteristics that go beyond the sporting activity itself. Green and Chalip (1998: 280) describe women's football as a sport subculture that 'gives participants much more than the opportunity to play together. It is a statement about who they are and the conventions by which they refuse to be constrained'. More generally, the adoption of subculture identity through sports is seen as a way of asserting cultural identity and a sense of community in a society fragmented by divisions of class, race and gender (Beezer & Hebdige, 1992). In many cases, such as surfing (Law, 2001) and snowboarding (Heino, 2000), sport subcultures represent a form of 'counter-culture' in that members deliberately distance themselves from the mainstream norms and practices of society.

Style incorporates the symbolic representations of subculture. This form of cultural capital has been found in the dress, hair and speech styles of surfers (Law, 2001), snowboarders (Heino, 2000), climbers (Donnelly & Young, 1988) and many other sport subculture groups. More generally, for the 'hard-core' members, these subculture symbols permeate all aspects of their lives:

> Participation in this (subculture) lifestyle is displayed in a range of symbols such as clothes, speech, car, and associated leisure activities; however, for the dedicated, often-obsessive participant, windsurfing participation is a whole way of life in which windsurfers seek hedonism, freedom and self-expression. For 'core' members . . . , windsurfing dictates their leisure time, their work time, their choice of career, and where they live. (Wheaton, 2000: 256)

Membership status within these subcultures is characterised by career stages that are based on the demonstration of commitment and prowess. These stages include (1) presocialisation or information-gathering about the subculture; (2) recruitment and selection by the subculture; (3) socialisation in the subculture; and (4) acceptance or ostracism from the subculture (Donnelly & Young, 1988). As a result, there is a variety of levels of membership in these subcultures, ranging from 'outsiders' who gather information so that they can obtain membership, through to the hard-core members who have achieved widespread acceptance. Membership and cultural identity within the group are, however, dynamic.

In the context of the mode of leisure experience framework (D. Williams *et al.*, 1992), sport subcultures tend to be more focused on activity and companionship than on place. Green and Chalip (1998: 275) arrived at this conclusion in their study of women football players participating in a tournament in Florida. They suggested that these particular sport tourists 'seek opportunities to share and affirm their identities as football players. It is the occasion to celebrate a subculture shared with others from distant places, *rather than the site itself*, that attracts them'. In this case, the host destination provided a social space for female football players to celebrate their subculture. Participants were able to distance themselves from their regular lives, they enjoyed a sense of camaraderie with their teammates and other members of the subculture, and they were given the opportunity to parade their subculture identities. The destination was described as facilitating the primary purpose of the visit to the tournament site.

At another level, sport subcultures are intimately connected and dependent on specific places for their sport. This is true of climbers, surfers, windsurfers, snowboarders and many other 'extreme' sport subcultures that are currently enjoying popularity. These groups tend to be very dependent on natural resources found in the periphery (Chapter 5). Their strong subculture commitment provides them with the motivations to overcome the constraint of distance.

Often, the spaces used by these subculture groups are contested. For instance, skiers did not welcome snowboarders when the sport was initially introduced to the slopes of the major ski resorts (Heino, 2000; Hudson, 1999). Due to financial necessity, effective management and on-site modifications, snowboarders and skiers increasingly share these slopes in harmony. Nevertheless, while the space associated with these sports is increasingly shared, subculture place identity may be quite distinct.

Subculture groups also recognise special places through access to 'insider information' (Donnelly & Young, 1988). As members of subculture groups progress through their subculture careers they become privy to information about 'special' sites in the context of their group. Experience at these sites may be closely tied to a member's status within his/her subculture. Place can become one with the activity. Hard-core subculture members will tend to live near to where they can be active in their sport and will use their vacation time to travel to destinations that are 'sacred' to their sport.

Marketing Place Through Sport

The tourism industry is in the business of selling places. Place is commodified through the process of marketing. The primary goal of a place marketer is to construct a new image of the place to replace either vague or negative images previously held by residents, investors and visitors (Page & Hall, 2003). In pursuing this goal, the tourism industry and the destination are actively trying to influence the meaning that is attached to a particular area.

The logic that underlies place marketing is twofold. First, it is based on an understanding of the way that place consumers, in this case sport tourists, make decisions about the destinations that they visit. Baloglu and McCleary (1999: 870) summarise this view, stating that destination

> image is mainly caused or formed by two major forces: stimulus factors and personal factors. The former are those that stem from the external stimulus and physical object as well as previous experience. Personal factors, on the other hand, are the characteristics (social and psychological) of the perceiver.

In place marketing, personal factors can be addressed through target marketing, while the stimulus factors can be modified through product development and promotion. The belief that destination image or place identity can be consciously manipulated is a fundamental assumption of place marketing (Gallarza *et al.*, 2002).

The second line of logic that explains increased attention to place marketing is that destinations are facing increasing competition from other places (Hall, 1998). Kotler *et al.* (1993: 346) argue that we are living in a time of 'place wars':

> The globalization of the world's economy and the accelerating pace of technological change are two forces that require all places to learn to compete. Places must learn to think more like businesses, developing products, markets, and customers.

Page and Hall (2003: 309) highlight the need to commodify particular aspects of place in the process of place marketing: 'In the case of urban [or regional] re-imaging, marketing practices, such as branding, rely upon the commodification of particular aspects of place, exploiting, reinventing or creating place images in order to sell the place as a destination product for tourists or investment.'

Sport is one of the most powerful ways of establishing place identity, as culture is one of the key factors in distinguishing places. By harnessing the cultural dimensions of sport, place marketers are able to commodify 'the ways of living' in a place. In a sport context, this can be done by developing (1) major facilities; (2) hallmark events; (3) focused tourism marketing strategies and policies; and (4) broad-based leisure and cultural opportunities within a destination (Hall, 1998).

Establishing a critical mass of visitor attractions and facilities has proven to be one of the most popular strategies for re-imaging a city. An obvious benefactor of this trend has been the real estate sector within the city, but the sport and tourism sectors have also been active promoters of this strategy. Belanger's (2000: 390) description of the development of a new home for the Montreal Canadians professional ice hockey team provides a good illustration of re-imaging a city:

> In 1996, the Montreal Canadians were poised to move to a new 'Temple' only this time christened with a corporate name: the Molson Centre. Completely financed by private capital and integrated into the 'revitalization' of the Windsor block in downtown Montreal, the construction of the Molson Centre was heralded as an all-Quebecois economic masterpiece. The creation of this new spectacular entertainment complex was promoted as a significant boost to Montreal's economy and as an act of bravery on Molson's part for solely financing this project in an unstable political and economic context.

Another high-profile strategy for re-imaging places is the hosting of hallmark events (Getz, 1997; Hall, 1992a). Sporting events are particularly attractive, given the media attention that they tend to attract. The Australian Tourist Commission actively tried to capitalise on the opportunity to re-image Australia in connection with the Sydney 2000 Olympic Games (Morse, 2001). They did this by developing a detailed strategy that included joint promotions with Olympic sponsors, a visiting media programme prior to, during and after the Games, the provision of logistical support for television broadcasters, the provision of press facilities for non-accredited media as well as accredited media, business development support, specially targeted promotions at high-yield markets and an assortment of other activities including a detailed post-Games strategy. At a broader level, Australia made a conscious attempt to reposition its overall brand. In fact, the International Olympic Committee's Director of Marketing stated:

> Australia is the first Olympic host nation to take full advantage of the Games to vigorously pursue tourism for the benefit of the whole country. It's something we've never seen take place to this level before, and it's a model that we would like to see carried forward to future Olympic Games in Athens and beyond. (Payne as cited in Brown *et al.*, 2002: 175)

A third popular approach to re-imaging places for tourism is non-event-related tourism marketing that attempts to capitalise on a positive association between sport and place. A recent example of this occurred in the 1998 New Zealand promotional strategy linking rugby to place. In announcing the campaign, the then Minister of Tourism stated that 'the upcoming promotion will leverage off the popularity of the All Blacks in rugby-mad South Africa to create an awareness of New Zealand and all its attractions' (New Zealand Tourism Board, 1998: 2). Sport-related marketing slogans, such as Edmonton's (Canada) 'City of Champions', also reflect this type of place-marketing strategy.

Finally, the widespread development of sport-related leisure and cultural services is a fourth type of approach used to sell places that is based on sport. This approach goes beyond the support of high-profile professional sports to the development of a sporting ethic within the place through such things as parkland and shorefront development that encourages active sporting pursuits such as jogging, cycling and sailing. Glasgow has used this approach to reposition itself as an active healthy community, both in terms of self-identity and in terms of destination image (Porteous, 2000; Hooper, 1998), as has Korea (Focus point 6.2).

Management Implications and Opportunities

The foregoing discussion suggests that tourism mangers have considerable opportunity to market 'place' through sport. This may be done indirectly by influencing the development of sport in a region, thereby impacting the sporting opportunities available and the way that region is viewed in terms of sport. However, a more direct approach to place-marketing through sport can also be taken. At a broad level, using sporting events or sport in general to foster a brand image for the destination offers the opportunity to benefit from sport's high profile in the media. A sport-based brand may serve as a primary draw for many potential visitors and is likely to serve as an important secondary attraction or appealing background context for others. Specific strategies can also be developed. Target marketing represents one such strategy that can capitalise on the existing sport resources that may be distinctive or unique to a place. This approach can be used to develop sporting opportunities, such as events or the designation of social spaces that attract mobile sporting subcultures.

A number of issues need to be considered in association with the numerous opportunities to market 'place' through sport. Bale's (1989) spectre of the trend towards homogenous sportscapes should certainly be of concern to sport tourism managers. Taken to its extreme, in a homogeneous sportscape, the need or desire to travel to different areas for sport is greatly reduced. Theoretically, sports leagues could be construed in a way in which geography is of little relevance. For example, the economies of scale associated with an elite competition in a centralised broadcast studio/sport facility would certainly alter travel flows for live viewing,

---

Focus point 6.2

Stadium Design in Korea

Korea co-hosted the world's most watched single sport event, the Fédération Internationale de Football Association (FIFA) World Cup in 2002. This event provided the opportunity to project the culture and way of life of Korea through the medium of stadium design, to those who attended games during the World Cup, and via television to a vast international audience. New stadia were designed and developed as a vehicle of image projection in the ten host cities in Korea. These stadia were designed to reflect the culture, natural surroundings and characteristics unique to each city. Seoul was the focal point of the Korean half of the tournament, where the opening ceremony took place prior to the match between defending champion France and their opponent, Senegal. The 65,856-seat stadium features an architectural design that symbolises a combination of Korean kites and octagonal serving trays. Munhak Stadium, a 50,616-seat facility in Incheon, has a sailboat-designed roof to reflect the city's historical role as Korea's leading maritime gateway. The traditional curved roofs at the stadium in Suwon are designed to bring to mind the ancient Hwaseong Fortress, a 5.1-km stone fortress completed in 1796. The Jeonju World Cup Stadium is also unique in its design, featuring the linear images of the strings of the Korean zither (Gayageum), the traditional fan (Hapjukseon) and the Sotdae, an image of a bird on a long pole facing the Pole Star. On the island of Jeju the World Cup Stadium takes full advantage of its surroundings, symbolising one of the island's many secondary volcanoes and the roof on one side representing a net flung from a fishing boat. These design features were incorporated with the intention of making the spectator experience of the stadia as memorable as the matches that they hosted, and to project the culture of Korea to a global television audience.

Source: http://fifaworldcup.yahoo.com/ed/

---

if not eliminate them. Under this scenario, team association could be based on a corporate entity (as is the case in Japanese club rugby) as opposed to geographic representation. Rather than spectatorship at the site of the competition, spectatorship would occur through home-based digital media.

Sport tourism managers must also think carefully about the integrity of their sport and avoid the temptation to sensationalise or spectacularise it in a way that changes its essence. This suggestion links closely to the issue of commodification (as discussed in Chapter 4). Sport tourism managers are clearly in the business of commodifying both place and sport. If the meaning associated with sport is destroyed in this process, then the meaning that sport provides to place will also be lost. What would be left are the disneyfied landscapes that Relph (1976) described.

Finally, it must be recognised that there are multiple views on place in tourism spaces (Schollmann *et al.*, 2001; Sherlock, 2001). Place marketers who use sport as a marketing tool need to appreciate the contrasting perspectives of place held by different groups. These distinct meanings are not just associated with hosts and guests, but with the complex array of subgroups that exist therein (e.g. in the case of alpine resorts: long-term, short-term residents, second home owners, skiers, snowboarders, climbers and numerous others). The failure of place marketers to account for these differences may result in conflicting views on place, which are non-optimal at the very least, and may in fact be non-sustainable in the long run.

Conclusion

This chapter highlights the importance of place in the context of sport tourism. Place may be defined as space which has been infused with meaning, and it is clear that tourism spaces are increasingly infused with meaning through sport. Sporting culture is particularly important in terms of three variations: sport and culture, sport as culture and sporting subcultures. Each can have major impacts on the way that sport tourists see and experience a destination. Given sport's powerful influence on the way place identity is understood, it is not surprising that it is manipulated to market tourism places. Place marketers attempt to use sport events, activities and nostalgic attractions to create desirable place images. One of the long-term challenges is to develop sport tourism in a sustainable fashion. Success in this endeavour requires not only that the integrity of sport be maintained at the destination, but that the resources on which it depends be protected and, where appropriate, enhanced.

Further Reading

Those readers who are new to the concept of place should consult Relph's (1976) seminal work on place and placelessness. Crouch's (2000) publication in this area reflects some of the most up-to-date and insightful perspectives on the way geographers are currently treating this concept. Examinations of the relationship between sport and culture in the context of place have also become increasingly prevalent. McGuirk and Rowe (2001) provide a particularly interesting assessment of the influence of rugby league on the culture in Newcastle, Australia. Similarly, Wheaton (2000) and Heino (2000) provide in-depth analyses of windsurfing and snowboarding (respectively) as contemporary sport subcultures. In a sport tourism context, Green and Chalip (1998) examine the subculture

associated with a women's football competition that attracts teams to
Florida from all over the USA. There is also a growing number of publications that focus on the way sport is increasingly being used as a tool
for the marketing of places. Silk and Andrews' (2001) study of re-imaging
national culture through sporting events represents a good example. In a
similar critical vein, Whitson and Macintosh (1996) examine the global
circus associated with international sport, tourism and the marketing
of cities.

Case study 6.1

Spaces of Identity and Places of Representation: Kuala Lumpur 1998

Michael Silk, University of Memphis, USA

In the eyes of the Asian Pacific Economic Council (APEC), Malaysia
is regarded as a developing nation, which has to 'prove' that it has
achieved 'developed' status by the year 2020 in order for it to enter
into free-trade agreements within the Council. Hosting the 1998
Commonwealth Games was a key element of the strategy to do this;
an event that could also demonstrate to the rest of the world, particularly the First World, that Malaysia is a place that can be an important
node within a network society (Castells, 1997) centred on the flow of
information, services and consumption. The Commonwealth Games
take place on a four-year cycle and, like the Olympics, host a multitude of sporting events. The Games are attended by participants from
over 80 countries, most of which were formerly part of the British
Commonwealth. The Games are therefore a major sporting event upon
which the world's media descend. Given that major segments of the
world's media were focused for two weeks on Malaysia, the Malaysian
government worked extremely hard through their control of key resources, particularly the government-owned Radio Television Malaysia
television network and the quasi-governmental organising committee
(SUKOM), to provide the world with an image of Malaysia that keyed
on place specific differences and hi-tech industrial investment that
could be used as competitive advantage in the race to attract investment and (corporate) tourists and perhaps mask structural inequalities
and human rights violations. In this way, we can see the strategies of
these important agencies in Malaysia as part of what Robins (1991, 1997)
has termed the 'new dynamics of relocalisation' – a return to the image
and profile of a given locale presented within the global economy.
Albeit temporarily, the city of Kuala Lumpur and the nation of Malaysia
competed in 'place wars' (Robins, 1991), presenting itself as a prefer-

ential location through the exploitation of local assets and resources. These strategies are summarised below:

Vision 2020: Political and Economic Conditions of Kuala Lumpur 98

The Games were a part of the Malaysian government's initiative to industrialise and develop Malaysia by the year 2020. This strategy, titled 'Vision 2020', set out to re-engineer the social, political and economic climate of Malaysia and stressed balanced economic growth, a high quality of life and the creation of national unity. The organising committee, SUKOM, saw the Games 'as an important step towards reaching the aspirations of Vision 2020' (SUKOM, 1996: 5).

Corporate Identities: The Games Signature

The Games Signature was the collective name for the logo, mascot, televisual and Internet graphics packages and merchandising for the Games. The signature was intended to symbolise the embodiment of strategic communicative values for the merchandising, consolidation and expansion of the Games and Malaysia (SUKOM, 1998). The logo, for example, draws its inspiration from Malaysia's national flower – the *Bunga Raya* or *Hibiscus*. The *Bunga Raya* indicates Malaysia's flag colour, red, blue and yellow, which, according to the organising committee, is a 'striking portrait of a confident, young, dynamic nation' (SUKOM, 1996: 13).

The Host Product: The RTM Broadcasts

The host broadcaster ensured that the production style, or 'look', of the Games was 'Made in Malaysia' (Host Broadcaster Consultancy, 1997). A butterfly design was chosen for the look as it reflected the blossoming or metamorphosis of Malaysia from the 'pupa' chrysalis stage through to the commercial, economic and cultural aspirations of Vision 2020 (SUKOM, 1998). In addition to the 'look', the graphics package and images used by the host broadcaster emphasised the commercial business district of downtown Kuala Lumpur. The graphic incorporated the Kuala Lumpur cityscape, the focal point being the tallest building in the world, the Petronas Twin Towers, and the Kuala Lumpur tower. These buildings, or the places of representation, were continually shown throughout the broadcasts as 'beauty shots', providing the dislocated viewer with a particular version of the city, a version that masked unfavourable images and highlighted the modern, the particular and the new cathedrals of consumption that promote the post-industrial image of Kuala Lumpur.

Event Scheduling: The Mines Resort and Langkawi Island

In constructing the event schedule, SUKOM decided that the shooting competition should take place away from Kuala Lumpur at the 'luxurious' tourist resort of Langkawi Island. Further, the boxing competition took place in the Mines Resort, an expensive and upmarket resort in the city of Kuala Lumpur. As such, following Whitson and Macintosh (1993, 1996), the scheduling of the shooting competition can be argued to have been an attempt to position Malaysia on the circuit of international tourism and showcase a particular destination image. As a further demonstration of the importance of spectacular places of representation, the government built a brand new 100,000-seat stadium and sports complex – Bukit Jalil. This was, in part, an effort to project an image of a prosperous, dynamic and robust economy to the world.

Bangsa Malaysia: The Opening Ceremony

Through the opening ceremony, the organising committee took every opportunity to refurbish and refine the cultural identity of Malaysia. The story of Malaysia was retold and stressed the establishment of a coherent (and of course false and inauthentic) national unity – Bangsa Malaysia. Following Relph (1987 in Dear & Flusty, 1999), Malaysian identities were reconstituted and, at the same time, reconnected with a particular version of the local. Thus, like Sennet (1999), place-making involved a search for the discovery, or at least a representation, of sameness in terms of a 'shared' Malaysian identity.

The Multi-media Super Corridor

Following Harvey (1989), Malaysia attempted to promote an image that could potentially establish a new corporate identity for Malaysia in the world marketplace and in the presentation of self in labour markets. This image centred on the new regimes of representation technologies that would allow Malaysia to become a node in the global economy. Specifically, throughout the Games, Malaysia referred to itself as the founder of the multimedia super corridor; as a place ready and able to compete within the new global informational economy.

In sum, Kuala Lumpur 98 was an opportunity to represent the culture, especially through spectacular landscapes and structures, such as the Twin Towers and new stadia. Following Firat (1995), these structures were extracted and abstracted from local culture and became the representations of Malaysia that were translated into marketable cultural meanings and extended beyond national borders. Kuala Lumpur and Malaysia were thus involved in a self-conscious exercise in promotion and marketing of their attractions to enhance the qualities of the city or locality (Morley & Robins, 1995). Specifically, cultural symbols were reframed as factors that enhance the quality of life for particular places.

Concrete signifiers of the particularising place commodification of Kuala Lumpur were served up through a global sporting event that emphasised meanings that made the host place an attractive location for investors and tourists alike.

Source: this Case study has been developed from an article that first appeared as Silk, M. (2002) 'Bangsa Malaysia': Global sport, the city and the mediated refurbishment of local identities. *Media, Culture and Society* 25 (4).

Further reading

Silk, M. and Andrews, D. L. (2001) Beyond a boundary? Sport, transnational advertising, and the reimaging of national culture. *Journal of Sport and Social Issues* 25 (2), 180–201.

Whitson, D. and Macintosh, D. (1996) The global circus: International sport, tourism and the marketing of cities. *Journal of Sport and Social Issues* 20, 239–257.

Chapter 7

Environment: Landscape, Resources and Impacts

Sport tourism's link to the environment is both as victim and as aggressor.
(Standeven & De Knop, 1999: 236)

Introduction

Sport tourism development is tied more closely to the geographical resource base at a destination than many forms of tourism. The extent to which tourists find a destination to be attractive is strongly influenced by the physical environment, including landscapes and climate (Boniface & Cooper, 1994; Krippendorf, 1986; Burton, 1995). Many sports are closely tied to the physical geography of a destination. For instance, Priestley (1995: 210) observes that single integrated golf resorts 'have mushroomed in the hotter climates where traditional sun, sand and sea tourism could or does exist.' In sports such as surfing, hang-gliding and scuba diving, there tends to be a hierarchy of destinations based on the experiential value of the physical environment. Destinations may be managed and promoted to develop new or exploit existing links to specific sports. For example, the development of integrated golf resorts in Spain capitalises on increasing levels of visitor demand for this sport in conjunction with the other attractions that exist in Spain (Priestley, 1995).

The sport tourism development potential of a destination is also determined by cultural influences on the landscape. Event sport tourism development at a destination requires, in most cases, constructed resources, including sport facilities and tourism infrastructure. Sports in central locations often use facilities that are purpose-built, such as stadia, marinas, sports halls and gymnasiums. Alternatively, sports may temporarily make use of buildings or infrastructures that are developed primarily for purposes other than sport. Examples include roads, central parks and urban tourism icons (e.g. New York's Central Park, Sydney Opera House), which may figure prominently as locations or backdrops to sporting scenes. An understanding of the spatial elements of sport tourism development is therefore incomplete without some consideration of the physical environment. This is an important starting point for understanding the resource requirements and impacts of sport tourism development. Natural and built resources for sport tourism, and impacts associated with each, are considered separately in this chapter.

Sport Tourism Landscapes, Environments and Resources

Landscape is an illusive term that is commonly associated with attractive scenery. Natural landscapes (and seascapes) are central to the pursuit of many sports. However, sports are not natural forms of movement and, therefore, 'the landscape upon which such body culture takes place is part of the cultural landscape' (Bale, 1994: 9). Even sports that rely on natural elements take place in environments that are subject to varying degrees of anthropogenic change. For instance, ski slopes are subject to change through the grooming of ski trails, the construction of facilities such as ski jumps and slalom courses, snow-making and the development of visitor services (Hudson, 1999). Golf courses, which are very 'green' in appearance, actually represent highly modified natural areas and are characterised by significant ecological impacts (Priestley, 1995).

While the popular use of the term landscape often implies naturalness, the landscapes of sport are, to varying degrees, cultural landscapes. The term sportscape is used in the geography of sport to describe the highly modified (e.g. modern stadium or arena) and technologised (e.g. corporate suites, closed circuit television) sports environment (Bale, 1994). Relph (1985: 23) notes that landscapes can 'take on the very character of human existence. They can be full of life, deathly dull, exhilarating, sad, joyful or pleasant.' This observation applies equally to the landscapes of sport. The manner in which the landscapes of sport are developed, and the impacts arising from the use of those landscapes, are important to sustainable sport tourism development.

The Landscapes of Sport

The values and interpretations associated with the landscape are highly subjective (Tuan, 1974). Sportscapes are no exception. Bale (1994) applies Meinig's (1979) 'ten versions of the same scene' to the landscape of sport in an exercise that is relevant to the study of sport tourism (Table 7.1). These 'versions' are important in understanding the resources and impacts of sport tourism. The development of resources and infrastructures for sport tourism should take place with consideration given to the values and interpretations of landscapes noted on Table 7.1.

Table 7.1 Interpretations of sport landscapes

Interpretations of sports landscapes	*Description*
1. Sport, landscape as natural habitat	It is possible for sport participants to encounter and utilise natural landscapes for certain sports events and, when the events are over, never return to them. They remain landscapes and never become sportscapes. Landscapes therefore may be used for sports but never 'sportised' in any permanent sense. Impressions of nature and environment are important elements of the athlete's experience.
2. Sport, landscape as human habitat	The sport landscape may also be regarded as part of the human habitat. Conscious decisions can be made for slopes, soils, elevations, sites and routes, channels or relief features to be used as homes for sport. Humans rearrange nature into sport-related forms; an adjustment rather than a conquest of nature.
3. Sport landscape as artefact	Many sport landscapes disregard the natural or semi-natural landscape upon which they are found. This view sees humankind as the conqueror of nature, with concrete, plastic and glass, totally flat synthetic surfaces and indoor arenas in which nature has been neutralised.
4. Sport landscape as system	Sport landscapes can also be viewed as part of intricate economic or physical systems. A sports stadium, for example, does not exist in isolation; it generates flows of people and spatial interactions over an area much greater than that of the stadium itself. For example, the Tour de France is part of an extensive economic system that affects the places through which it passes. Sports events are also part of physical systems. Snow conditions influence performance in ski races and rain may deter attendance at sports events.
5. Sport landscape as problem	The excessive dominance of sport over nature may be seen to lead to social or environmental pollution, erosion and visual blight. Problem landscapes occur in a variety of sports in quite different ways. Traffic congestion and crowding can result from hosting a sports event in an inner-city stadium. Erosion of soil and damage to plant cover on ski pistes in alpine regions are also examples. Impacts also differ in terms of their permanence. When the sport landscape

Table 7.1 continued

	becomes perceived as a problem it can lead to political activism and the rejection of sporting events that might have induced landscape change.
6. Sport landscape as wealth	The sport landscape may also reflect the view that land is a raw material. The long-term returns of lands given over to sport are important. So, too, are the significant economic benefits that one-off events generate in local areas. Sport may be a form of place-boosting for purposes of attracting investment, and may influence rental profits. The sport landscape is littered with advertising hoardings and other evidence of sponsorship.
7. Sport landscape as ideology	The sport landscape may be viewed as a reflection of various ideologies. Sport landscapes may be explicit responses to nationalism. New national sports may be introduced to countries from more dominant neighbours. The stadium may be an expression of modern technocentric ideology.
8. Sport landscape as history	The present day landscape of sport is a result of the cumulative processes of historical evolu-tion. Sport landscapes are often accumulations. Size, shape, materials, decorations and other manifestations tell us something about the way people have experienced sport over time.
9. Sport landscape as place	This view sees landscape as a locality possessing particular nuances, unique flavours and a sense of place. For the sports participant – athlete or spectator – the experience of place, therefore, could be argued to contribute to the overall sporting experience.
10. Sport landscape as aesthetic	Landscapes can possess aesthetic qualities predisposing the observer towards one and against another. Aesthetics are related to the artistic quality of the sport landscape. The aesthetics of the sport landscape are also portrayed in paint, film, photograph and print. Such portrayals may be accurate representations of what exists in the physical landscape. It is also possible that landscape icons may become mythical landscapes (e.g. the landscapes of English cricket and American baseball).

Source: adapted from Bale (1994: 10–13)

The resource base for sport tourism

The potential for sport tourism development at a destination is determined by the existence of requisite sport and tourism resources and infrastructures. A sport tourism resource analysis may include natural environments, constructed sports facilities, tourism transport and infrastructure and information services. These need to be provided in the required balance and combination, or developed in a planned and coordinated way as determined by the development goals of the destination. The importance of coordinated planning and development arises from the considerable overlap that exists between the resource requirements for sport and those for tourism (Standeven & De Knop, 1999). Domestic and international airline services are used by travelling sports teams and leisure travellers for the same purpose, whereas both use stadia, albeit for different reasons (sports competition and sport spectatorship respectively). The existence, or systematic development, of sport and tourism infrastructures is required for any location to function as a sport tourism destination (Table 7.2)

Considerable opportunity exists, therefore, for sport and tourism resources to be developed in a synergistic fashion that maximises the mutual benefits of the stakeholders. Event sport tourism, for example, offers the potential for the inner-city resource base for sport, recreation, entertainment, retail and service to be transformed in a planned and coordinated manner. This course of strategic development may generate the advantages of enhanced profile and destination image vis-à-vis sport tourism, thereby improving the standing of the destination in the hierarchy of sport tourism locations (Chapter 5). The status of a ski destination, for example, is a function of high-quality ski facilities, in combination with the required tourism services and infrastructure (see Case study 7.1 on pp. 136–138).

The reproducibility of sports

The tourism resource base may be classified in various ways. One approach draws on the distinction between those that can be reproduced, or transported, and those that are non-reproducible (Boniface & Cooper, 1994). Resorts, theme parks and stadia are readily reproduced and can be developed in a variety of locations. In contrast, natural landscapes and cultural heritage are generally non-reproducible. Sports resources may also vary on the basis of their transportability. Nature-based sports, such as downhill skiing and rock climbing, tend to be dependent on certain types of landscapes or specific landscape features. Attempts to create artificial ski slopes in central locations have met with moderate commercial success. The reason for this is that the experiential value of the mountain

Table 7.2 Resource base for sport tourism development

Tourism industry resource requirements	*Sport sector resource requirements*
Natural features: national parks, scenery, lakes, mountains, rivers, coastlines	Natural features: national parks, open amenity spaces, wilderness areas, geographical features (mountains, rocks, spas, coast-lines, marine environments)
Facilities and infrastructure: transport services, places of accommodation, dining, entertainment	Facilities and infrastructure: stadia, arenas, sports halls, transport infrastructure, dining, entertainment.
Built amenities: public toilets, parking facilities, signposts, shelters	Built amenities: public toilets, parking facilities, signposts, shelters
Tourist information services: visitor information services, Internet-based information services, booking and ticketing services, travel agents	Sport services: coaching and leadership, equipment/clothing hire and/or purchase, storage and management, supervision and safety, hiring, operations, training facilities, injury prevention and medical facilities, science and research facilities
Tourism organisations: planning and development, strategic planning, destination image, tourism marketing, place promotion, visiting media programmes, tourism research, industry coordination and liaison	Sport organisations: sports clubs, volunteer and community groups, administration, facility development, funding, sponsorship, information services, marketing, merchandising
Transport services: road, rail, air, sea (domestic and international), plus scenic journeys, gondolas, tourist routes, rides, heritage rail tourism, historic routes, tour coaches, hot air balloons	Transport services: road, rail, air, sea (domestic and international)
Entertainment and activities: attractions, casinos, cinemas, zoos, shopping, nightlife, nightclubs	Entertainment and activities: sports halls and venues (ice rinks, leisure centres, gymnasiums, swimming pools, climbing walls), golf courses, marinas, sports museums, halls of fame, shopping, nightlife

Source: adapted from Sandeven and De Knop (1999: 67–73)

environment, which forms an important part of the ski experience for many sport tourists, is not transportable. The same is true of indoor climbing walls. While they present an exciting new variation of rock-climbing, they cannot duplicate the unique challenge of outdoor climbing sites. Green sports are those that are dependent on the integration of a physical activity with specific environmental attributes (Bale, 1989). Sports such as surfing, cross-country skiing, windsurfing, sailing, mountain-climbing and orienteering are examples of green sports, as they are built around specific features of the natural environment as sources of pleasure, challenge, competition or mastery. A case in point is the way that hang-gliding, parapenting and windsurfing harness the natural forces of air and sea. As a result, participants enjoy a heightened sense of environmental awareness due to the role it plays in their performance. The experiential value of these sports is largely dependent upon the mood of the landscapes where they are performed. These landscapes are inherently non-transportable.

In contrast, other sports are more readily transported. Indoor sports such as ice-skating have been successfully transported from the high to mid and equatorial latitudes with the development of improved ice-making technology and expanding markets. Indeed, indoor arenas have transformed sports like ice hockey from outdoor to indoor activities, impacting their spatial and temporal distribution (Higham & Hinch, 2002a). Spatially these sports have spread from high to low latitudes and temporally from winter sports to year-round activities. Outdoor winter sports such as ski jumping may also be transported from peripheral to central locations in the high latitudes to capture the advantage of proximity to markets. The Holmenkollen (Oslo, Norway) and Calgary 1988 Olympic (Canada) ski jumps are examples of constructed ski jump facilities that have been developed adjacent to central locations.

Many sports, such as competitive swimming, diving, squash and racket ball, are performed in indoor sports centres and have become very transportable. These sports are also characterised by highly prescribed spatial rules and standards. Other sports that are traditionally played in outdoor settings can also be transported and performed in indoor sports centres and arenas. Examples include tennis, netball, athletics and even equestrian activities. These sports demonstrate what Bale (1989: 171) refers to as the 'industrialisation of the sport environment', which relates closely to the concept of transportability. Indoor cricket, for example, is a sport that takes place in air-conditioned centres that are typically housed in unused industrial buildings and warehouses located in industrial landscapes (Bale, 1989).

The application of technology to the modern stadium demonstrates the height of sport transportability. The reproducibility of the sportscape facilitates the transportation of sports and the sport experience. For instance, in 2002 the Australian Rugby Union (ARU) considered hosting the 2002 Mandela Trophy test match between the Wallabies (Australia) and the Springboks (South Africa) in Hong Kong (China) rather than one of the Australian state capitals. Rugby is an example of a transportable sport that offers opportunities for generating new markets and revenue. Viewed another way, sports facilities may be built, permanently or temporarily, at locations designed to maximise market access. Such developments offer the potential to enhance the status of sports such as snowboarding and beach volleyball through increased public awareness and spectatorship (Focus point 7.1). However, the transportability of sports also presents the threat of the displacement of a sporting activity from its original location. The importance of retaining and enhancing the idiosyncrasies and elements of uniqueness associated with a tourism site is an important strategy to mitigate this threat (Bale, 1989: 171).

Focus point 7.1

Wanaka Snowfest: Bringing extreme Nature-based Sports into the Urban Environment

The town of Wanaka, New Zealand, hosts an annual winter sports festival, which includes a series of events such as the World Heli Challenge and the Wanaka Snowfest. The World Heli Challenge, which has, since its inception in 1995, been at the cutting edge of modern winter sports competition, involves 70 skiers and boarders who are transported by helicopter to remote alpine regions to contest extreme, free-ride and downhill competitions. The Snowfest features Masters ski races at ski fields in the Wanaka region. These events take place in the surrounding alpine environments. Other events, such as snowboarding, ski jumping and acrobatic competitions, have proved to be relatively transportable sports. The culmination of the two-week World Heli Challenge and the Wanaka Snowfest is the 'Pulsate Wanaka Big Air'. This event 'brings the snow to the town, with over 8000 spectators, international headline bands and a host of the world's premiere new school aerialists'. These sports are contested in the main street of Wanaka. This requires the development of a temporary extreme ski facility, featuring snow-making equipment. Streetlights provide floodlighting and the shops and sidewalks become galleries for spectators. For the duration of the festival, the streetscape of downtown Wanaka becomes a snowscape for extreme sport. This innovation has brought significant benefits to sports such as acrobatic snowboarding due to enhanced spectator access. The status of Wanaka as a tourist destination has also been enhanced by the success of the annual Wanaka Big Air event.

Source: http://www.lakewanaka.co.nz/The_Big_Events.html

Environmental Impacts of Sport Tourism

From a geographical perspective, 'the environment is the totality of tourism activity, incorporating natural elements and society's modification of the landscape and resources' (Mitchell & Murphy, 1991: 59). An understanding of the impacts of sport tourism, and of management techniques appropriate to those impacts, is central to sustainable sport tourism development. 'Inevitably, the growth and continuing locational adjustments made by modern sports have created significant changes in the landscape' (Bale, 1989: 142). Many such impacts are fleeting, or temporary. Triathlons, marathons, cycle races, car rallies and festival or exhibition sports are often conducted on circuits, courses or courts that may be constructed temporarily in urban areas. The impacts of these sports, which may include a sizeable body of spectators, are rapidly dispersed at the conclusion of the contest. The immediate negative consequences of stadium-based sports may include traffic congestion and crowding, and undesirable impacts such as vandalism, antisocial behaviour, littering and breaches of security. These impacts are generally short-term, but they can cause disruption to a great number of community residents (Bale, 1994). They may also result in aversion effects upon visitor flows into or within a destination as non-sport tourists choose to visit other destinations or cancel their intended visit (Faulkner *et al.*, 1998).

Other sports may have a longer-term, or indelible, impact in cases where naturalness forms an important, perhaps central element of the sport tourist experience. While environmental impacts in natural areas may be 'permanent but, paradoxically annoying to few' (Bale, 1994: 11), one significant consequence may be a compromise of the quality of the sport tourist experience. This is illustrated by the stagnation of ski markets in Europe and North America as a demand-led response to the unsustainable management of environmentally sensitive alpine environments (Flagestad & Hope, 2001).

Sport Tourism in the Built Environment

Much of the existing literature on the environmental impacts of sport tourism has focused on natural areas (Standeven & De Knop, 1999). However, sport tourism development in urban areas presents unique environment, resource and impact issues that require informed consideration. Sport tourism in the urban context may include:

(1) active sport tourism in the technologised sports landscape (e.g. hotel gymnasiums, squash, badminton and tennis courts, swimming pools), recreational running along urban parks, and developed littoral zones;
(2) recreational or club sport in dedicated sports fields or improvised settings (e.g. skateboarding, street basketball);

(3) recreational or competitive sports that take place in the unmodified (e.g. kayaking, surfing) or modified (e.g. fishing in waterways) natural environments on the urban fringe; and

(4) event sport tourism.

Active, recreational and competitive sports in the urban context generate relatively benign impacts, although they may require management of social impacts or recreational conflict between participants. Sport tourism events that takes place in central locations, in the form of elite or non-elite sports that require dedicated or temporary facilities, offer considerable potential for impact, both positive and negative. The impacts of event sport tourism in the built environment are a function of the scale of the event and the infrastructure capacities of the destination.

Issues of scale in event sport tourism

Scale, be it global, regional or local, is critical to the study of sport tourism in central locations. 'The idea of scale, or geographical magnitude, keeps in focus the area being dealt with, and can be likened to increasing or decreasing the magnification on a microscope or the scale of a map' (Boniface & Cooper, 1994: 3). The capacity for locations to accommodate flows of tourists is determined in large part by the scale of the destination and its capacity to absorb tourists. The tourist function index, for example, employs the number of tourist beds and the total resident population of a destination as indices of tourist capacity. The concept of tourism-carrying capacity considers the maximum level of tourist activity that can be sustained without adversely impacting the physical environment, or the quality of the visitor experience with consideration given to the views of the host community (Mathieson & Wall, 1987; Archer & Cooper, 1994).

'[M]ega-events are short term events with long term consequences for the cities that stage them' (Roche, 1994: 1). Unfortunately, interests in the impacts of event sport tourism are often restricted to economic development (Burgan & Mules, 1992), positive image and identity, inward investment and tourism promotion (Getz, 1991; Hall, 1992a). This focus ignores the potential for sporting events to create negative impacts, which tend to increase with the scale of the event (Olds, 1998; Shapcott, 1998). Where the scale of a sports event is too great for the social and infrastructure capacities of the host city, significant potential for negative impacts arise (Hiller, 1998). Host community displacements and evictions (Olds, 1998), increases in rates and rents (Hodges & Hall, 1996), the disruption of daily routines due to crowding and congestion (Bale, 1994), security issues (Higham, 1999) and the exaggerated behaviour of 'sports junkies' (Faulkner *et al.*, 1998) may be associated with large-scale sporting events. Shapcott (1998: 196), for example, reports that

720,000 room-renters [were] forcibly removed in advance of the 1988 Olympics in Seoul, thousands of low income tenants and small businesses forced out of Barcelona before the 1992 Games [and] more than 9000 homeless people (many of them African-American) arrested in the lead-up to the 1996 Olympics in Atlanta.

Sporting events and competitions of more modest scale include regular season domestic sport competitions, national/regional championships and non-elite sports events. At these levels of sport, the potential for negative impact is reduced (Higham, 1999). Crowding and infrastructure congestion are less likely to occur and are more rapidly dispersed. Nonetheless, the positive impacts of sports events of more modest scale are, within the geographical parameters of the destination, precisely the same as mega-events (Hall, 1993). The issue of scale in event sport tourism mirrors the 'alternative tourism/mass tourism' debate (Wheeler, 1991; Krippendorf, 1995), which links closely to the concept of sustainable tourism development. The achievement of a match between the capacity constraints of host cities and the scale of the sports events that they seek to host represents an important element in achieving sustained success in event sport tourism.

Managing the compatibility of sports in the built environment

Consideration of the compatibility of multiple sport demands is an important sport tourism management issue in the built environment. Different sports may be viewed as:

(1) Compatible: sports that can use the same area of land or water at the same time.
(2) Partially compatible: sports that can use the same area of land or water, but not at the same time.
(3) Incompatible: sports that cannot use the same area of land or water and need to be zoned into exclusive spaces.

The extent to which different sports demonstrate compatibility with other landscape users varies considerably. For example, motor sports and sports involving dangerous equipment (e.g. field archery) are essentially incompatible with other sports. The incompatibility of sports generally increases at higher levels of competition. Competitive or elite levels of sport often require specialised and sometimes exclusive use of facilities. The sports manager, then, must be mindful of the required balance between specialisation and multiple use in the design of sports facilities. The Montreal stadium developed for the 1976 Olympic Games is an example of a specialised facility which has proved inappropriate for subsequent use due to its sheer size (OCA, 1997c).

The development of multiple-use facilities, particularly those that cater for sports at various levels of competition (ranging from local/recreational to international/ championship), may diversify and expand the user and spectator market catchments for a facility. Consideration should be given to both the spatial (e.g. dimensions of the playing surface, parking and spectator capacities) and temporal (e.g. daily/week use patterns, sport seasonality) compatibility of sports that may derive mutual benefit from the use of a single multiple-use facility. In some cases, however, the development of generalised or multiple-use facilities can cause unacceptable compromises to the sport experiences of both participants and spectators. Stadia with running tracks, for example, typically are characterised by non-optimal viewing for a high proportion of spectators (Bale, 1989).

The issue of compatibility in the built landscape extends to reconciliation of sport/non-use interests, particularly at sites that are designed primarily for purposes other than sport. For example, the marathon and distance running boom, with race fields exceeding 20,000 in some cases, has 'put pressure on municipal authorities to control and redirect traffic on race days' (Bale, 1989: 163). Streetcar rallies, cycle races and a host of festival sports may also cause disruption to normal use of the urban landscape (Focus point 7.2). Such impacts, however, tend to be short-term and rapidly dispersed. They do, however, require that sport managers and event organisers consider security, safety and liability issues relating to their sport.

Focus point 7.2

Sport Tourism in Environments that are Designed for Other Purposes

Athletes crossing Tower Bridge during the London marathon and Formula One motor racing cars competing in the streets of Monaco provide some of the most compelling place-based images in modern sport. During the 2000 Olympic Games, Sydney Harbour and the Sydney Opera House served as tourist attraction markers (Chapter 2) when they formed the backdrop for the men's and women's Olympic triathlons. These are examples of sports that have taken place in built landscapes that were designed for purposes other than sport. The running of the bulls through the streets of Pamplona and the New York marathon are sports events that are associated with the distinctive heritage and cityscapes where they take place. Perhaps the best example of this is the Tour de France cycle race, which features over 2000 miles of public roads, town and village high streets and city boulevards, culminating in a sprint to the finish up the Champs-Elysées in central Paris. These events and others of lesser scale highlight the tourism profile of the event location and serve as destination markers via media exposure. They may also have significant impacts on the lives and daily routines of community residents. Such impacts need to be carefully managed to serve the interests of residents, competitors and other visitors.

Landscape to sportscape: The impacts of sport facility development and design

It has been noted that 'the search for regional diversity in the land-scape has remained an important motive for travellers, despite the standardisation and homogenisation of the tourism industry' (Mitchell & Murphy, 1991: 61). There exists an evolutionary tendency to confine and homogenise the sporting environment. The transition from landscape to sportscape represents one aspect of standardisation and homogenisation in sport tourism. The modern stadium has an ancient history and has evolved through phases that have been influenced by the formalisation of sports rules and the imposition of spatial limits in sport, which allowed the development of facilities for spectators to observe games at close proximity (Bale, 1989).

More recently technological developments, such as video screens, virtual advertising, floodlighting and retractable enclosures, have been imposed on the modern stadium (Bale, 1989). This course of development may significantly alter the overall sporting experience, from the view-point of both competitors and spectators. One implication may be erosion of 'the cultural mosaic that encourages tourism' (Williams & Shaw, 1988: 7). The potential contribution to sport tourism development of unique stadium design, contiguous markers, distinctive elements of the destina-tion and the natural elements that differentiate destinations must be carefully considered in relation to the design and development of sports resources.

Sport Tourism in the Natural Landscape

Natural features are central to sport tourism experiences in peripheral areas. They also present a distinct range of management issues. 'Sports like hang gliding create pressure on rural hill and scarp country, surfing on beach areas, skiing has placed pressure on mountain regions and water sports compete with one another for precious room on the limited amount of suitable inland water space' (Bale, 1989: 163). These landscapes can be quite fragile and sensitive to disturbance (Hall & Page, 1999). Sport activ-ities on these landscapes, therefore, need to be managed in order to mitigate negative impacts (Weed, 1999).

The challenge of sustainable sport tourism development in natural areas arises for a variety of reasons. One reason is the dynamic nature of sport as reflected by the speed with which new sports are developed and diffused. The transition from an emerging sport pursued by relatively few to a mass participation phenomenon may take place in a short space of time (Standeven & De Knop, 1999). Recreational running, which emerged and developed in popularity in the 1970s, is a case in point. Other sports that have demonstrated a rapid rise in popularity include mountain biking, snowboarding, scuba diving, windsurfing, triathlon, jet-skiing and kite-surfing. This dynamic presents fascinating development opportunities at tourist resorts and destinations, but it also requires proactive intervention to establish and implement appropriate policies and management strategies to protect the natural resources at activity sites. In some cases the development of participation sports has taken place in the absence of a relevant legislation framework, management structure or administrative authority. Sports such as BASE jumping and bungee jumping demonstrate the challenge that management agencies may encounter with the development of new sports innovations. Extreme sports such as these may defy a single management authority (Mykletun & Vedø, 2002).

The management of the impacts of sport tourism in natural areas is a complex task. Indeed, simply measuring the impacts of tourism is fraught with difficulty. Rarely do baselines exist from which to measure change, and the impacts of tourism can seldom be disaggregated from the direct or indirect impacts of other human activities (Mathieson & Wall, 1987). The impacts of littoral sport tourism on marine flora and fauna, for example, are difficult to distinguish from those of fishing, aquaculture, or the inappropriate dumping of waste materials from towns, industries, agriculture and forestry (Bellan & Bellan-Santini, 2001). The impacts of sport tourism in fragile alpine ecologies may, due to extremes of altitude and climate, require extended recovery and regeneration timeframes (Flagestad & Hope, 2001). Although the visual impacts of development may be immediately apparent, more subtle changes on fragile alpine flora, growth and regeneration rates, water regulation (May, 1995) and the breeding success of rare alpine bird species (Holden, 2000) require intervention programmes and long-term monitoring.

While it is sometimes possible to identify positive and negative impacts within the social, cultural, economic and environmental contexts of the destination, these impacts are connected in a complex web of relationships. The acceptability of different impacts in combination is also viewed subjectively by different stakeholder groups, and by different individuals within stakeholder groups (Mathieson & Wall, 1987; McKercher, 1993; Hunter & Green, 1995). The extensive literature on sustainable tourism development and impact management is of high relevance to sport and tourism managers, who should be cognisant of the environmental impacts of sport tourism (Hunter, 1995; Cantelon & Letters, 2000).

The compatibility of sport tourism in the natural landscape

Hunter (1995) observes that sustainable tourism development requires reconciliation of human needs, as well as environmental limitations. Human needs and the benefits and costs of tourism accrue to two main groups: the hosts and the guests (Archer & Cooper, 1994). The excessive or inappropriate promotion of sport development interests over the stewardship of natural areas may give rise to congestion and crowding, social and environmental impacts, or modification of the landscape in ways that are unacceptable to the host community. The sustained quality of the visitor experience must also enter into considerations of the appropriate direction and level of sport tourism development.

Sports that are pursued in the natural landscape may also demonstrate varying degrees of compatibility with other sports. Incompatible motivations and goals of participation in sport may give rise to symmetric or asymmetric conflict between participants in *different* sports (Graefe *et al.*, 1984). Symmetric conflict describes a situation in which participants in two sports feel the existence of social conflict arising from the presence of the other. Jet-skiers, surfers and swimmers may experience symmetric conflict, giving rise in some cases to situations of physical danger. Asymmetric conflict arises when participants in one sport are adversely impacted by the presence of those engaging in a second sport, while participants in the latter may be oblivious to, or even welcome, the presence of those engaged in the former. The intrusion of technologies such as global positioning systems and cellular telephones in nature-based sports is an increasingly common cause of social impact and conflict between sports participants (Ewert & Shultis, 1999). Sports such as orienteering and downhill skiing may be compatible with other sports, if segregated in space and/or time through appropriate management techniques. Sports that take place in coastal environments include diving, surf-skiing, swimming, jet-skiing, windsurfing, kayaking and recreational fishing, which offer varying degrees of compatibility. Consumptive (e.g. hunting) and mechanised (e.g. jet boat racing) sports are fundamentally incompatible with other uses, as they may either irrevocably compromise alternative sporting pursuits and/or present physical danger to participants in other sports. This issue dictates that sports that take place in the sport tourism periphery must be carefully managed to reduce conflict.

The psychographic profile of the sport participant (Chapter 3) also determines the compatibility of different sports, and of different participants in the same sport. Conflicts may arise between participants *within* a sport if the motivations of participants are incompatible. Wilderness cross-country skiing and surfing are sports that take place in environments that can be contested by numerous participants when conditions are favourable. Access to waves is managed within the surfing community by an unwritten surfing etiquette (Wheaton, 2000). The reconciliation of conflicts between incompatible sports requires careful management to mitigate potential conflicts. Once again, the compatibility of sports in the natural landscape decreases with the seriousness of the participant or competitor. Yachting and canoeing are compatible at the recreational level, but not at the higher levels of competition (Bale, 1989). Similarly, recreational skiing cannot take place simultaneously on the same runs as competitive forms of skiing.

The Impacts of Event Sport Tourism: A Paradigmatic Shift

Events hosted in central and peripheral locations offer similar opportunities to foster environmental interests, as well as to implement negative impact mitigation techniques. The legacy of the 1992 Albertville (France) Winter Olympic Games is one of considerable and irreversible disfigurement of the natural environment due to intense and poorly planned development (May, 1995). By contrast, the 1994 Lillehammer Winter Olympic Games have been coined the 'Green-White Games' because new approaches to environmental management were pioneered in the planning of that event (Kaspar, 1998). In all aspects of capacity and scale, Lillehammer, a town of only 24,000 residents, would generally be considered ill-equipped to host a large-scale event like the Winter Olympic Games. Obvious challenges included traffic congestion, crowding, waste management and irreversible environmental impacts. Commitment to an environmental plan was articulated in a joint statement issued by the Chief Environmental Officers of Lillehammer and Oppland County. It stated in reference to Project Environmental Friendly Olympics (PEFO) that

> [any] development must conform to the natural and cultural landscape and other regional features. In the long run this will be crucial in preserving and enhancing qualities that are already assets to tourism. For local people it will be most important to construct the arenas and other buildings needed for the event in an environmentally friendly way. (Chernushenko, 1996: 66)

Event-planning and innovation in the design and development of sports facilities and tourist infrastructure were central to this success, despite the existence of conflicts and compromises in the planning of the event (Lesjø, 2000). The Olympic Environmental Charter, as ratified in 1996, now requires that Olympic organising committees articulate and implement an environmental protection policy. This Charter was used for the first time in the planning of the 1998 Winter Olympics in Nagano (Japan). Cantelon and Letters (2000: 294) argue that 'it was the widespread environmental damage at the 1992 Albertville and the Savoie Region Games, and the subsequent Green Games of Lillehammer, Norway (1994), that were the historical benchmarks for the development of this policy'.

The Sydney 2000 Olympic Games represents an entrenchment, but also a significant advancement of the environmental achievements of Lillehammer 1994. Conservation, ecological restoration and the remediation of industrial sites formed an integral part of the Sydney Olympic

Games development programme (OCA, 1997a,b). These sport tourism events provide evidence of new perspectives on the sport tourism–environment nexus. The environmental legacies of the 1994 Winter (Lillehammer, Norway) and 2000 Summer (Sydney, Australia) Olympic Games represent a paradigmatic shift from impact mitigation to proactive environmental stewardship and habitat creation associated with event sport tourism (Chernushenko, 1996; Cowell, 1997).

Management Implications and Opportunities

These discussions raise various sport tourism management issues relating to landscape, resources and impacts. It is clear that different sports, and levels of competition within a sport, interact with and respond to the landscape in various ways. Bale's (1994) theory of sport landscapes lends itself well to this discussion. The development of sport landscapes as artefacts, for example, must be negotiated carefully by sports managers, as it brings with it implications for the sport experiences of active and event sport tourists and, therefore, the potential of a sport to function as a tourist attraction. The unique qualities of 'sport landscape as place' and 'sport landscape as aesthetics' are also worthy of consideration in terms of their relevance to place promotion (see Chapter 6). The view of 'sport landscapes as systems' has considerable management utility. Different sports, and sport landscapes, operate within systems that vary in terms of market range, travel patterns, flows of commerce and impacts. The Volvo Round the World Ocean Race, 2002 FIFA World Cup (Japan and Korea), Tour de France cycle race, and domestic sport competitions offer examples of sport tourism events that are global, international, national and regional in the landscape systems that they embrace. The landscape systems associated with spatially dispersed sports, multiple and single-venue sports differ in all aspects discussed in this chapter, with implications for the management of these events and for the sport tourism development opportunities that they offer.

The relationship between event scale and impacts provides important insights into the opportunities, potential and sustainability of sport tourism development. An understanding of the sport tourism environment, however, also affords insights into the alleviation of threats that exist in sport tourism development. The transportability of sports provides a case in point. On one hand, the relocation of a sport to enhance public awareness or market access may result in its transformation into a high participation and/or spectator sport. On the other hand, transportability presents the threat of relocation, with implications for the status of a destination within the hierarchy of sport and sport tourism locations (Chapter 5).

A review of the resource base for sport tourism illustrates the common and peculiar resource requirements for sport and tourism. It is the peculiar resource requirements of sport and tourism that may place limitations on sport tourism development at a destination. For instance, development of the sport resource base at a destination does not, in itself, present opportunities in the field of sport tourism. Rather, it must be coordinated with development of the tourism sector at the destination, to ensure that adequate transport networks, accommodation and tourist and information services exist to allow sport tourism development at a destination to meet its potential. The proactive treatment of environmental and resource issues through planning and management has emerged as a key element of sport tourism development.

Conclusion

Sport tourism environments and resources form an important part of the foundation upon which sport tourism development occurs. Landscape and climate are key determinants of the attractiveness of tourist destinations. They also bear considerable influence on the sport and recreational activities that tourists associate with a destination, thereby influencing destination image. The relationship between sport and the environment is a dynamic one. By understanding this relationship, sport tourism managers achieve a competitive advantage in harnessing trends that offer opportunities and, equally, in recognising those that may pose a threat to sport tourism development. Reproducible, or transportable, sports offer a valuable example in this respect. The development of sport technologies, which may challenge established views of the reproducibility of sports, should be a concern of sport tourism managers. This chapter also considers the sharp distinction that lies between sport tourism development in the built (central) and natural (peripheral) environments. The importance of this distinction lies in the contrasting sport tourism impacts and management issues that apply to sport tourism in these differing contexts.

Further Reading

Mathieson and Wall (1982) provide a seminal work on the impacts of tourism and this is an important starting point for those beginning their study of the dimensions of social, physical and economic change that tourism development may bring to a destination. Christaller (1955, 1963/1964) presents a classic analysis that highlights the relevance of core/peripheral location in understanding the manifestations of tourism and tourism development within the European context. Standeven and De Knop (1999) offer valuable insights into the physical impacts of sport tourism, although the natural environment is the focus of much of their writing, to the general neglect of sport tourism in urban settings. Manifestations of sport tourism in the urban environment are less broadly considered in the sport tourism literature, although it must be noted that Bale (1994) provides a critical analysis of the landscapes of modern sport with a significant degree of consideration given to sports in the urban environment. Studies that focus on the environmental dimensions of specific sports are presented by Priestley (1995) and Hudson (1999).

Case study 7.1

The Impact of America's Cup 2000 on the City of Auckland, New Zealand

Mark Orams, Massey University, New Zealand

The America's Cup is reputed to be the world's oldest international sporting competition. It has been contested between yachts representing sailing clubs of foreign nations since 1851. Team New Zealand, representing the Royal New Zealand Yacht Squadron, successfully challenged for the Cup off San Diego, California in 1995. In March 2000, on the waters of the Hauraki Gulf off New Zealand's largest city, Auckland, the America's Cup was successfully defended by Team New Zealand. This is the first time the Cup has been successfully defended by a country other than the USA.

The hosting of this sporting event presented an enormous challenge for a small, isolated nation like New Zealand. Eleven syndicates (five from the USA, four from Europe, one from Japan and one from Australia) competed for the right to challenge Team New Zealand for the Cup. The infrastructure needs of these challenging groups (and the defender), the huge influx of visitors over the Cup competition and the logistics of managing a large maritime sporting event were far beyond anything New Zealand had hosted before. In addition, the hosting of the America's Cup event had significant economic impacts for the surrounding region and for New Zealand as a whole.

The immediate challenges after winning the America's Cup in 1995 were, first, how the new Cup holders (the Royal New Zealand Yacht Squadron) could maximise the chances to successfully defend it and, second, how to host the event itself. The requirements of America's Cup-class yachts are significant – they are over 20 metres long and need a minimum depth of 7 metres. In addition, these yachts do not carry their own engines and, therefore, are towed to and from the sailing area (as a result they require a large 'turning' area). Furthermore, they must be removed from the water each day and stored on land, where maintenance and development activities are carried out. As a consequence, the water space, docking areas and 'hardstand-compound' areas needed to host an America's Cup syndicate must be large, deep, sheltered and provide all tide access. In 1995, when New Zealand first won the Cup, there was nowhere in the country where all these requirements could be met. In order to allow the development of such facilities and to permit the many different agencies needed to help run the event time to get organised, Team New Zealand CEO Sir Peter Blake announced that the thirtieth defence of the America's Cup would be held in the summer of 1999/2000. This caused some controversy because, in recent times, the Cup had been competed for on a three-year cycle. A five-year gap between Cups was a significant departure from this routine. However, the decision allowed much needed time for preparation, particularly for the redevelopment of the downtown waterfront 'viaduct basin' into the 'America's Cup Village'.

Thus, the hosting of this sporting event prompted a $NZ60 million redevelopment of what had been a seldom-used and poorly presented boat harbour into an attractive recreational, residential and commercial centre for tourists and residents alike. The America's Cup Village not only contains America's Cup competitors' bases, but restaurants, cafés, retail outlets, upmarket apartments and a small stadium used for concerts and special events. It is also a venue for marine tourism operators, such as water taxis, charter yachts and hospitality boats. In addition, the hosting of the thirtieth America's Cup involved the securing of international commercial sponsors and large numbers of local volunteers to help with the funding and running of the event. Central, regional and local government were involved in planning and initiatives to cope with the estimated additional 405,000 (35,000 international and 370,000 domestic) visitors to the city of Auckland during the competition. In addition to the increased tourism, an estimated 720 people directly involved with each of the 11 challenging syndicates became long-term residents in the Auckland area, establishing 'mini-communities'. These people included sailing crew, boat builders, sail makers, maintenance staff, weather specialists, designers, team management and, in many cases, their families. Supporters, friends and sponsors of challengers also visited for extended periods. Furthermore, over 1500 media representatives from over 40 countries, three cruise ships and 80 'super-yachts' (50–120 metres in length) were hosted over the five-month duration of the event. The international exposure for New Zealand was estimated to be worth as much as $NZ90 million. Economic impact studies estimated that the Cup event was worth in excess of $NZ640 million of added value to the nation's economy and that it supported 10,620 full-time equivalent years of employment. Team New Zealand's successful defence in 1999/2000 means that these financial and other benefits increased further as New Zealand hosted the subsequent Cup event in 2002/03.

This case illustrates the significant impacts that the hosting of a major sporting event can have on a host location's infrastructure, economy and arguably even its nightlife, culture and self-image. The America's Cup presented an enormous challenge and an unprecedented opportunity for New Zealand. This sporting event had impacts that went far beyond its attraction for tourists or its financial benefits. It lifted the profile of this small island nation on the world stage and contributed to the redevelopment of the downtown waterfront in its largest city. In addition, the successful defence against representatives from major developed world nations, such as the USA, Italy, Japan and France, fostered a positive sense of self-worth and national pride among New Zealanders. Most particularly, however, it confirms the opportunities that sports competition may offer in terms of landscape and resource (re)development with significant implications for interests in sport and tourism development.

Further reading

McDermott Fairgray Group and Ernst and Young (2000) *The Economic Impact of the America's Cup Regatta, Auckland 1999–2000.* Wellington: Office of Tourism and Sport, New Zealand Government.

Orams, M. B. (1999) *Marine Tourism: Development, Impacts and Management.* London: Routledge.

Orams, M. B. and Brons, A. (1999) Planning for a major sport/tourism event: The America's Cup 2000, Auckland, New Zealand. *Visions in Leisure and Business* 18 (1), 14–28.

Part 4: Sport Tourism Development and Time

Chapter 8

Sport and the Tourist Experience

Sport is seen to be an important factor in many decisions to travel, to often feature prominently in the travel experience, and to be an important consideration in the visitor's assessment of the travel experience.

(Hinch & Higham, 2001: 48)

Introduction

This chapter considers sport tourism themes in the short term and, in doing so, focuses on the tourist experience. The tourist experience represents the sum of several distinct processes that unfold in five phases: anticipation, travel, visitor experiences at the destination, travel back and recollection (Clawson & Knetsch, 1966; Manfredo & Driver, 1983). The anticipation phase of the tourist experience requires an understanding of information search, decision-making, planning and the formulation of expectations, each of which are affected by travel motivations. Travel to the destination forms an important part of the tourist experience as it influences length of stay and the infrastructure and service needs of the tourist. The activities, feelings and behaviours of sport tourists are key dimensions of their visitor experiences. These may vary significantly with, for example, the relative priority placed on the pursuit of sport and other touristic activities at a destination. The experience concludes with processes of evaluation and recollection. Visitor experiences at the actual destination, therefore, form only one part of the subject of this chapter.

The Anticipation Phase

Information search, decision-making, planning and the formulation of expectations are important aspects of the visitor experience in the anticipation phase. The typology of sport tourists presented in Table 8.1 serves as a starting point from which to consider the pre-trip phase of the sport tourist experience. Different sport tourist types are likely to vary considerably in terms of information search, decision-making and planning.

Table 8.1 Sport tourist typologies

Sport tourist typology (Glyptis, 1982)	Parallels with subsequent typologies
General holidays with sport content	Incidental (G. Jackson & Reeves, 1997) Incidental (Reeves, 2000)
Specialist or general sport holidays	Sport activity holidays (Standeven & De Knop, 1999) Independent sport holidays (Standeven & De Knop, 1999) Sporadic (Reeves, 2000) Occasional/regular (G. Jackson & Reeves, 1997) Occasional sports (wo)men (Maier & Weber, 1993) Mass sports (Maier & Weber, 1993)
Upmarket sport holidays	Organised holiday sports (Standeven & De Knop, 1999) Occasional/regular (G. Jackson & Reeves, 1997)
Elite training	Top performance athletes (Maier & Weber, 1993) Dedicated/driven (G. Jackson & Reeves, 1997)
Spectator events	Passive sports on holiday (Standeven & De Knop, 1999), including casual and connoisseur observers Passive sport tourists (Maier & Weber, 1993)

Information sources and decision-making

Use of a diverse range of information sources is typical of the way most tourists plan for their trips, but different types of tourists use different search strategies (Page *et al.*, 2001). Information may be obtained through word of mouth, via advertisements and promotions and through professional outlets such as travel agencies and information centres. The information requirements of different sport tourist types and, therefore, avenues of information search in the pre-trip phase, stand in significant contrast. Elite athletes, for example, tend to focus on the availability of competition and suitable high-quality training facilities, while destination choice may be determined by acclimatisation or altitude-training requirements (Maier & Weber, 1993). In this context, destination requirements are focused around the pursuit of sport performance. Requisite information is likely to be sourced from specialised packages that are developed by sports managers and disseminated through targeted niche marketing. The travel information needs of elite athletes include competition schedules and training itineraries that are usually developed by national sports bodies through initiatives such as reciprocal international training programmes. Relatively little autonomy in destination choice exists within this market segment (Reeves, 2000), although differing philosophies towards training may be associated with alternative training venues and destinations.

The processes of decision-making for specialist or general sport holidays offer several notable contrasts. Access to sports training facilities of high standard, diversity or uniqueness may be an important consideration in the planning processes relating to this market (Maier & Weber, 1993). However, access to holiday regions, tourist attractions and activities may also feature prominently in the decision-making process. This is a consequence of the high autonomy in destination choice enjoyed by this market segment (Reeves, 2000). Those who pursue specialist or general sport holidays demonstrate a greater propensity to use standard tourism information services, such as travel agents and destination brochures, in the decision-making and travel-planning processes. They are also more likely to respond to attraction markers, both contiguous and detached (Chapter 2), to establish or raise awareness of a destination. For tourists within these market segments, sport may be one of a variety of activities pursued while on holiday (Getz & Cheyne, 1997). Differences between sport and touristic interests in the planning phase are important points of distinction.

Sport tourism and visitor expectations

Visitor expectations may vary significantly among participants within a given sport (Chapter 3). Expectations and desired experiences are a function of the lifestyles, attitudes and personalities of individual sport tourists and are likely to vary considerably with demographic profile, travel career stage, sport experience and/or recreational use history (Schreyer *et al.*, 1984; Watson & Roggenbuck, 1991; P. Pearce, 1988). The study of tourist expectations relating to sport is in its infancy, although notable contributions have emerged in relation to a small number of activities, such as golf, skiing and scuba diving (Priestley, 1995; Hudson, 1999; Tabata, 1992). Little or no attention has, as yet, been paid to the visitor expectations of event or nostalgia sport tourists (Gibson, 1998a; Gammon, 2002). Sport tourism development at a destination requires the further commitment of national and/or regional tourism organisations to understand and monitor the expectations and desired experiences of tourists within target market groups.

Sport and the Study of Tourist Motivations

Research into tourist motivations is concerned with why people travel, the benefits that they seek and the experiences that they pursue to satisfy their needs and desires (Cooper *et al.*, 1993). Tourist motivation is a function of self-perceived needs of the traveller, which drive the decision-making process and the purchase of tourism products (Collier, 1999). The motivational profile of the traveller is a combination of intrinsic and extrinsic factors. These factors have been described in terms of push (psychological) and pull (cultural) factors (Dann, 1981). The former are intrinsic and unique to each tourist, as they are determined by the personality and attitude of the individual. Pull factors include price, destination image and marketing and promotion. Destination image, which is a function of physical and abstract attributes (Echtner & Ritchie, 1993), plays an important part in the formulation of expectations. Physical attributes include attractions, activities, sporting facilities and physical landscapes. Abstract attributes are less readily measured and include atmosphere, crowding, safety and ambience. These pull factors may also influence the perceived needs of tourists in the anticipation phase of the travel experience.

Sport tourism, like other forms of travel, entails a set of motivations that are established in anticipation of the fulfilment of desired needs. B. Stewart (2001) identifies a range of factors that motivate fans to travel to support their teams and these fall within the gambit of push and pull factors. Push factors include release from everyday life, the search for camaraderie, the need to develop friendships and a sense of belonging, emotional release and the opportunity to do things that cannot be done at home. In contrast, pull factors that may motivate event sport tourism include the atmosphere and excitement of a highly charged match and the tension associated with the uncertainty of the outcome. Tourist motivations are critical to understanding why people do or do not travel, their choice of destination and other aspects of tourist behaviour.

The sport of golf demonstrates the diverse range of tourist motivations held by sport participants. Approximately 150 million people travelled internationally to golf destinations in 1999 (Bartoluci & Čavlek, 2000). The motivations underpinning this travel and, as a consequence, the sport tourism experiences of golfers, differ between distinct sport tourist types (Table 8.2). These cannot be generalised directly to other sports because of the unique rules, competition structures and elements of play that characterise each sport (Chapter 2). However, an understanding of the motivations that sport tourists hold towards their chosen sports is critical to success in developing sport tourism destinations. Similar studies that examine the tourist motivations associated with specific sports are certainly justified.

Table 8.2 Sport motivation profiles of sport tourists who play golf

Sport tourist types (Glyptis, 1982)	Primary motivations	Destination attributes	Secondary activities
General holidays with sports content	Various business or leisure travel motivations	Vary with primary motivations (existence of a golf course is incidental)	Playing golf, among other things
Specialist sport holidays	Pilgrimage to the heartland of golf; emulating icon players	Grand slam and other championship courses	Nostalgia sport tourism
General sport holidays	Golf as one part of a suite of visitor activities	Single integrated resorts	Family-based activities
Upmarket sports holidays	Golf as a specialised visitor activity	High degree of luxury; second home developments adjacent to golf courses	Domestic and social activities
Elite training	Seeking competition and challenge from a range of golf courses	Networks of golf courses forming golf regions	Coaching clinics; professional advice; purchase of equipment

Source: adapted from Glyptis (1982); Priestley (1995)

It is useful to consider the relative importance of sport and tourism motivations held by sport tourists (Gammon & Robinson, 1997). Those motivated by elite training are unlikely to concern themselves with other touristic activities available at a destination. The focus of elite athletes is on preparation and performance. They may be oblivious to the experiential opportunities arising from being a tourist, at least in advance of and during the period of competition. In some cases, however, 'the touristic element may act to reinforce the overall experience' (Gammon & Robinson, 1997: 8), even when there is an intense focus on competition. On the other hand, those who pursue general holidays with a sport content hold a quite a distinct motivational profile, such that sport tourist activities may be incidental or secondary to other tourist experiences that form the primary travel motivation.

Sports fans also vary in the extent to which they are motivated to travel in support of a sports team. For some fans, involvement in the sport itself is the dominant travel motivation. Social identity can be constructed and reinforced through fandom in which 'sport becomes a pivotal means of signifying loyalty and commitment, producing enduring leisure behaviour' (I. Jones, 2000). B. Stewart (2001) has developed a typology of Australian team sport watchers, which demonstrates the diversity that exists within this travel market. The motivations held by each of these fan categories influences visitor experiences at the host destination:

(1) *Passionate partisans*: hardcore supporters who attend games regularly, regardless of inconveniences; their moods and identities are closely linked to the successes and failures of their team.
(2) *Champion followers*: less fanatical, they change their allegiance or their allegiance remains held in abeyance until their team starts winning some games.
(3) *Reclusive partisans*: their interest in the game and commitment to the team is strong, but they attend games infrequently. Interested in the team, more than the game.
(4) *Theatregoers*: they primarily seek entertainment through sport, but are not necessarily attached to a particular team.
(5) *Aficionados*: Attracted to exciting games, and also to games that involve star players, they are interested in the demonstration of skill, tactical complexity and aesthetic pleasure, which take priority over the outcome of the game.

Sport tourists who attend other types of sports events may demonstrate quite different motivations and preferences (Pyo *et al.*, 1988). Delpy Neirotti *et al.*, (2001) examined the motivations of event sport tourists attending the 1996 Atlanta Olympic Games. They distinguished factors that motivated the decision to attend from motivations that evolved after the decision to attend had been reached. The former centred on the event offering a once-in-a-lifetime opportunity. Respondents reported that, having arrived at the decision to attend, experiencing firsthand the excellence of athletic competition, the international party atmosphere, the cultural experience and the historical significance became important motivations. The potential to combine sports travel with other leisure activities at the destination is evident in this case. In contrast, spending time with family may be an important travel motivation for those who participate in small-scale sport events (Carmichael & Murphy, 1996). This motivation is particularly applicable to female participation in sport, which is more likely to take place with other family members (Thompson, 1985).

In many sports, consumer identification with a sport subculture may be an important travel motivation (Chapter 6). Green (2001: 5) notes that 'interactions with others are at the core of the socialisation process and provide avenues through which values and beliefs come to be shared and expressed'. Sport tourism may, therefore, be motivated by a celebration of subculture through participation, or, equally, through non-sport activities at the destination (Green & Chalip, 1998). This discussion confirms the importance of understanding the motivations that exist within sport tourism market segments and the tourist experiences that they mediate.

Sport Tourism Visitor Experiences

The visitor experience can be described and studied in various ways. At one level, it is important to understand the tourist experience in terms of length of stay, the activities pursued and general tourist behaviour. It is also important to note that the visitor experience is a combination of tangible (physical attributes) and intangible (emotions and feelings) elements. The experiential approach to studying the visitor experience involves understanding the emotions and feelings that comprise the visitor experience. These emotions may include joy, relief, exhaustion, euphoria and dejection, which arise from victory, defeat, camaraderie or simply through participation in physical activities. Visitor experiences are a function of the motivations and desired experiences of the tourist, but are also influenced by the sport and tourism systems at a destination. The three sections that follow examine the elements of the sport tourism visitor experience illustrated in Figure 8.1.

Travel and Tourist Experiences

Time/cost/distance travel thresholds and length of stay

The investment of time, money and energy in accessing a destination will generally influence length of stay and, as a consequence, most aspects of the visitor experiences (Collier, 1999). For example, the distance decay

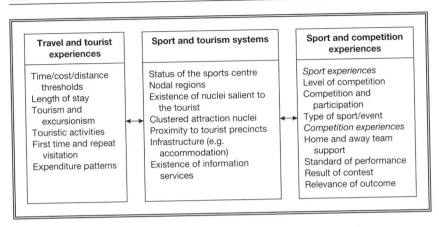

Figure 8.1 Factors influencing the sport tourism visitor experience

function associated with different modes of transportation influences
levels of accessibility and the use of tourism infrastructure. Similarly, the
standard and capacity of transport infrastructure, including the perceived
security and efficiency of transit and arrival procedures, influence the
travel phase of the tourist experience and visitor satisfaction. Moreover,
the travel time/cost/distance function of tourism may be modified by the
development of transport nodes, infrastructure and services. The rapid
rise of budget airline services and the development of a new generation
of rail services have greatly influenced time/cost/distance travel thresholds in Europe (Page *et al.*, 2001). Proximity to transport nodes and
services may reduce time/cost/distance constraints, resulting in altered
spatial travel patterns and desired visitor experiences.

Tourism and excursionism

Length of stay at a destination relates closely to visitor engagement in
tourist activities at a destination. The status of the sport tourist as tourist
or excursionist influences the visitor experience. Nogawa *et al.* (1996)
define sport excursionists as day trippers who do not stay overnight at a
destination. Their study identified statistically significant differences
between sport tourists and sport excursionists in terms of engagement in
non-sport activities while on their trip. The former were more likely to
undertake tourist activities such as sightseeing, even in cases where the
length of stay at the destination was a single night. Participation by
sport tourists in touristic activities at a destination may be fostered, then,
where extended length of stay can be encouraged, and where appropriate
planning facilitates participation in such activities.

Touristic activities and visitor expenditures

Sport events offer significant potential to generate tourist activity at a destination. Stevens (2001) identifies that, on baseball game days at Oriole Park (Baltimore, USA), double- and triple-digit percentage increases in trade are experienced by tourism businesses in the city. Spectatorship at professional baseball games in Baltimore was found to generate a 20% increase in hotel occupancy rates in the vicinity of the stadium. This sport was also found to generate significant increases in business for various attractions and activities, including the Babe Ruth Museum, Balls Sports Bar, the Baja Beach Club, the National Aquarium and the Maryland Science Centre (Stevens, 2001). Engagement in touristic activities and patterns of expenditure differ between local fans, event sport tourists and event sport excursionists (Bale, 1993a). A study of the expenditure patterns of spectators at Atlanta Falcons American Football games revealed that the costs of purchasing tickets represented 77% of the total expenditures of local spectators, as opposed to 41% of the expenditures of non-local spectators (Schaffer & Davidson, 1985). The majority of expenditures engaged by non-local spectators were directed towards food and entertainment, accommodation, transport and parking, concessions and shopping. Law (2002) notes that the greatest contribution of the stadium to tourism will be felt in cases where stadia are developed in close proximity to attractions, tourism services and infrastructure. It is not surprising, therefore, that there is a trend to integrate contemporary stadia developments with malls, plazas, hotels and other sport and entertainment facilities, such as theme parks, halls of fame and cinemas (Stevens, 2001).

First-time and repeat visitation

Visitor experiences and expenditures differ between first-time versus repeat visitors. While sports may offer great variety, uncertainty of outcome and authenticity in the tourist experience (Chapter 2), Godbey and Graefe (1991) observe that, in the case of college football, the spectator experience for repeat visitors may take on a predictable routine:

> The drive to the college community in question, choice of lodging and dining, the institution of 'tailgating' (eating, drinking and socialising in parking lots or other areas close to the stadium before or after the game), the choice of travel companions, even the people sitting in adjoining seats may not change radically from game to game. (Godbey & Graefe, 1991: 219)

This situation may influence spending patterns in two ways. On one hand, the likelihood of repeat visitation may be eroded due to lack of novelty in the visitor experience. Alternatively, the sport tourist may combine the sport experience with new activities or events at the destination to achieve the level of novelty and stimulation required to warrant repeat travel. Godbey and Graefe's (1991) study of non-local season ticket holders visiting the Pennsylvania State University to experience college football identified a strong negative correlation between repeated attendance at football games and levels of visitor expenditure (Table 8.3). It seems evident, therefore, that sports producers and tourism managers need to innovate and perhaps collaborate to offer novel experiences for repeat visitors.

Table 8.3 Average visitor expenditures ($US) at state college football games

Expense category	Number of games attended						
	1	2	3	4	5	6	7
Restaurants	20.78	13.92	11.14	10.83	8.79	6.61	6.44
Retail food and beverages	2.94	4.34	1.59	1.76	1.90	1.77	1.50
Admission fees	0.45	0.36	0.41	0.35	0.30	0.26	0.25
Night clubs/bars	6.15	4.30	3.34	2.59	2.94	1.90	1.79
Games clothing and equipment	6.67	3.24	2.19	2.07	2.57	2.18	2.24
Other retail shopping	19.60	10.44	7.20	5.23	6.23	4.45	4.77
Lodging	12.85	12.82	12.14	11.63	6.50	5.07	4.18
Personal health expenditures	0.11	0.03	0.11	0.06	0.26	0.15	0.09
Private auto expenses	6.00	6.83	4.17	3.67	3.02	3.59	2.52
Commercial transportation	3.52	7.42	5.29	0.95	0.91	0.34	0.08
Baby sitter fees	0.21	0.82	0.00	0.15	0.03	0.10	0.05
Equipment rentals	0.00	0.00	0.00	0.17	0.06	0.03	0.02
Charitable donations	0.41	0.30	0.43	0.35	0.32	0.27	0.22
Total per game expenses	79.69	64.82	48.01	39.81	33.83	26.72	24.15

Note: n=1600, surveyed over a one year period
Source: based on Godbey and Graefe (1991: 221)

Sport and Competition Experiences

The sport experience

The defining qualities of different sports mediate the sport tourist experience in various ways. This experience also varies with levels of competition and types of involvement in sport (Chapter 2) (Figure 8.1). Tourist experiences and expenditures vary between levels of competition, particularly between amateur and professional sports (Reeves, 2000). Professional sports attract a wider catchment of sports fans and, potentially, the interest of other businesses and sponsors. As may be expected, 'travellers who go to a youth sports championship . . . tend to spend less than those who are attending a major event such as a Super Bowl' (Loverseed, 2001: 35). In general, expenditure patterns associated with event sport tourism are similar to other forms of leisure-based travel. However, the magnitude of the expenditure is likely to vary between competitive and non-competitive events.

The competitiveness of the active sport tourist influences the tourist experience. Competitive sports are usually pursued with a single-minded focus, but, if time allows, touristic activities may be pursued at the conclusion of competition. By contrast, recreational participation in sports is often free of rigid time constraints, which offers the opportunity for engagement in a wide variety of touristic activities through the duration of the visit.

Opportunities for event and active sport tourists to engage in touristic activities at a destination also differ between sports. Sports that take place in natural areas offer quite different leisure and touristic opportunities compared to those that are contested in urban tourism destinations. The timing, pacing and duration of an event or sport contest may also facilitate or inhibit engagement in other touristic activities at a destination. The visitor experience and economic impacts of the 1999 Rugby World Cup (Wales), for instance, was inhibited by the spatial and temporal planning of the event. C. Jones (2001: 247) notes that 'the low gate receipts and visitor expenditure in general, were due in no small part to the fact that only eight of the 41 games were held in the Principality (of Wales)'. This effectively compromised the efforts of marketing and tourism agencies to portray the event as 'Welsh'. It also resulted in 'fixture gaps' (periods of up to 12 days between games scheduled in any host city), which contributed to a lack of atmosphere at the host destinations (C. Jones, 2001).

Gratton *et al.* (2000) present an economic impact study of six sports events hosted in British cities and towns in 1997, which provides valuable insights into the varied visitor experiences and tourism impacts associated with different sports. Their study included the World Badminton

Championship (Glasgow), European Junior Boxing Championship (Birmingham), England versus Australia Ashes cricket test (Edgbaston), International Amateur Athletics Federation (IAAF) Grand Prix (Sheffield), European Junior Swimming Championship (Glasgow) and Women's British Open Golf Championship (Sunningdale). These sports events were placed on a continuum to illustrate the extent to which each was competitor- and/or spectator-driven. Cricket and golf were identified as being spectator-driven, while badminton and swimming were competitor-driven. Swimming, badminton and boxing attracted a variety of competitors, officials and representatives from governing bodies. The extent to which these different types of sport tourists are able to leave their sports event and take free time to experience the destinations that they visit stand in significant contrast.

The duration of sports events also influences the visitor experience and the economic impacts of the event (Gratton *et al.*, 2000). The boxing and swimming championships lasted nine and four days, respectively, while the IAAF Grand Prix was completed in less than five hours. Different sports, contested at different levels, offer different degrees of opportunity to engage in touristic activities at a destination. International test match cricket is a sport that includes long days of play and practice sessions on days of non-play. The duration of an amateur boxing contest stands in marked contrast to test match cricket. The opportunities for competitors in these sports to engage in leisure activities at a destination differ accordingly. However, the relative degrees of constraint that these sports impose upon their participants do not necessarily apply to spectators.

The profile of sport tourists also varies significantly between sports. Popular organised sports, such as soccer and baseball, are dominated by spectator markets made up of young males. These markets are generally characterised by low disposable incomes when contrasted with the more mature spectator markets associated with sports such as golf and test cricket (Loverseed, 2001). Gratton *et al.* (2000) report that international cricket generated the greatest economic impact of the six study events, due to high spectator appeal, the relatively long duration of the contest (five days) and the high spending profile of attendees.

The competition experience

The status of a competition, stage of the season and outcome of a contest may also influence the visitor experience (Figure 8.1). Sports that are contested within a league (or within divisions of teams) provide, at different stages of the competition season, varied opportunities to foster and encourage leisure and touristic activities at a destination. 'Big time North American college football each fall provides the impetus for lots of tourism and considerable monetary spending' (Godbey & Graefe, 1991:

219). This potential varies from week to week with the circumstances of different games. While event sport tourists generally travel to support a team that is playing away from home, it is also the case that sport tourists may travel considerable distances to support their team at home. This point is clearly illustrated by Case study 8.1, (see pp. 160–162) in which Gibson demonstrates that sport tourists may perceive themselves as 'host resident' or 'visitor', based on the team that they support, with implications for the visitor experience (Gibson *et al.*, 2002). The standard of a team or individual performance, which may be worthy of celebration or condemnation, and the competitive outcome of a contest may also influence the overall visitor experience, especially at higher levels of competition. A famous victory may be followed by days of street celebration (Focus point 8.1), whereas an ignominious loss may send fans hurrying for the first train home.

Focus point 8.1

Celebration of France's FIFA World Cup victory: Paris, 12 July 1998

The 1998 FIFA World Cup was hosted, and the final won in front of the home crowd, by France. The path that the French team negotiated to the final was a tenuous one. Their quarter-final against Paraguay was won in extra time by a 'golden goal'. In the semi-final France was victorious over Italy, a two-time champion, in a game that was level after full time and extra-time, and decided in a nail-biting penalty shootout. In the final, on 12 July 1998, the French team administered the *coup de grâce*, in a complete performance 'defeating the ultimate adversary, the football nation of legend, Brazil' (Dauncey & Hare 2000: 344) by the convincing margin of 4–1:

> On the night of 12 July . . . there was an outpouring of joy and sentiment that was unprecedented since the Liberation of 1944 . . . Huge numbers of people poured onto the streets in spontaneous and good-humoured celebration. In Paris, hundreds of thousands gathered again on the Champs Elysées the next day to see the Cup paraded in an open-topped bus. For all, the victory was an unforgettable experience. (Dauncey & Hare, 2000: 331)

A global television audience of nearly 40 billion, the largest television audience for a single sport, watched these events unfold. Based on the knife-edge quarter- and semi-final victories of the French team, it is clear that the width of a crossbar can bear heavily on the emotions, experiences and behaviours that occur spontaneously in response to the performances and outcomes of football championships (Dauncey & Hare, 2000).

Sport and Tourism Systems

The visitor experience of sport tourists is influenced by the sport and tourism systems at a destination. The spatial distribution and accessibility of sports facilities and venues in central and satellite areas influence the sport experience for both hosts and guests. Bale (1982) makes reference to 'sports nodes' that are functionally delineated areas where the sport experience takes place. These nodal regions can be managed to minimise negative impacts, such as congestion, noise and unruly behaviour, as well as to enhance the sport and tourist experience. The 'tourism system' that serves sports nodes is equally important. Tourists often embark on a trip with one attraction, or one particular experience in mind (Leiper, 1990). In sport tourism, as in any other form of tourism, tourists typically engage in combinations of attraction nuclei that are salient to the desired experiences of the tourist. The importance of the tourism system in fostering the visitor experience is emphasised by Leiper's (1990) concept of 'clustered nuclei'. Clusters of symbiotic attraction nuclei are a significant element of the contemporary tourism system. Leiper (1990: 375) explains that 'tourists' precinct seems a useful expression for describing a small zone within a town or city where tourists are prone to gather because of clustered nuclei with some unifying theme'.

The development of stadia within tourist precincts illustrates the potential for tourist experiences to be fostered in association with event sport tourism (Stevens & Wootton, 1997). A unifying force exists where sports facilities are developed in association with sports bars, museums, halls of fame and other forms of entertainment. The development of complementary activities (e.g. non-sport entertainment) and tourist services (e.g. transport nodes, accommodation, banking and information services), enhance the status of the tourist precinct. These developments may or may not be permanent. The temporary creation of tourist precincts is a strategy that attempts to leverage sports events to encourage a wider experience of the destination. Nash and Johnston (1998), for instance, describe the development of exhibitions, promotions and community events in the cities of Liverpool and Leeds, which hosted the 1996 European Football Championship.

The visitor experience is also influenced by external tourism systems. Main entry points to a destination region may act as major points of concentration for tourists. This was the case during the 1994 Lillehammer Winter Olympics, which generated economic benefits for the gateway city of Oslo, more so than it did for the host town of Lillehammer (Teigland, 1999). Where event sport tourism takes place in a major urban tourism destination, such as the Sydney Olympic Games (2000), the reverse may occur. Nearby secondary sport tourism centres can leverage the event in their own tourism development interests (Chalip, this volume, Case study 3.1;

pp. 52–54). It is apparent, then, that 'intervening attractions along major travel corridors, and competing tourist destinations' may influence the visitor experiences (Teigland, 1999: 308).

Sport Tourism and Visitor Behaviour

An understanding of the visitor experience is incomplete without consideration of the manifestations of sport tourist behaviour. The theory of planned behaviour states that tourist behaviour can be predicted based on attitudes and subjective norms (Ajzen & Driver, 1992). Tourist behaviours are evaluated based on instrumental costs and benefits, as well as the positive or negative feelings that the behaviour may bring about. Studies that investigate the motivational characteristics of sport tourism niche markets may be extended to the tourist behaviours that are associated with sport tourism in its various forms. Tourist behaviour is a critical element for sustainable sport tourism development. Individual sports are characterised by sport tourist behaviour profiles that may or may not benefit the tourist destination. Active sport tourism is generally constructive in the immediate outcomes of participation, including exertion, fitness, camaraderie, social contact and subcultural identity.

The behaviours associated with sports team fans and spectators are highly varied and in many cases unpredictable (Giulianotti, 1995b, 1996; Getz & Cheyne, 1997; Weed 2002) (Focus point 8.2). Bale (1989) describes team-based contests, such as soccer and ice hockey, as ritualised conflict. Team sports foster the emotional involvement of spectators, bringing rival fans together into an intense setting (the stadium or arena) that can give rise to confrontation and antagonism. The manifestations of such behaviour may be displayed by players (e.g. ice hockey, baseball), coaches (e.g. basketball, American football) and/or spectators (e.g. soccer, cricket).

Team sports may be associated with tourist behaviours that vary in the extreme. The behaviours of spectators at the International Rugby Board Hong Kong Sevens contribute to a carnival atmosphere, while the passionate support of football clubs may produce behaviours that are confrontational and violent. Manifestations of sport tourist behaviour influence visitor experiences, expenditures and social impacts at a destination. The management and regulatory responses to these behaviours include restrictions on movement (segregation), alcohol bans and heavy police presence. Individual sports, such as tennis, golf and surfing, offer the contrasts of entertainment and demonstrations of individual skill. Appreciation of individual performance is commonly associated with these sports, which may still be the subject of collective behaviour, but are less likely to be associated with antagonistic behaviour on the part of participants or spectators.

Focus point 8.2

Team Sports and Visitor Behaviour

The behaviours associated with team sports vary considerably between sports, and between regions and countries. Cricket in Australia and New Zealand has in recent years been associated with instances of unruly crowd behaviour, as have test matches between India and Pakistan. By contrast, in England cricket is a sedate and traditional affair, while in the West Indies cricket is a sport of carnival and celebration. Rugby spectatorship in England is closely tied to social class and is generally a refined and serious spectator experience. Rugby and Rugby League in the South Pacific, Australia and New Zealand have occasionally been associated with political demonstrations, unruly crowd behaviour and rioting, although these generally pale alongside the more serious occurrences of football hooliganism. Professional soccer has, since 1908, been associated with acts of football hooliganism in over 30 countries in Europe, Asia, Africa and South America (Dunning, 1999). Yet Giulianotti's (1996) ethnographic study of Ireland's football fans at the 1994 World Cup Finals in the USA was notable for the absence of football hooliganism and, instead, the presence of 'carnival fandom' and the promotion of a fresh sense of Irish identity beyond nation-state boundaries.

Disorderly sport spectator behaviours may have negative effects on host communities and raise the potential for host/guest conflict (Weed, 2002). I. Jones (2000) applies the concept of serious leisure to football fandom in an attempt to explain the behaviours of football fans as part of the social identity process. The characteristics of serious leisure in this context include longevity in the support of a chosen team, strong identification with the chosen leisure activity, investment of significant personal effort and the existence, in some cases, of a career path involving stages of achievement and recognition. Modelling is an important aspect of this form of social identity construction, whereby 'the neophyte member begins to deliberately adopt mannerisms, attitudes, and styles of dress, speech and behaviour that he or she perceives to be characteristic of the established members of the subculture' (Donnelly & Young, 1988: 223). Two important behavioural consequences of serious leisure identification include 'in-group favouritism' and 'out-group derogation'. The preferential and derogatory attitudes of each are based on group membership, rather than the individual characteristics of members of the group. 'Hostility towards out-groups may be demonstrated if the goals of the two groups are seen to be mutually exclusive' (I. Jones, 2000: 291).

It is apparent that spectators at sports events can either foster or counter tourism development interests through individual and collective behaviours. Event sport tourists can create a carnival atmosphere and bring colour, excitement and atmosphere to a destination that is attractive to tourists, or generate noise, security risks and create offence that may be repulsive to them (Higham, 1999; Weed, 2002). 'Sports junkies' are tourists whose behaviours are indicative of a strong commitment to their sport or support for their team. The behaviour of these sport tourists may create aversion effects (Faulkner *et al.*, 1998), while contributing to accommodation shortages that displace other forms of tourism, such as corporate, business and conference travel. These varied and contrasting manifestations of tourist behaviour demonstrate the importance of considering all aspects of the sport tourist experience along with the economic impacts of different forms of sport tourism at a destination (Higham, 1999).

Recollection and Visitor Satisfaction

Travel home and recollection form an important part of the visitor experience (Clawson & Knetsch, 1966). Visitor satisfaction influences whether the experience will predispose a visitor to return to the destination or explore new places (Ryan, 1995). Multiple criteria are assessed in the recollection process, and the weighting of criteria varies between different forms of sport tourism. Satisfaction with spectator events may be based on an assessment of its drama, standards of performance and the behaviour of other fans (Bale, 1989). Touristic experiences, such as crowding and congestion, standards of service and uniqueness of the destination, may also feature prominently in the recollection phase.

Event sport tourism experiences, if satisfactory, may promote and generate tourist activity beyond the timeframe of the initial event. 'People who attend the event may return for a vacation, or those who watch the event on television may decide to visit the destination later' (Gibson, 1998a: 60). One of the most comprehensive research studies addressing this aspect of the sport tourist experience was conducted by Webb and Magnussen (2002) following the 1999 Rugby World Cup (RWC) hosted by Wales. Their initial research phase estimated that the short-term impact of the RWC was £82.3 million. A follow-up survey of non-Welsh respondents conducted in 2002 indicated that 44% of the sample had subsequently returned to Wales and 77% had recommended Wales as a place to visit. Over one third (36%) of recommendations had resulted in visits to the destination (Webb & Magnussen, 2002). Carmichael and Murphy (1996) provide one of the few empirical studies into behavioural intentions towards a destination following small-scale sports events. They provide insights into the various forms that repeat travel to a destination may take, including investment, the development of business interests and retirement, as well as leisure travel. Furthermore, they raise important questions regarding the role of small-scale sports events in tourism. These include:

(1) the significance of the event itself, as against other factors that may influence future travel to the destination;
(2) the relative significance of sport and touristic elements of the event experience that influence future travel intentions; and
(3) the translation of travel intentions into future travel actions and the decay of travel intentions generated by sports in the weeks and months following an event.

The factors that feature in the recall phase of the sport tourism visitor experience remain poorly understood. These factors are certain to differ between sport tourist types. High-performance athletes are likely to be influenced by the standard of training facilities, personal performance and the outcome of the sport contest (Maier & Weber, 1993). Sport experiences may be judged on uniqueness by casual spectators, while more serious sports fans will judge them by opportunities that they provide to enhance social identity and self-concept (Gibson, 1998a). By contrast, those pursuing general holidays with some incidental sport content may assess the uniqueness of the touristic experience of the destination in the recollection phase (Glyptis, 1982). In each instance, perceptions of the destination, and the propensity for repeat travel, are influenced by different factors.

Management Implications and Opportunities

The sport tourism experience takes place in several phases. The motivations and expectations of sport tourists, which are subjective and difficult to generalise, influence each phase of the visitor experience. Sport managers need to understand the motivations and expectations that define distinct sport tourism market segments, and how they influence all aspects of the visitor experience (Gammon & Robinson, 1997). Visitor experiences pursued by specific market segments, which may be redefined during the actual experience, are notable for their diversity. Successful completion of competition, or the elimination of a team during the preliminary rounds of an event, will alter the focus of visitor experiences. The extent to which sport tourists engage in other touristic activities at a destination is influenced by two important factors. These include the travel profile of the visitor (e.g. distances travelled, mode of transport, length of stay) and the sports and/or competitions that sport tourists experience at a destination (e.g. scheduling of the sport, standard of the performance, outcome of the contest). Sport tourism development interests will be well served by an appreciation of the tourist experiences that visitors seek to fulfil at a destination (Gibson *et al.*, 2002). The ability to accurately profile visitors in terms of their travel characteristics, combined with an appreciation of the unique qualities of the sport(s) and/or sporting interests in which they intend to engage, will assist in understanding and enhancing the desired visitor experience.

The sport tourism experience is also mediated by the sport and tourism systems at a destination. Success in the integrated planning of sport nodes and tourism precincts offers great potential to facilitate and enhance the visitor experience at a destination (Stevens & Wootton, 1997). Sport and event planning, production and management also contribute to this goal. For example, sports event planning may be directed towards effective marketing and tourism promotion, the creation of atmosphere at a destination or the enhancement of the visitor experience (C. Jones, 2001). It is important, therefore, that sport managers give careful consideration to the timing, scheduling and pacing of sports and sport events, the development of ancillary activities and entertainments, and links to the wider tourism product at the host destination. Enhancement of the visitor experience may be one outcome of these strategies, thereby contributing to the sustainability of sport tourism development.

Conclusion

This chapter considers the short-term temporal dimension of sport tourism development. It addresses how sport may influence the frequency, timing and duration of sport tourism experiences, and how different aspects of sport and tourism mediate visitor experience at a destination. One of the pressing challenges in the academic study of sport tourism is to develop insights into the relationship between sport tourist motivations/expectations and tourist experiences/behaviours at the destination. The fact that sport tourism experiences and, as a consequence, patterns of visitor expenditure, can be influenced by planning and management strategies in sport tourism is an important point that emerges from this discussion. Scheduling and programming of sports events and competitions have direct implications for the tourist experience. The creation of tourist precincts, permanent or temporary, through the provision of ancillary entertainment and complementary attractions and services is another important management strategy that may contribute towards this end. Success or failure of sport tourism development initiatives will be determined to a large degree by the effectiveness of these strategies to enhance sport tourist experiences at a destination.

Further Reading

Two useful resources for those initiating study into the tourist experience are Clawson and Knetsch (1966) and Manfredo and Driver (1983).

Further insight into sport tourist motivations and preferences is provided by Gammon and Robinson (1997), Pyo *et al.* (1988) and Delpy Neirotti *et al.* (2001). Chalip *et al.*'s (1998) research into sources of interest in travel to the Olympic Games is also highly recommended. For a more in-depth discussion of the diversity that exists within active sport tourism experiences, readers should consult WTO and IOC (2001).

Donnelly and Young (1988), Dunning (1999) and Giulianotti (1996) provide strong reviews of the experiences associated with football hooliganism. Barker (2004) offers valuable insights into the wider issues of crime associated with sport events. Within the context of sport tourism, these publications may be read in association with Murphy's (1985) insights into tourism in host communities and Weed's (2002) considerations of football hooligans as sport tourists. Faulkner *et al.* (1998) offer insights into the wider visitor experiences associated with different sport tourism niche markets. Similarly, Gratton and Taylor (2000) and Gratton *et al.* (2000) provide valuable insights into the economics of sport and sport tourist experiences. Chalip (2004) considers the means by which destinations may leverage sports events in the pursuit of economic benefits. The development opportunities of relevance to urban sport tourism experiences are explored thoroughly by Stevens and Wootton (1997) and Stevens (2001).

Case study 8.1

US College Football: The Sport Tourism Experience

Heather Gibson, University of Florida, USA

In the USA, thousands of people travel each week to watch college-level competitions in a wide variety of sports, from tennis and swimming to baseball and basketball, yet the tourism potential of these travellers is largely unrecognised (Irwin & Sandler, 1998). Division 1A football in the USA draws large crowds from late August until the beginning of January for those teams who are invited to the bowl games (championship games). One of the football teams with a large following is the University of Florida Gators. The University of Florida (UF) is located in the city of Gainesville, approximately 80 miles (129 km) west of Jacksonville and 100 miles (161 km) north of Orlando. On average 84,000 fans attend each of the five or six home football games each season, of which 50,000 are non-students and almost 80% of whom travel from outside the county to attend games (University Athletic Association, 2000). In addition to football, the University has 17 other sports teams that attract fans to Gainesville throughout the year, although not on quite the same scale.

In the autumn of 1999, prior to three home football games, a sample of 181 Gator fans who travelled from outside the county were surveyed. Two-thirds of these fans attended four or five home football games per season and 61% attended the Orange and Blue Game each spring, which is an intra-squad scrimmage and provides the fans with a preview of the team for the coming season. In addition, 66% reported they occasionally attended other Gator sports events which entailed additional trips to Gainesville. The data were analysed to investigate the suggestion that sport tourists (those who stay overnight) differ in their behaviours in comparison to sport excursionists (day trippers) (Nogawa *et al.*, 1996) – 47% percent of the fans stayed less than 24 hours (sport excursionists) while 48% stayed at least one night (sport tourists). On average, sport excursionists travelled 94 (152 km) miles each way to attend home football games, while sport tourists travelled 192 miles (309 km). During each of these visits to Gainesville, sport excursionists spent an average of $US114.82, whereas sport tourists spent an average of $US293.38 on food, accommodations and tailgate supplies.

Tailgating is a major part of attending a football game in the USA. Starting three to four hours before a game, fans gather in the car parks surrounding the stadium and eat, drink and socialise with friends and family. Some tailgates are quite elaborate with satellite television and professionally catered food; others are simpler affairs consisting of barbecues and sandwiches. Fans reported that arrangements for their tailgate are put in place the week before a game. This often entails coordinating the food, making sure they have all the equipment and supplies they need and contacting their friends and family. The major differences between sport excursionists and sport tourists were that most sport tourists paid for accommodations (mean $US76.84) and spent more on meals (mean $US66.05). Almost 36% of the sport excursionists spent the night in Gainesville in a range of accommodations from hotels/motels, bed and breakfasts, campers and the homes of friends and family.

In the fall of 2000, in-depth interviews were conducted with 20 Gator fans. These were long-time fans, many of whom had been Gator supporters for over 20 years. They were all season ticket holders and attended most, if not all, of the home football games as well as some away games and a range of other Gator sports. The 1999 survey provided valuable information about the tourist-related behaviours of the fans when they attended football games. The interviews offered the opportunity to ask more detailed questions about their trips to Gainesville.

The interviews revealed, in line with other studies (e.g. Faulkner *et al.*, 1998), that, while attending home games, the Gator fans tended to be motivated by one thing, that was to see the game and to tailgate with their friends and family. While they spent money in local bars and restaurants and some spent some time shopping, none mentioned visiting any of the other tourist sights in Gainesville. Whereas, when they travelled to away games they frequently turned their trips into 'mini vacations', often adding a day or so before or after the game so that they could see the sights associated with the area. Indeed, many fans indicated that they take vacation days from work so they can travel to see the Gators.

It is apparent that, while Gator fans are tourists and contribute to the economy in Gainesville largely through expenditures on food and accommodation, because they tend to be motivated by one thing, to see the game, they are not very interested in other activities. Perhaps the lesson for communities wishing to benefit from small-scale event sport tourism generated by college sports is to concentrate on the visiting fans. It might be recommended that local tourism agencies actively market their communities to visiting fans, making them aware of the local attractions before they plan their trips so that they might arrange to spend extra time at a destination. Moreover, communities should leverage the sports event by arranging for other events to be held in conjunction with the game. For example, on Friday nights before a game, events could be held in Gainesville to attract the visiting fans to spend another night in town and to showcase the historic downtown area. As Irwin and Sandler (1998) suggested, this would take much more cooperation between the local tourism agencies and the universities than exists at present. It is also recommended that the University Athletic Association (UAA) web site add a hotlink to the Gainesville Visitor and Convention Bureau's web site, which lists community events and attractions as well as providing information about accommodation, transportation and other tourism-related services and products. The UAA should also investigate the possibility of other tourism attractions, such as organised tours of the stadium, fantasy football camps, where the fans would get a chance to scrimmage with players under the direction of the UF coaching staff, and a Gator Hall of Fame showcasing the history of the team. In so doing, University of Florida football would attract all three types of sport tourists: event, active and nostalgia (Gibson, 1998a), while adding to the suite of visitor experiences that could be achieved by the diverse range of visitors who are referred to generically as sport tourists.

Further reading

Gibson, H. (1998a) Sport tourism: A critical analysis of research. *Sport Management Review* 1, 45–76.

Gibson, H., Willming, C. and Holdnak, A. (2003) Small-scale event sport tourism: Fans as tourists. *Tourism Management* 24 (2), 181–190.

Irwin, R. and Sandler, M. (1998) An analysis of travel behavior and event-induced expenditures among American collegiate championship patron groups. *Journal of Vacation Marketing* 4 (1), 78–90.

Chapter 9

Seasonality, Sport and Tourism

It is not known with any certainty whether tourists travel in peak season because they want to, because they have to, or because they have been conditioned to.

(Butler, 2001: 19)

Introduction

Seasonality is the mid point on the sport tourism development temporal framework (Chapter 1). In the context of this chapter, seasonality is defined as 'a temporal imbalance in the phenomenon of tourism, which may be expressed in terms of dimensions of such elements as numbers of visitors, expenditure of visitors, traffic on highways and other forms of transportation, employment and admissions to attractions' (Butler, 2001: 5). It is one of the most common characteristics of tourism, yet probably one of the least understood. More often than not, it is viewed as a problem that needs to be fixed.

Seasonality is not generally seen as a major issue in sport (Higham & Hinch, 2002a). It is dynamic though, with sport seasons changing and, in most cases, expanding dramatically over the past 30 years. The purpose of this chapter is to examine the way that sport influences tourism seasonality with an emphasis on how sport can be used to alter tourism seasons in targeted destinations. This will be done by examining seasonal patterns and issues in a tourism context and then in a sporting context. Consideration will be given to the factors that influence these patterns, followed by a review of sport-based strategies that have been used in an attempt to alter tourism seasonality. The Case study presented at the end of this chapter considers the impact of professional rugby union on seasonal patterns of tourism in New Zealand (Case study 9.1; see pp. 180–183).

Seasonal Patterns and Issues in Tourism

BarOn's (1975) pioneering study of tourism seasonality consisted of an analysis of tourism data from 16 prominent tourism destination countries covering a period of 17 years. His work confirmed 'most statistical series of arrivals and departures of tourists, bed-nights in accommodation, employment in hotels and other branches of the tourist industry show considerable fluctuations from month to month due to seasonality and other predictable factors, which can be measured' (BarOn, 1975: 2). Similar patterns have been confirmed subsequently in Europe where it was found that

> thirty eight per cent of all the trips made outside their own countries by adult residents of the Common Market end in the three months July to September. If there were an even distribution of trips across the year no more than twenty five per cent would end in these months. (Dutch Ministry of Economic Affairs, 1991: 17)

In Canada, Stanley and Moore (1997) confirm that a peak travel season exists in July and August, with a decline in the autumn, followed by slight upswings in December and February. They also found distinct seasonal patterns associated with tourists travelling for pleasure, to visit friends and relatives, on business, and for conventions. In contrast to those travelling for leisure purposes, convention and business tourists demonstrated a propensity to travel in the spring and distributed their trips relatively evenly during the rest of the year, except for a marked decline in July (the high point in the leisure travel season). Similar seasonal travel patterns throughout Canada have been confirmed, with slight variations on the basis of trip purpose (business or leisure), location (urban or rural, province/region) and market segment (families, group tours, meetings/conventions) (Canadian Tourism Commission & Coopers and Lybrand, 1996; J. Murray, 1996). Weighill (2002) found that event sport travellers in Canada were more likely to travel from January to March, while active sport travellers were busiest during the July to September period.

Tourism seasonality tends to be more exaggerated in peripheral areas than in urban areas (Jeffrey & Barden, 2001). One of the reasons for this is that the central place characteristics of urban areas mean that there is a greater concentration of year-round attractions in cities than in peripheral areas (Murphy, 1985). These attractions include museums, art galleries, historic buildings, shopping and entertainment venues, many of which are indoor facilities that offer protection from the natural elements. Sporting events, facilities and programmes represent a significant part of this suite of attractions (Chapter 5). In contrast, peripheral areas are characterised by a much narrower range of attractions (Butler & Mao, 1996) that are also sensitive to weather and climatic conditions. They are also remote by definition, which may present a variety of access problems at certain times of the year (Baum & Hagen, 1999).

Seasonality as a problem

The prevailing view of tourism seasonality is that it is a problem that should be resolved by destination managers. Advocates of this position point out that tourism seasonality has many negative effects on the destination (Allcock, 1989; Jefferson, 1986; Laws, 1991; Lockwood & Guerrier, 1990; Poon, 1993). McEnnif (1992: 68) captures the essence of the view that seasonality is a problem by highlighting

> underutilisation of capacity at one end of the scale and congestion, environmental damage, saturation of transport infrastructure, increased risk of road accidents, higher prices and a negative impact on the quality of the tourism product at the other. Although some countries suffer from traffic congestion and damage to ... tourism products through overutilisation, most are chiefly concerned with off-peak underutilisation of capacity.

Different regions of the world report many of the same problems associated with seasonality, despite experiencing quite different patterns of seasonal variation. For example, Great Britain's high season occurs in the summer months of July and August, with a marked decline in tourism during the winter months. Jamaica, in contrast, has a busy winter season, but a slow spring season (Robinson, 1979). Despite contrasting visitation patterns, both destinations report that seasonality has negative environmental, economic and social consequences.

With a few notable exceptions (e.g. Ball, 1988, 1989; Butler, 1994; Mourdoukoutas, 1988), little attention has been paid to the possible benefits that may be attributed to seasonality. Hartmann (1986: 31–32), however, argues that tourist low seasons offer 'the only chance for a social and ecological environment to recover fully. A dormant period for the host environment is simply a necessity in order to preserve its identity.' Similarly, Butler (1994: 335) suggests that, 'while areas may experience very heavy use during peak seasons, in the long run they may well be better off than having that use spread more evenly throughout the year'. In fact, the off-season has been described as having a 'fallow effect' in that it offers the destination a period of recuperation (Baum & Hagen, 1999).

The dynamic nature of tourism seasonality

Although tourism seasonality implies that the variations in tourism activity over the course of a year are relatively predictable, they are also dynamic in the longer term (Kennedy & Deegan, 2001). Two significant factors that may influence long-term patterns of tourism seasonality are globalisation and climatic change. In the first instance:

[The] relative level of affluence of residents of industrialized countries, coupled with legislated free time and ease of transportation has meant that many tourists can overcome real seasonal (climatic) problems and pursue the sun or snow at whatever time of the year they prefer, often creating inverse seasonal peaking in destinations with different climates to that of their home region. (Butler, 2001: 14)

However, rather than balancing out seasonal patterns in their home regions, these tourists are exacerbating seasonal peaking in the destination areas. An example is downhill ski enthusiasts from northern hemisphere countries who follow the ski season to the southern hemisphere in June, July and August.

Climate change may have the effect that, as some areas of the world become warmer, their summer seasons will be extended and winter seasons shortened (Harrison *et al.*, 1999). In the latter case, even a slight warming trend may have quite dramatic effects on the viability of ski resorts (Tuppen, 2000). A recent study of the potential impacts of climatic change on winter recreation in Ontario, Canada, highlighted the vulnerability of four major activities (Scott *et al.*, 2002). Even relatively small increases in temperature were shown to result in major decreases in Nordic skiing, snowmobiling, ice fishing and downhill skiing activities. The least affected of these activities was downhill skiing, due to the availability of snow-making equipment that increases the range of temperatures for which snow cover can be guaranteed. Even with this technology, however, a relatively small increase in temperature was shown to reduce the average ski season by between 21% and 34%. Given the dispersed nature of the other activities, current snow-making technology was not seen as a feasible way to mitigate the potentially drastic impacts of global warming in this area.

Seasonal Patterns and Issues in Sport

A significant part of the dynamic evolution of sport over the past 30 years has been the expansion of traditional sporting seasons. While the reasons for this development include an assortment of technological innovations, changing social conditions and general forces of globalisation, one of the most significant factors has been the professionalisation of many sports at the elite level of competition. In conjunction with this trend, partnerships with broadcast media have generated pressures to increase the length of the competitive season (McPherson *et al.*, 1989). In many cases

the restrictions of functioning within a traditional sports season have ... been cast aside. The professional development of numerous sports, where teams compete virtually year round has, in those cases, largely eliminated the notion of sport seasonality. (Higham & Hinch, 2002a: 183)

European football is one of many examples that illustrate this trend. The professional football season in Europe has been transformed, through the development of international league competitions, from a domestic winter sport into an international club sport that takes place across most of the calendar year. Other examples exist where sport seasons have been altered to revolve around the summer rather than winter months. The Norwegian Football League, which takes place in summer to exploit favourable playing and spectator conditions, is one example. Similarly, the development of the Super League realigned rugby league from a winter to a summer sport in the UK and France as part of a strategy to develop a global competition season involving teams based in the northern and southern hemispheres.

Figure 9.1 illustrates the expansion of the rugby union competition season in New Zealand from 1975 to 1999. Using data drawn from New Zealand rugby union statistics published on a season-by-season basis in the *New Zealand Rugby Almanac*, the dramatic expansion of the rugby season is evident. This expansion of the sport season was advanced by the professionalisation of rugby union in the southern hemisphere in 1996 (Higham & Hinch, 2002a), with various implications for tourism (Case study 9.1; see pp. 180–183).

The development of all-season sports facilities represents another change that has facilitated the extension of sport seasons. Examples include summer skiing facilities in Scandinavia (Focus point 9.1), the all-season Millennium Stadium in Cardiff (Wales) and the proliferation of smaller-scale leisure sports facilities that effectively provide climatically controlled environments or ones dominated by new technologies (Bale, 1989). For sports that are conducted in the outdoors, an assortment of equipment and clothing innovations have expanded the range of climatic conditions in which they may be comfortably pursued.

Notwithstanding these changes, it is evident that seasonal patterns still exist in sport. This is most obvious in the case of winter sports, such as those that require snow, or summer sports, such as sailing and scuba diving, which are much more attractive to participants in warm-water conditions. The reality of these sport seasons has a direct impact on the seasonality of sport tourism.

Sport as a factor of tourism seasonality

At a general level, tourism seasonality has been attributed to 'natural' and 'institutional' factors (BarOn, 1975; Hartmann, 1986; Frechtling, 1996). Natural seasonality refers to regular temporal variations in natural

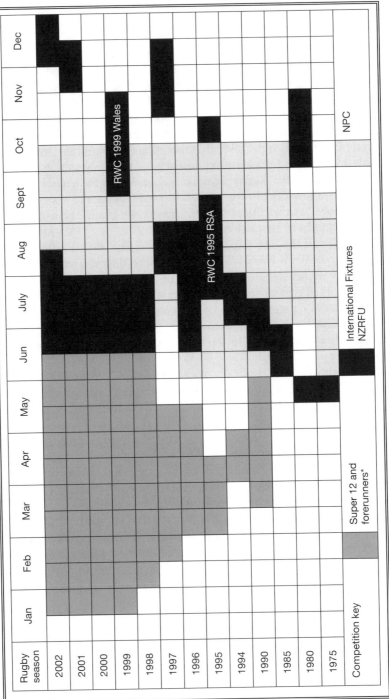

Figure 9.1 The expansion of the New Zealand representative rugby season (1975–2002)

Notes: * Rugby Super 12 (1996–), Super 10/CANZ (1990–1995); includes pre-season warm up games. NPC: National
            Provincial Championship. RWC: Rugby World Cup. Years prior to 1994 are not continuous

Focus point 9.1

The Vuokatti Ski Tunnel (Finland)

The Vuokatti Ski Tunnel is an indoor cross-country ski track, located 600 km north of Helsinki in Vuokatti, Finland. The ski tunnel, which is 1212 m in length and features significant changes in elevation, was developed in close association with the tourist infrastructure of Vuokatti. Its starting point is the Vuokatti Sports Hotel and Sotkamo-Vuokatti tourist information area. The Sports Hotel provides the service centre for skiers, reception and information services, refreshments, ski waxing and sport shops. For reasons of landscape management, the ski tunnel is partly subterranean and covered with a protective and concealing layer, so that from the exterior the ski tunnel has the appearance of a ridge that is typical of the surrounding landscape. The air and snow temperature inside the ski tunnel, as well as the air-conditioning, are monitored and controlled by computer. The inside air is normally maintained between −5° and −9° Celsius but can be dropped to −18° Celsius as needed. Tunnel air is totally exchanged every four hours. The tunnel's snow-making system consists of high-pressure cannons which replenish the trail surface at night when required. The ski trails are groomed mechanically. This ski training facility has positioned Vuokatti as the world's leading training centre for Nordic ski disciplines and an all-season ski destination. Vuokatti is the training centre where Finnish and foreign skiers prepare for the coming winter championships and world cup events. A network of above-ground cross-country ski tracks complements the tunnel track. The whole complex caters for a wide range of skill levels, thereby targeting recreational as well as elite skiers. The Vuokatti Ski Tunnel demonstrates the potential for technologised sports facilities to unlock the seasonal constraints of sports such as skiing, thereby opening significant opportunities for sport tourism development throughout the calendar year.

Source: http://www.skitunnelvuokatti.fi/eindex.html

phenomena, particularly those associated with cyclical climatic changes throughout the year (Allcock, 1989; Butler, 1994). For example, climate is of fundamental importance to sport tourism in higher latitude destinations, although it is often considered as a nuisance factor or constraint to tourist development. Kreutzwiser (1989: 29–30) contends:

Climate and weather conditions . . . influence how satisfying particular recreational outings will be. Air temperature, humidity, precipitation, cloudiness, amount of daylight, visibility, wind, water temperature, and snow and ice cover are among the parameters deemed to be important. . . . In summer, air temperature and humidity can combine to create uncomfortable conditions for vigorous activities, while wind and temperature in winter can create a wind chill hazardous to outdoor recreationists.

These climatic variations are closely correlated with other cyclical events in the natural realm, such as plant growth and animal migration, the latter of which has a direct bearing on sport hunting.

By contrast, institutional factors reflect the social norms and practices of society (Hinch & Hickey, 1996). These include religious, cultural, ethnic, social and economic practices as epitomised by religious, school and industrial holidays. Two of the most prevalent institutional constraints on the scheduling of sport travel are school and work commitments (Butler, 1994; McEnnif, 1992). Tradition also plays a large part in the scheduling of these vacations. Changing religious views, social norms, transportation options and technological advances may moderate these forces.

Butler (1994, 2001) has identified three additional causes of seasonality. The first of these is social pressure or fashion, which is usually set by celebrities and other privileged classes within society. A sport example of this factor would be media attention given to celebrities at yachting regattas and horse racing meets. Inertia or tradition is a second seasonality factor. People tend to be creatures of habit and, if they have traditionally taken their holiday during a given time of the year, they will likely continue to do so. For example, even upon retirement, many individuals will tend to take an 'annual vacation' during the same period that they were previously constrained to due to their jobs. Finally, the scheduling of sporting seasons is a factor in its own right. Butler (2001) makes the case that sport seasons have a direct impact on tourism seasons. Winter sports such as skiing, snowboarding and snowmobiling are perhaps the most obvious examples, but summer-based activities such as surfing and golf also influence travel patterns as tourists search for the best seasonal conditions for the pursuit of their sporting passions. Climatic conditions appear to be influential in all of these examples, yet even sports that are played within climatically controlled settings, such as competitive basketball, normally have distinct seasons. If an inclusive definition of the 'institutional' category of determinants was adopted, then the sporting season would seem to be closely associated with this category. Indeed sport sociologists have long argued that sport is a social institution (McPherson *et al.*, 1989).

Butler (2001: 8) has suggested that

> [it] is the interaction between the forces determining the natural and institutionalized elements of the seasonality of tourism in both the generating and receiving areas as modified by actions of the public and private sector which creates the pattern of seasonality in tourism that occurs at a specific destination.

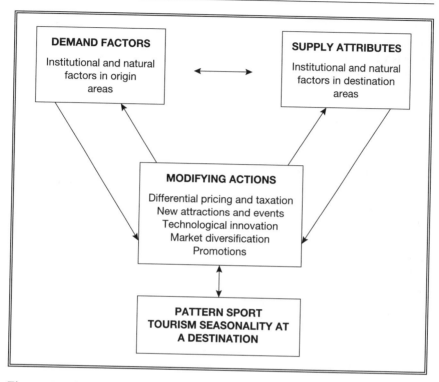

Figure 9.2 Sport influences on patterns of tourist seasonality
Source: based on Butler (2001)

While the interactions between the factors that influence seasonal patterns of sport tourism visitation are complex, their basic relationship is relatively straightforward (Figure 9.2). Institutional and natural factors influence tourism demand as well as tourism supply. Sport tourism managers may intervene in this process by modifying supply attributes through strategies such as the development of climatically controlled sport facilities. They may also modify institutional and natural factors on the demand side through such strategies as promotional information that dispels misconceptions that potential tourists might have about sport participation during the off-season. A strategic approach to the manipulation of these factors can have a significant impact on when sport tourists visit particular destinations.

Differential influence across the hierarchy of sport attractions

The degree to which a sporting activity influences tourism seasonality is in part determined by the placement of that sport within the traveller's hierarchy of attractions (Chapter 2). Trip behaviour varies on the basis of the centrality of sport as the tourist attraction or how prominently the sport features as a travel motivation. Where sport is the principal focus of the trip (i.e., the primary attraction), travellers demonstrate a greater propensity to travel in the tourism 'off-season' (WTO & IOC, 2001). More casual sport tourists (i.e. those who see sport as a secondary or tertiary attraction) show higher levels of seasonal variation in their travels. Where sport is the primary motivation, sport tourists are willing to negotiate through institutional and natural constraints that might otherwise be insurmountable for more casual sport tourists (Hinch *et al.* 2001).

For example, outbound tourists from Germany, the Netherlands and France who have a strong sport focus are more likely to travel from January to April than are outbound tourists with a more casual approach to sport. The latter group is much more likely to travel from May to August (Table 9.1)

In the case of casual sport tourists (Table 9.1), a single peaked pattern of seasonality emerges that reinforces typical summer peaks for general tourism visitation to destination countries. A similar pattern was found for sport tourists in Canada (Weighill, 2002).

The degree to which a sporting activity is dependent on natural resources is also an important factor in terms of seasonal patterns of activity. Sports such as skiing and sailing are directly tied to specific natural attributes such as snow and wind conditions respectively. Other sports, even though they occur outdoors, may be enhanced by natural attributes, but these attributes are not necessarily central to the experi-

Table 9.1 Seasonal travel patterns of outbound sport tourists with both strong and casual sport focus from Germany, the Netherlands and France (1999)

Country	Jan.–April	May–Aug.	Sept.–Dec.	Total (%)	Trips (1,000s)
Strong sport focus					
Germany	44	32	24	100	11,000
Netherlands	39	46	15	100	7000
France	40	51	9	100	500
Casual sport focus					
Germany	11	57	32	100	21,000
Netherlands	10	70	20	100	3000
France	20	57	23	100	3000

Source: abstracted from WTO and IOC (2001)

ence. In the latter case, natural factors like weather may serve as the general context, rather than having a direct bearing on the essence of the sporting performance. In cases such as mountain biking and beach volleyball, natural conditions which deviate from what is perceived as the ideal may be a significant deterrent to sport tourism at certain times of the year. Alternatively, advantageous or extreme weather conditions (e.g. leading to snow melt and high river flow volume) may be promoted as a positive characteristic for many types of extreme sports (e.g. white water rafting, kayaking).

Strategic Responses

Tourism managers have tried to address issues of seasonality in numerous ways. These responses have included attempts to lengthen the main season and/or establish additional seasons by diversifying markets, using different pricing and tax incentives throughout the year, encouraging the staggering of holidays, encouraging domestic tourism in off-seasons and providing off-season attractions such as festivals and conferences (Butler, 2001; Baum & Hagen, 1999). Strategies that have the most relevance in a sport tourism context are changes to the product mix along with market diversification.

Changes to the sport product mix

Individual sports are characterised by their own patterns of seasonality. By capitalising on these unique characteristics, it is possible to manipulate seasonal patterns of tourism visitation in a destination. Two sub-types of sport-based product mix strategies are particularly prominent. The first is the introduction of sporting events during the off-peak tourism periods and the second is the introduction of new or improved sport facilities and programmes.

The introduction of new events and festivals is one of the most common strategies for altering seasonal tourist visitation (Hinch & Jackson, 2000). Many special events do not require large capital expenditures, are relatively transportable and can be targeted to specific, or combinations of, market segments. Sporting events may offer the additional advantage of utilising existing facilities and infrastructure at off-peak times in the destination. A good example of product diversification through the introduction of sporting events is provided by the Isle of Man (Baum & Hagen, 1999). The Isle of Man has traditionally been a popular summer tourist destination in the UK, but a sharp decline in the 'sun seeker' markets in the early 1980s prompted the development of a product diversification strategy designed to increase sport tourism in the shoulder seasons. Two new sporting events were introduced. The first was the development of the Manx TT road race, scheduled during the shoulder tourism period of late May and early June. Recent event evaluations show that it attracts approximately 37,000 visitors who spend in excess of £15 million at the destination. This major event is supported by a series of other motor sport events throughout the year that each attract between 3000 to 6000 visitors.

The second type of sporting event that was introduced on the Isle of Man to increase visitation during the tourism low season was the Student Festival of Sport. This festival was

> started in 1985 as part of the Isle of Man's 'Year of Sport'. In its inaugural year, a total of 1000 participants were welcomed; by 1997, this number had increased to 2700, taking part in a wide range of sporting activities (archery, badminton, basketball, cricket, cycling, fencing, field hockey, netball, rugby, soccer, shooting, ten pin bowling, triathlon, swimming and water polo). (Baum & Hagen, 1999: 306)

The Student Festival of Sport was reported to have cost the local government £29,100 to run in 1997 with a return of 7884 bed nights and £500,000 in direct visitor spending. A distinguishing feature of both of these sports events was the close collaboration of the sport and tourism sectors. For example, a budget-priced inclusive package for sea travel to the island and one week of accommodation proved to be very successful for the Student Festival of Sport.

Product diversification designed to modify seasonal visitation can also take the form of physical development. In a sport context, a classic example of this type of strategy is the development of all-weather resorts, such as Centerparcs in Europe, which provide year-round sport-based facilities for family groups. Golf developments have also been used effectively to modify seasonal visitation. For example, Baum and Hagen (1999: 309) report that

> [the] development of Prince Edward Island, Canada, as a recognized golf resort with in excess of a six month season (compared with the traditional two to three month beach season), is the result of a planned strategy, public and private sector investment and a focus on quality outcomes in all aspects of the development cycle.

This development was accompanied by targeted promotions to senior and retired markets interested and able to visit during the shoulder seasons.

Perhaps the best example of this type of strategy can be found at ski resorts (Tuppen, 2000). In the face of falling visitation in the 1980s, ski resorts in North America and Europe made a concerted effort to improve and diversify their products. One of the key improvements was a major expansion in snow-making equipment, which allowed heavily used runs between the upper slopes and the base of the resort to open sooner and close later in the year, thereby facilitating an extended season. Just as importantly, it built consumer confidence within active sport tourism markets that there would be snow at the resorts during what had previously been considered a very marginal period. Many resorts also expanded the range of winter-based activities that visitors can partake in through the provision of indoor sports and fitness centres, plus facilities for other types of winter sports, such as snowboarding, cross-country skiing and snowshoeing. Some, such as the resort of Whistler, British Columbia, Canada, developed summer attractions like golf courses to provide all-season attractions.

Notwithstanding these successes, Baum and Hagen (1999) advise caution in the use of product diversification through facility development as a strategy for addressing seasonality. Careful financial analysis is required, especially in the case of peripheral destinations, to verify that an adequate return on investment will be achieved. The lower initial costs of product diversification through the introduction of new events goes a long way to explaining the popularity of this approach over more expensive facility redevelopment strategies.

Market diversification

For product diversification strategies to work there needs to be a corresponding demand in the market place. It is, therefore, necessary to verify market needs prior to investing in product development. In a tourist seasonality context, there are a number of market segments that are traditionally recognised as having fewer constraints relating to the timing of travel. These groups include senior citizens, conference delegates, incentive travellers, empty nesters, affinity groups and special interest tourists (Baum & Hagen, 1999). The success of Prince Edward Island's product expansion into golf was due, in large part, to their parallel strategy of marketing to seniors and empty nesters who have greater flexibility to travel outside the peak summer months. While there are many market segments that have relevance in terms of sport tourism seasonality, one of the most promising is the special interest segment (Hall & Weiler, 1992). Individuals who are passionate about a given sport, including members of sporting subcultures (Chapters 3 and 6), will be much more motivated to overcome constraints to travel during the off-season than general tourists. They represent niche markets (Chapter 3) that can be targeted during the off-season and who are willing to travel long distances to pursue their sporting passions. The development of the World Wide Web as an information source for tourism and sport enables communication with what is potentially a widely dispersed market.

Another form of market diversification addresses the institutional constraints that sport markets face at different times of the year. A good example of this type of approach to the resolution of a seasonal visitation problem is illustrated by the use of geographic market segmentation by Eurocamp (Klemm & Rawel, 2001). This company specialises in self-drive holidays in Europe that feature active sporting amenities at the campgrounds en route. Initially, the company targeted British families, but, due to the institutional constraint of school holidays, bookings were concentrated in August. A conscious strategy to promote their product to other European countries that had different school holiday periods was successfully pursued over a 15-year period. The outcome of the market diversification strategy was a consistently high level of bookings from May to September, rather than in the single month of August.

Leisure constraints theory

Notwithstanding the successes reported above, seasonal variations in tourism remain a prominent feature of the industry. The 'stubbornness' of these patterns has led to the suggestion that more attention should to be paid to the needs and behaviours of the consumer (Baum & Hagen, 1999). Leisure constraints theory represents one framework that provides additional insight into this area (Hinch & Jackson, 2000; Hinch *et al.*, 2001). This theory considers what prevents non-participants from taking part in the leisure pursuits. In the context of sport tourism seasonality, leisure constraints theory raises the question, 'What is it that inhibits people from travelling for sport at certain times of the year?' The answers to this question would provide a better understanding of sport tourist seasonal behaviour and would identify constraints that can be targeted by managers.

Hudson and Gilbert (1998) have used a leisure constraints framework to examine non-participation in downhill skiing in Britain. Their framework is positioned in a tourism context and operationalises the hierarchical model of leisure constraints (Crawford *et al.*, 1991) to identify management options designed to increase participation in downhill skiing. For example, one of the constraints that they found was that non-skiers were afraid that they would be cold and uncomfortable on the slopes. A logical management response to this is to raise consumer awareness of technological advances in the manufacture of winter clothing that will allow enhanced ski comfort.

Figure 9.3 has been modified from the hierarchical model of leisure constraints (E. L. Jackson *et al.*, 1993) to emphasise its relevance in the study of sport tourism seasonality.

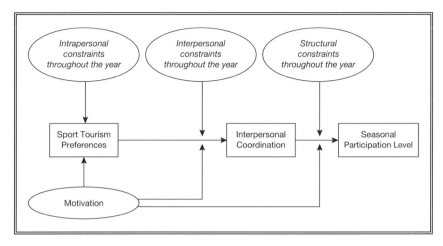

Figure 9.3 Hierarchical model of seasonal sport tourism constraints

Source: based on Jackson *et al.* (1993)

One of the key characteristics of this model is the order in which seasonal constraints are encountered and negotiated. In the context of sport tourism seasonality, sporting preferences are the starting point. A major consideration at this stage is the centrality of seasonal factors in terms of the motivations for travel. In cases where natural seasonal factors like climatic conditions are the primary attraction or motivation for the sport tourists (e.g. sunny warm conditions for casual sport tourists, favourable snow conditions for serious skiers), their absence in a destination during a given time of the year will be a major and perhaps insurmountable constraint. E. L. Jackson *et al.* (1993) have labelled these as intrapersonal constraints. Where these constraints do not exist, sport tourists proceed to the interpersonal constraint level. Team sports, or those that are enhanced by fellow participants, require the potential sport tourist to coordinate his or her travel plans with others. Potential sport tourists who seek travel and sport companions but cannot find them, will fail to participate even though they have the initial motivation. Finally, structural constraints consist of things such as high travel costs, lack of accommodation and school or work commitments. Ways around this last level of constraints may be negotiated by the potential sport tourist, although they too may prove to be insurmountable. Innovative packaging by the host destination can facilitate this negotiation process throughout the year. By understanding this leisure constraint framework, sport tourism destinations can identify appropriate seasonal target markets and help them to negotiate the particular constraints that they face at various times of the year.

Management Implications and Opportunities

It is clear from the foregoing discussion that sport tourism is not only a factor in tourism seasonality, but that it can potentially be harnessed as a means to modify tourist visitation patterns over the course of a year. Lengthening competition seasons for spectator sports and scheduling sport events during tourism shoulder seasons are direct ways of increasing visitation to a destination during these periods. Active sport tourism also represents an opportunity to consciously influence tourism seasonality in a destination. This is especially true for sport tourists who are members of sport subculture groups. Destinations should consider the resources that they have in their region during the tourism shoulder seasons that may be attractive to specialised sport subcultures. Those destinations that offer a unique blend of attributes can adopt a niche marketing strategy that effectively attracts a geographically dispersed but passionate group of visitors during non-peak times of the year. Finally, while nostalgia sport tourists have not been discussed in depth in the chapter, the tourism literature on seasonality highlights the potential for museums and similar types of facilities to attract visitors outside the summer months (Stevens, 2001).

Nostalgia sport tourism offers this same opportunity in terms of sport museums, stadium tours and halls of fame. Indeed, stadium tours are rarely conducted on days when sports or events take place and, as such, largely take place outside competition seasons. Programmed nostalgic experiences, such as fantasy camps and reunions, also offer considerable flexibility in scheduling throughout the year, thereby presenting significant potential strategies for managing the seasonal distribution of sport tourism.

While tourism managers have long pursued the economic benefits of modifying seasonality, sport managers are increasingly adopting a similar approach. There are financial benefits for sports that can attract sport tourists at non-traditional times of the year. While some of these benefits may be collected directly at the gate of the sporting venue, others can be leveraged through the tourism industry. For example, sport tourists travelling during the off-season are likely to enjoy lower rates for accommodation due to higher vacancy rates. These benefits can be maximised if collective action on the part of a particular sport can demonstrate that there are substantial numbers of sport-related visitors arriving during this period. Group rates and adjoining travel packages can then be negotiated.

The positive side of tourism seasonality mentioned at the beginning of this chapter should not be lost in the search to solve the 'problem' of seasonality. Sport tourism destinations can benefit from a 'fallow period' that allows for the regeneration of natural and human resources.

Notwithstanding the tendency for many sport seasons to expand schedules to the point where they are almost year-round pursuits, there may be a downside to this. Spectators and athletes may 'burn out' if they do not have a chance to re-energise during an off-season. Sports offer their most powerful function as tourist attractions when the enthusiasm of participants is at its peak – yet this peak cannot be prolonged indefinitely. In the interest of the sustainability of the sport, sport tourism and the destinations where this activity takes place, it may be strategically prudent to maintain some form of seasonal variation over the course of a year.

Conclusion

This chapter has demonstrated that both tourism and sport are characterised by seasonal variations during the course of a year. Whereas these variations are generally seen as undesirable in a tourism context, there has been relatively little concern about seasonal variation in a sporting context. Somewhat paradoxically, seasonal patterns of tourism tend to be stable despite ongoing attempts to modify them, while sporting seasons have undergone extensive change – especially in terms of their extension throughout the year. A variety of factors influence seasonality in both of these realms, but this chapter highlights the considerable interaction that exists between the seasonal patterns of sport and the seasonal patterns of tourism.

Sport has been identified as one of numerous factors affecting the seasonality of tourism, but one of increasing significance. As such, the scheduling of sporting events, the redevelopment of sporting facilities and the targeting of selected sport markets are strategies that can be used to modify patterns of tourist visitation at destinations throughout the year. Leisure constraints theory provides a powerful tool for developing systematic strategies to influence sport tourism seasonality. Notwithstanding these points of discussion, it should be noted that providing rest or 'fallow periods' in sport and tourism patterns may play a significant part in the sustainability of many forms of sport tourism development.

Further Reading

Baum and Lundtorp's (2001) collection of papers on seasonality and tourism represents a rich source of information on this topic. Highlights include Butler's chapter, which is based on an earlier paper of his published in 1994. This chapter emphasises the relevance of seasonality in a tourism context and identifies sport as one of the key determinants of seasonal variations in the tourism phenomenon. Baum and Hagen's (2001) chapter in this volume is also recommended as it highlights some of the key strategies used to modify seasonality in peripheral tourism areas. Further insight into applicable strategies is found in Klemm and Rawel's (2001) chapter, which examines marketing approaches designed to extend the active season for a tourism product with a significant sporting dimension. Beyond the Baum and Lundtorp volume, Higham and Hinch's (2002a) article on sport, tourism and seasons provides a focused examination of seasonality and sport tourism. Finally, in partial response to Butler's (1994) criticism that little is actually known about the causes of seasonality, Hinch and Jackson (2000) present leisure constraints theory as a way of understanding the seasonal behaviour of tourists, which demonstrates considerable relevance to the study of seasonality in sport tourism.

Case study 9.1

The Otago Highlanders and Seasonal Patterns of Travel

James Higham, University of Otago, New Zealand, and Thomas Hinch, University of Alberta, Canada

The Otago Highlanders, who represent the southern half of the South Island of New Zealand, compete in Rugby Super 12, a professional competition involving regional teams from New Zealand, Australia and South Africa. This Dunedin-based franchise was created in 1995 as part of the professionalisation of rugby union in the southern hemisphere. Given the commercial orientation of this competition, the entertainment value of the sport has been emphasised. For example, the rules governing the competition were modified to encourage a faster style of rugby that rewarded attacking play (e.g. bonus point systems apply to tries scored and margins of victory). As a result of these initiatives, a new tourist attraction was created which changed the seasonal pattern of visitation to Dunedin.

One of the more significant changes heralded by Rugby Super 12 was the scheduling of the competition. Historically, rugby union was a winter sport, but this changed with the introduction of a professional league. The rugby season in New Zealand, formerly limited in its amateur days to 12 winter weeks (June–August), was extended across 10 months of the calendar year (February–November). The season now begins with Rugby Super 12, followed by international fixtures, a national provincial championship and, in most years, end-of-season international tours.

Rugby Super 12 consists of a 14-week competition that involves regular season play followed by semi-finals and a grand final. It begins in late February and ends in early June. In the context of tourism seasonality, the scheduling of this competition is an institutional factor that influences the timing of sport tourist visits. Creating the Super 12 schedule involved an arbitrary set of decisions made by owners, managers and sponsors based on their assessment of the availability of players and the inclination of spectators and television viewers to follow the competition.

The seasonal tourism development potential of Rugby Super 12 centres on its capacity to generate intra- and inter-regional visitor activity throughout its 14-week season. More specifically, the addition of the Otago Highlanders franchise in Dunedin has led to:

Additional Visitors from Within the Franchise Region During the Autumn Shoulder Period

The Super 12 competition attracts many visitors from across the franchise region to attend home matches. These travellers are generally not rescheduling an otherwise planned trip, but rather they are travelling more frequently to Dunedin so that they can attend Rugby Super 12 games.

Additional Domestic Visitors From Beyond the Franchise Region During the Autumn Shoulder Period

Rugby Super 12 generates inter-regional domestic tourism. When neighbouring franchises meet, this potential is greatest. In March 1999, for example, the Crusaders from Christchurch visited Dunedin to play the Highlanders. The domestic travel component of this fixture is confirmed by the *Otago Daily Times* (1999), which reports that 'almost 10,000 Canterbury Crusaders fans are expected to be among a crowd of 30,000 for the Super 12 rugby match on Friday night (9 April 1999)'. In actual fact, this game produced a record crowd of 36,120 for a regular season non-international fixture. The *Star Sunday Times* (11 April 1999) reported that 'on Friday afternoon the traffic was slowed to 10 km/h on the Kilmog, the range to the north of Dunedin, as an estimated 8,000 Canterbury fans drove south'.

Changed Travel Patterns and Behaviours of International Visitors

While there does not appear to be a significant direct increase in international travel flows during the regular season, semi-final and final matches are likely to result in such visitation when the visiting team is from South Africa or Australia. More commonly, international visitors who are already in this region (e.g. Queenstown resort area) may be influenced to spend an extra day in Dunedin to attend one of the Highlander matches.

New Travelling Groups

Women, families and young people are more likely to travel to watch Rugby Super 12 than the amateur rugby competitions that preceded it. The combination of the changed nature of the competition and its scheduling during warmer months (i.e., late summer and autumn) has contributed to a new spectator fan base willing to travel to support their team. Those who travel significant distances tend to stay the night in Dunedin, especially after an evening fixture.

Potential to Link Sport Attendance With the Wider Local Tourism Product

The Super 12 season coincides with periods of late season activity in the local tourism attractions sector. For example, the nature-based tourism product in Dunedin has traditionally been closed to visitors during the winter sports season due to low demand, but this appears to be changing as general visitation increases during the autumn season. The presence of additional visitors within the area has increased the critical mass of potential visitors to these other attractions.

Shoulder Season Marketing Tool

The Highlanders generate increased media exposure for Dunedin during a normally slow time of the year. Television broadcasts and media reports related to the Highlanders raise the profile of Dunedin and create an exciting urban image for the city during the autumn months.

Multi-purpose Stadium Development

The development of multi-use stadium facilities at the Highlander's franchise headquarters (Carisbrook, Dunedin) provides the opportunity to host other sporting and non-sporting events at different times of the year.

This case demonstrates the impact that the development and scheduling of sport can have on seasonal variations in tourist visitation. Clearly, the introduction of the Highlanders franchise in Dunedin served the mutual interests of the sport and tourism sectors. While significant benefits were realised by both of these sectors, little direct consultation aimed at leveraging sport and tourism opportunities in a coordinated manner took place between them. If the full benefit of sport is to be captured as part of a strategy to modify seasonal patterns in visitation then sport and tourism managers must work closely with each other.

Further reading

Higham, J. E. S. and Hinch, T. D. (2002a) Sport, tourism and seasons: The challenges and potential of overcoming seasonality in the sport and tourism sectors. *Tourism Management* 23, 175–185.

Higham, J. E. S. and Hinch, T. D. (2002b). Sport and tourism development: Avenues of tourism development associated with a regional sport franchise at an urban tourism destination. In S. Gammon and J. Kurtzman (eds) *Sport Tourism: Principles and Practice* (pp. 19–34). Eastbourne: Leisure Studies Association.

Higham, J. E. S. and Hinch, T. D. (2003) Sport, space and time: Effects of the Otago Highlanders franchise on tourism. *Journal of Sports Management* 17 (3), 235–257.

Chapter 10
Evolutionary Trends in Sport Tourism

In some respects, it was tourists [to France] who thus passed on mountaineering to sports enthusiasts in the 18th and 19th centuries, before the latter, the mountaineers, then offered tourist skiing in return during the 20th century.

(Bourdeau *et al.*, 2002: 23)

Introduction

The relationship between sport and tourism is as dynamic in the long term as it is in the short and medium terms. Sport influences destination life cycles and tourism influences sport life cycles. The first part of the chapter examines these types of interactions. Nostalgia sport tourism, which is motivated by a desire to reconnect to the sporting past, represents a special case in which sport heritage serves as a tourist attraction. Examples include sport halls of fame, sites of past sporting events and imagined pasts played out through fantasy sport camps and programmes. This emerging area of sport tourism is the focus of the second part of this chapter. Neither the interaction between life cycles nor nostalgia sport tourism occurs independently of other forces operating in the broader environment. A dynamic web of local, national and global trends influences these phenomena. The third section of the chapter presents a discussion of these trends. Finally, Butler's Case study of the interaction between tourism and the sport of golf at St Andrews, Scotland illustrates how the development of a sport has had a direct bearing on the way that its birthplace has evolved as a tourist destination (Case study 10.1; see pp. 200–203).

Cyclical Relationships in Sport and Tourism

Destination and product life cycles are dominant features of tourism (Christaller, 1963/1964; Plog, 1972; Doxey, 1975; Stansfield, 1978). Butler's (1980) tourist area life cycle model epitomises this idea with its six stages of exploration, involvement, development, consolidation, stagnation and either rejuvenation or decline. In revisiting Butler's model, Johnston (2001a) suggested that the early part of this cycle could be classified as the pre-tourism era in that some other institutional framework besides tourism dominates the destination. Similarly, the latter stages of stagnation and decline can be described as a post-tourism era as tourism is succeeded as a dominant or important sector of the destination economy. The general pattern of these cycles is one of increasing visitation until the destination's resources are adversely affected, at which point visitor numbers begin to decline (Chapter 4). A variety of management implications emerge from these cycles, with the most obvious being that management intervention is needed to sustain tourism resources so that the destination's life span can be prolonged.

Sport attractions play a significant role in the life cycles of many destinations. For example, in his detailed analysis of the destination life cycle of Kona, Hawai'i, Johnston (2001b) noted that the original 'Ironman' race was transferred from Honolulu to Kona in the early 1980s. This shift corresponded to the last period of Kona's development phase and served as an image maker for the destination. It marked a critical point in the development of Kona by replacing the 'way of life' image with a sports theme. Other destinations have used sport as a tourism development strategy in a similar fashion (Focus point 10.1).

The evolutionary dynamics of sport

Sport is increasingly being used as the focus of strategies to rejuvenate tourism destinations. Successful implementation of this strategy requires that tourism managers are informed about sport life cycles:

> Like tourism products, individual sports, sports disciplines and sport events have their own life cycles. They too go 'out of fashion'. And they increasingly find themselves having to compete against other leisure activities and events. . . . In sport too there is a constant need for the adaptation of individual sports and events to the changing requirements of sportsmen and sportswomen, as well as spectators. (Keller, 2001: 4, 5)

Just as a primary measure of the tourism destination life cycle is the number of visitors to a destination, a primary indicator of sport life cycles is the number of participants and spectators involved. Other measures of the status of a sport within its life cycle include the sophistication of rule structures that characterise a sport, the level of skill development and physical performance and, increasingly, the extent of commodification and professionalisation.

The dynamics of sport have been clearly illustrated in recent years by the slower growth of many highly structured team sports and the ascent

Focus point 10.1

Marine Sport and the Evolution of 'Cold Water' Resorts

During the late nineteenth and twentieth centuries, seaside towns and villages in England developed as coastal resorts serving a domestic visitor market. The lifespan of many English coastal resorts ended in the 1960s with the advent of chartered air travel and the preference of many British tourists to undertake cheap mass travel to the 'warm water' coastal resorts of the Mediterranean. In latter years, the rejuvenation of 'cold water' resorts of northern and western Europe has been attempted through, in some cases, the development of coastal and marine sports. Newquay, which is situated on the north coast of Cornwall, England, is a case in point. The rise and fall of Newquay as a tourist destination has been followed in the last decade by its rejuvenation as England's premier surfing destination. This one-time fishing village and coastal tourist resort has transformed itself into a sport tourism destination. Surfing is a sport that takes place all year round in Newquay. Newquay's reputation as a surf destination has been enhanced through the development of a series of sport events. Since 1981, Newquay has hosted the Rip Curl Newquay Boardmasters, which has evolved from a regional surf contest into a world-class lifestyle festival, where sport, music and youth culture are blended together in a nine-day beach extravaganza. This event has developed into the largest lifestyle sports festival in Britain. The Newquay Boardmasters is the only British event that forms part of the Association of Surfing Professionals (ASP) World Tour and attracts over 80,000 party people, and over 200 international surfers, including some of the icons of the sport. The British Bodyboard Club also holds their annual 'Airshow' at Newquay's Tolcarne Beach over a weekend in mid July, with back-up dates in mid and late August to ensure that the contest takes place in reasonably sized surf. Newquay provides a vivid illustration of the potential that sport tourism development offers in the evolution and, in this particular case, the rejuvenation of a tourist destination.

Source: http://www.surfnewquay.co.uk

of individualised and extreme sports (de Villiers, 2001; D. Murray & Dixon, 2000; Thomson, 2000). Keller (2001: 13, 14) states:

> The membership for organized types of sport is on the decline, as are the proving grounds from which top-level sports traditionally draw new blood. The new generation is a sliding, gliding and rolling generation. Their sports are freestyle events like 'inline skating', 'street basketball' and 'snowboarding', which in many cases are associated

with a youthful subculture. Performance and rankings no longer play any role. What counts are the aesthetic, 'feel-good', atmospheric effects.

Increasingly, extreme sports have emerged for people who wish to get away from someone else's rules and regulations and set up their own renegade groups. Yet, even these sports are part of an evolutionary process. As sports institutions, media, equipment and clothing manufactures and the tourism industry interact, extreme sports tend to shift from subculture to mainstream. Hoffer (1995) suggests that the cycle is perpetuated in that, as the process of commodification intensifies, structures and rules begin to form to ensure the activity is managed in a way that facilitates commodification until some group once again breaks away to begin something new.

Snowboarding provides a good illustration of this process. It emerged as a subculture activity in resistance to the dominant culture of alpine skiing. Initially, it was characterised by a non-traditional view of sport. Yet the initial radical nature of snowboarding has been steadily moderated through the pressures of commodification. The development of snowboarding as a commercial television product by ESPN illustrates this point (Focus point 10.2). Another benchmark in the evolution of snowboarding from a subculture to a mainstream sport was the inclusion of snowboarding in the 1998 Winter Olympic Games.

The evolutionary dynamics of tourism

Tourism cycles also influence the development of sport. For example, over the past two decades, golf has been introduced to many hot climate destinations as a tourism development strategy (Priestley, 1995; Bartoluci & Čavlek, 2000). In the process of this development, opportunities to participate in the sport of golf have been extended to, and taken up by, local residents (Case study 10.1; see pp. 200–203). A reciprocal relationship also exists in that tourism provides

> an opportunity for leisure activities to be popularized. With increased popularity they have developed into formally organized sporting activities. Some even progressed from leisure activities to Olympic disciplines. Beach volleyball and snowboarding are two good examples of this. (de Villiers, 2001: 13)

Tourism not only introduces sport to new areas, it also fosters innovation within sport. Figure 10.1 illustrates that change in sport occurs in recreational and competitive settings, the former being more conducive to major innovation than the latter. Both settings are influenced by external trends associated with the economy, politics, society, technology

Focus point 10.2

Snowboarding: From Non-competitive Sport to High Entertainment Drama

The consumption of sport through media involves processes of commodification of sport to enhance its entertainment value, to the point that sports may become a branch of show business. The popularity of snowboarding as a participation sport is exceeded by the popularity of snowboarding as consumed through media. Capturing spectator markets, those who do not actively engage in a sport, increases the superficiality of consumption due to spectator demand for sensationalism over subtlety (Heino, 2000). This point is recognised by television producers:

> In 1997, ESPN hosted its first Winter X (eXtreme) Games. They invented a new snowboarding competition for these games titled 'Boarder X'. Instead of just one snowboarder racing down the mountain or being judged on his or her tricks in the halfpipe, ESPN put six snow boarders on a course at once. The snowboarders raced up 20-foot side embankments, over bumps; and around sharp curves, and launched off a 40-foot jump at the end. The simultaneous action of six snowboarders getting air, doing tricks, and pushing off each other as they race down the course was quite sensational. It was spontaneous and unpredictable rather than rigid and controlled. The moment everyone recalls from that competition was the act of one snowboarder passing another one in the air while doing a back flip off the forty foot jump. The fairly noncompetitive sport of snowboarding, with just the rider, his board, and the mountain, was transformed into high-drama entertainment. (Heino, 2000: 186)

and the natural environment. Sport innovations often originate from external environments. The reason that recreational sport is more conducive to innovation is that experimentation is encouraged in most leisure and tourism settings. Keller (2001) also argues that the change in location and uninterrupted free time that tourists enjoy while on holiday provide a setting that is fertile for innovation in sport pursuits.

In competitive settings, the focus is on performance in terms of recognised physical skills and rules. These are structured in ways that preclude radical change. Major innovations in recreational sport settings are shaped by leisure patterns that may be unique to specific geographic regions. In contrast to the lack of constraints in a recreational context, a variety of sporting institutions act as gatekeepers to change in competitive sport environments. The spatial and institutional dissemination of

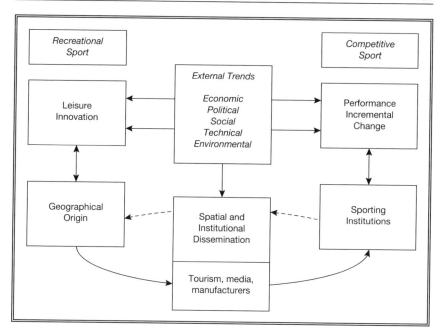

Figure 10.1 Innovation in sport

Source: adapted from Keller (2001)

major innovations and incremental change in sports occurs through the broadcast of entertainment and news programmes by a range of media and by the marketing efforts of sporting goods manufacturers. Tourists also act as significant agents of innovation and dissemination. They introduce new sporting interests to tourist destinations and may, in turn, be exposed to new sports while they are there.

Nostalgia Sport Tourism

Nostalgia sport tourism is a unique manifestation of the positioning of sporting heritage as a tourist attraction. It provides tangible evidence of the way that sport life cycles can have a direct impact on tourism in the form of sports halls of fame and museums, high-profile sporting venues and a range of thematic programmes, all of which take on the mantle of tourist attractions in their own right (Delpy, 1998). In general terms, nostalgia 'involves a bittersweet longing for an idealised past which no longer exists' (Goulding, 1999: 2). As such, sport has always been closely associated with nostalgia, perhaps because it connects people to their youth when they were typically more active (Gammon, 2002). Snyder

(1991: 229) builds on this idea by suggesting that sport nostalgia can trigger reflections on our own mortality, which often result in an idealisation of the past:

> On the surface it appears that halls and museums attract people because of their fascination with sport, including the idolized figures and memorabilia from the past. But this is only part of the explanation; the attraction may also be based on the contrasts in incongruity between past and present. This juxtaposition of the past with the present creates the context for feelings of nostalgia.

Past sporting experiences may become reference points from which sport-oriented people derive meaning for their lives. This meaning results from both collective and individualised views of the past. In the case of the former, popular media and various sporting institutions celebrate an assortment of sporting victories, events and personalities in a way that impresses them upon the popular consciousness. In the latter case, sport nostalgia is linked to the benchmarks of an individual's sport involvement and identity at different points in their life. This combination of collective and individualised nostalgia creates a powerful force that is increasingly being mined by the sport and tourism industries in order to create economic development opportunities.

As could be expected, people of middle age or older are often seen as the primary cohorts for nostalgia-based tourism. Snyder (1991: 238) suggested that

> for many people sport triggers feelings of longing for the past when they had pleasant experiences associated with sport. This reflection is most evident for the middle-aged and elderly, who have had more sport experiences, but perhaps more important, this is a period of their lives when concern about their own mortality is salient in their self-reflections. Consequently, for those involved in sport, nostalgia may provide a source of consolation and a means of adjustment to the uncertainties of their lives.

More recently, Gammon (2002) has argued that nostalgia is also of interest to youth, as reflected in the popularity of retro television and radio shows.

Sport museums and halls of fame are probably the primary manifestation of nostalgia sport tourism (Redmond, 1991). The first reported example of a sport hall of fame is the National Baseball Hall of Fame located in Cooperstown, New York. It was opened in 1939 and currently attracts approximately 400,000 visitors per year (Gammon, 2002). The induction of new members is a high-profile annual media event in the USA. Clearly, the National Baseball Hall of Fame is a major tourist attraction.

Past, current and, in some cases, future sites (e.g. designated Olympic sites) of sporting events and activities are a second type of nostalgia sport tourism attraction (Bale, 1993b). The essence of these sites is their inherent appeal as special places where heroes played and legends were made (Stevens, 2001). This aura fosters an emotional nostalgic experience, which focuses on the connection between place and sporting performance. However, tensions between heritage and modernity are common. For example, the Montreal Forum, a site of many historic sporting events in Canada, was replaced in 1996 by a new spectacular entertainment and professional sport centre. In an attempt to retain some of the nostalgic aura of the Forum, an elaborate campaign was carried out to imbue the new Molson Centre with a sporting (ice hockey) heritage. This campaign included a 'living legends' game in the new centre as well as a closing commemorative ceremony at the Forum (Belanger, 2000). Another approach to capturing nostalgia is the inclusion of sport museums and halls of fame in new facilities. For example, the sport museum at FC Barcelona (football stadium) attracts a purported 500,000 visitors a year.

Fantasy sport programmes are a third and particularly intriguing variation of nostalgia sport tourism. They range from mock training camps to themed cruises, restaurants and bars. However, one of the most exciting variants of this type of programme is the sport fantasy camp, where

> for a mere few thousand dollars, fans can spend a week, or a weekend, training with and finally competing against the legends of the game. The allure of being that close to one's heroes is so powerful that these camps have taken off in popularity. (Schlossberg, 1996: 110)

Gammon (2002) suggests that there are five main motivations to travel to these camps as reflected in promotional literature:

(1) the desire to be associated with a famous event;
(2) the opportunity to train in a famous or meaningful facility;
(3) to increase identification with a particular team or club;
(4) to be closely associated with sporting heroes; and
(5) general interest in the sport and in skill development.

For the nostalgia sport tourist, these camps enable participants to escape from the routine of their day-to-day existence. They provide nostalgia sport tourists with the opportunity to relive or recreate their sporting histories.

Major Trends Affecting Sport Tourism

Strategic planning is a critical aspect of sport tourism development, albeit one that is fraught with challenge. Few phenomena are more problematic in forecasting than trends in sport and tourism, both of which are ultimately discretionary activities. Trend analysis does, however, provide general insights into probable future scenarios in sport and tourism demand.

A variety of predictions have been made about sport tourism. Most foresee continued growth in demand for sport and tourism experiences (Getz, 1998; Delpy, 2001; Standeven & De Knop, 1999; Turco *et al.*, 2002). However, this growth is unlikely to take the form of a simple linear extension of existing sport tourist participation patterns. Table 10.1 summarises trends in sport that are currently affecting sport tourism. Bourdeau *et al.* (2002) see the underlying trend in sport as one of diversification, with a shift towards individual sports. New sporting opportunities will continue to emerge in urban settings, but peripheral areas will also grow in stature as sport places of uncertainty and risk.

Table 10.1 Key trends in sport

Trend	*Description*
1. The increasing development of individual sports as opposed to collective sports	This view is consistent with a societal change in mentality towards 'neo-individualism' and personal development. Participants may gravitate towards other individuals who share their sporting passion, but this will likely be done outside of the traditional sporting institutions.
2. Diversification of sports participation models	People will generally be willing to try a broader range of sports activities than they have in the past. Similarly, sports disciplines will tend to open up their membership to a wider spectrum of participants.
3. Exaggerated segmentation of sports disciplines	An increasing variety of sport hybrids and specialisations will emerge as new sporting experiences are sought.
4. Adaptation of sports activities to the constraints of urban life	The experiences associated with outdoor adventure sports will be simulated in the city where they are accessible to urbanites constrained by time from pursuing these activities in natural settings. A recent example is the emergence of indoor climbing facilities in urban areas.
5. Development of a mythology of adventure in a natural environment	Natural environments will grow in significance in real and symbolic terms as places where sport tourists confront uncertainty, risk and destiny.

Source: adapted from Bourdeau *et al.* (2002)

These trends are themselves rooted in more general tendencies in the broader context in which sport and tourism exist. Economic, political, societal and technological trends form the context for participation in both sport (Collins, 1991) and tourism (Hall, 2000b). Environmental trends and issues as addressed previously in Chapter 7 are also critical.

Economic trends

Globalisation is perhaps the most dominant economic trend that has emerged from the latter part of the twentieth century (Chapter 4). It has exerted increased pressure for the commodification of sport and tourism. Of particular significance is the tendency towards the convergence of tourism, leisure, sport and entertainment. This is especially true of elite organised sport, where the trend towards professionalism and 'show business' is already evident (de Villiers, 2001; Keller, 2001).

The media plays an important role in this process. Popular media has had a long association with sport, inclusive of the golden ages of newspapers, radio and television. It is the last of these forms of media, however, that is perceived as having the greatest impact on elite sport (McKay & Kirk, 1992). From the outset, the television broadcasting of sport generated concern that fans would stop going to the actual competition in favour of viewing sports from the comfort of their homes. At the root of this concern was the belief that sport revenues would shift from traditional sporting institutions to the broadcasters:

> The economics of sport were founded on the principle of persuading large numbers of people to leave their homes, to travel to enclosed sporting venues and to pay for entry in order to view professional performers engaged in various forms of structured, physical competition. (Rowe, 1996: 569)

History has shown that broadcasters have indeed enjoyed substantial financial rewards, but they have also generated significant financial benefits for owners and administrators of televised sports, as well as the destinations where these sports take place. Television revenues for professional sport now far exceed gate revenues. Despite this changing economic context, there are still concerns that the media have subverted sport for their own purposes and, in the process, have eroded the integrity of these sports. For example, as Rowe (1996: 573) noted:

> Television has progressively exerted pressure on sports to be played at times convenient to broadcast schedules and to modify rules in order to guarantee results, to prevent events going too far 'over time', and to overcome any dull passages that might tempt viewers to reach for the dial (later the remote control). The global spread of

sports television has created its own severe pressures on sport by, for example, demanding that wherever possible 'live' sports should be transmitted at a time convenient for the largest and most lucrative TV markets.

Interactive technology in the form of pay-per-view television, the Internet and video games presents substantial challenges for sport tourism. Some authors have speculated that the increasingly interactive experience of watching sport from the comfort of home may eventually result in the need to pay spectators to attend televised games in order to create an exciting atmosphere in the sporting venue (Johnson, 1991). The overall benefits of the on-site experience for sport tourists must clearly exceed the costs associated with the trip. It is also important for sport tourism managers to advocate the retention of the things that make sport unique. While pure entertainment can be a very powerful tourist attraction, sport as entertainment is unique. The inherent authenticity of sport provides a competitive advantage to many tourism destinations that may be lost if the nature of the activity shifts to staged entertainment.

The influential role of the media is not limited to mainstream sports. Subculture sports can also be closely tied to the media. In today's post-modern society, 'the specialized press ... plays a fundamental role in initiating participants to techniques, equipment, cultural codes and languages which lay the foundations for the identity of the sports "tribes"' (Bourdeau *et al.*, 2002: 27). This medium is, therefore, of particular interest to sport tourism managers as it influences where subculture members travel in pursuit of their sporting passions.

Political trends

Changing balances of power and influence drive political trends. The emergence of free-trade agendas highlight changing power configurations throughout the world. The economic benefits of free trade are unlikely to be evenly distributed. Hall (2000b: 88) predicts that there will be

> increased conflict between developing and developed countries over global economic development strategies as it becomes apparent to large numbers of the population in developing countries that they will never be able to have western lifestyles due to population and resource constraints.

The repercussions of such sentiments and other political grievances are already being felt in terms of protest activities that have direct impacts on tourism and sport.

Terrorism is not a new challenge in tourism (Hall, 2000b; Sonmez *et al.*, 1999), nor is it alien to sport (Wedemeyer, 1999). Perhaps the most notable terrorism incident in a sport tourism context was the fatal attack on Israeli athletes at the Munich (1972) Olympic Village (Wedemeyer, 1999). Yet, despite the high profile of sporting events as terrorist targets, there have been surprisingly few politically motivated attacks on sport. Indeed it has been suggested that sport tourism was one of the more resilient types of tourism in the aftermath of the terrorist attacks in America on 11 September 2001 (WTO, 2001).

The most obvious implication of this is that major sporting events are going to require high levels of security. An increase in preference for off-site spectatorship over on-site consumption of the event may also occur. Active sports characterised by dispersed spatial patterns of participation may increase in popularity relative to major event sport tourism. Similarly, nostalgic tourism may increase as traditional patterns of event sport tourism consumption are altered.

Socio-demographic trends

Socio-demographic trends are also likely to exert considerable influence over the future of sport tourism (Delpy, 2001). Of particular significance is the aging population of developed countries. For example, downhill skiing has been directly impacted by this trend:

> People born between 1946 and 1964 make up almost a third of the North American population and they started switching to more gentle winter sports such as snowshoeing and cross-country skiing, because their aging bodies could no longer handle the rigours of alpine runs. High-tech computer designed skis and equipment, which make it safer and easier for even aging outdoor lovers to learn or continue to enjoy the sport, have halted that trend somewhat in recent years. (Loverseed, 2000: 53)

In the face of this trend, sport tourism operators have to adjust their products to match the needs of their markets. This adjustment will involve a shift from hard adventure activities to less physically demanding soft adventure outdoor sport activities. An aging population will become more health conscious and, therefore, seek sport activities that will help them to retain and perhaps regain their health rather than put it at risk.

The shift from a modern to a postmodern society is also mediating the context of sport tourism. At one level, this shift has its economic roots in the rejection of the welfare state and regulated markets in favour of competition, free trade and globalisation (Stewart & Smith, 2000; Merkel *et al.*, 1998; Coalter, 1999). Niche markets, individualism, flexibility, time fragmentation, new technologies, innovative communication networks and commercialisation all characterise today's society. The role of place in postmodern sport is also changing. Local tribal loyalties based on the

Table 10.2 A comparison of modern and postmodern sport

Dimension/component	Modern sport	Postmodern sport
Game structure	Rules are sacred	Rule modification and experimentation
Team leadership	Conservative	Adventurous
Values and customs	Amateurism, respect for authority, character building	Professionalism, innovation
Organisation and management	Central control	Diffusion of authority
Financial structure	Gate receipts	Sponsorship, television rights, gate receipts, sport as business
Venues and facilities	Basic seating at stadia	Customised seating, video support
Promotion	Limited	Extensive
Viewing	Live match attendance	TV audiences dominate
Spectator preference	Display of traditional craft	Eclectic blend of entertainment
Fan loyalties	Singular and parochial loyalty	Multiple loyalties – all spatial scales
The sports market	Undifferentiated mass market	Fragmented and niche markets
Coaching and training	Rigid, repetitive practices	Blend of science and naturalistic practices – variety

Source: adapted from Stewart and Smith (2000)

'home team' have tended to be replaced by attachments to corporate identities or brands. Table 10.2 summarises the changing face of organised sport from the modern to the postmodern era. Murray and Dixon (2000) have argued that the emergence of 'instant sports' is the result of the shift from modernity to postmodernity. This is consistent with the emphasis on consumer orientations over citizenship orientations and unstructured over structured sports in western society.

Technological trends

Technological innovations have irrevocably changed the face of sport and tourism. They have improved sporting performances and enriched tourism experiences. Moreover, technology has further blurred the line between sport and tourism. For example, the development of the Internet has resulted in the creation of a multitude of sport-related web sites that vary from the static provision of basic information about a sport to interactive sport sites that can form the basis of a leisure experience in their own right (E. L. Jackson, 1999). Virtual reality or cyberspace is having direct impacts on the way that people experience leisure (Bassett & Wilbert, 1999). The extent that sport experiences in cyberspace can substitute for sport experience in real space remains a matter of speculation. Current examples of sport experiences that take place in cyberspace include live on-line sports commentaries, sports gambling on-line, real-time viewer surveys during sport broadcasts, and instant progress updates and live digital video images of sports contests. On another level, many computer games conform closely to definitions of sport (Chapter 2), with the exception of the physical activity requirement, but there is no reason that this has to remain the case. Physical activity could be incorporated into these games much more extensively than it is at present.

Past technological advances in transportation have played a key role in tourism development and they are likely to continue to do so. The anticipated introduction of a new generation of long-haul, wide-bodied and multiple-level jet aircraft will increase access and reinforce 'hub and spoke' transportation patterns (Hall, 2000b). Continued advances in space travel will result in increased access to weightless environments, which may spawn a whole new generation of sport. Similar developments in marine environments are likely to present dramatic new opportunities for sport tourism in that realm.

Recently, a variety of environmentally controlled sport facilities have been built, such as the Skydome in Toronto with its retractable roof. This trend goes beyond major spectator sports to sporting activities that were once the exclusive domain of the outdoors and wilderness areas:

> Sports-oriented theme parks are all the rage with free climbing, water slides, hydrospeeding, golf training or skateboarding. In the United Kingdom and the Netherlands there are ski domes where beginners can test their ability at skiing and experienced skiers can get into shape before the season starts. . . . Generally speaking leisure parks and theme parks do not rely on any [natural] landscape. They are in fact genuine industrial zones for sport-related enjoyment. (Keller, 2001: 15)

These facilities tend to be constructed in urban areas, where participants have easy access in terms of time (i.e. they can ski after work on a week day) and in terms of space (i.e. they can participate in their preferred sporting activity close to home) (Chapter 5). If these urban-based artificial sporting environments were perfect substitutes for the same activities in natural settings, then it is logical to predict that there would be fewer visits to peripheral areas. In reality, these artificial environments are not exact substitutes. They may in fact serve as demand shifters in that more people will be introduced to the sport and may eventually seek out traditional activity sites. In the foreseeable future, the original natural settings are likely to remain the preferred location for the vast majority of participants.

Management Implications and Opportunties

Sport tourism managers should consider the cycles of different sporting events as they attempt to influence the life cycle of the tourist destination. Care must be taken to avoid compromising the essence of sporting events, as doing so may lead to the stagnation or decline of the sport and the loss of competitive advantage at a destination. It should also be recognised that the media is a major player in the life cycles of sporting events. Technological advances and the increasing sophistication of sport broadcasting are clearly making spectatorship from the comfort of one's home an increasingly competitive alternative to attending live sport. On-site spectatorship should go beyond simply keeping pace with interactive media technology available to the stay-at-home audience. The personal link between the athletes and the spectators must be safeguarded and enhanced, as should the unique experience of place. Sport managers must treat spectators as an integral part of their sport, which they are (Hornby, 1996), and foster opportunities to encourage spectators to see themselves as such.

Active sport tourism appears to be a significant area of potential growth, given a broad-based shift from traditional sports to individualised activities such as health activities and extreme sports. Sport tourism managers need to monitor the emergence of new sports and develop a good understanding of the motivations that underlie participation in these activities. The life cycles associated with them should be carefully considered, with particular attention paid to whether the sport appears to be destined for a long or a short life cycle.

Sport tourism managers should develop separate strategies for 'alternative' versus 'mainstream' sports. For example, the independence of extreme sport athletes means that they may travel more like 'independent' than 'group' travellers. Given that the travel experiences sought by extreme athletes are distinct from those sought by mainstream athletes, they are likely to be attracted by different promotional messages, use different modes of transportation or fare structures, stay in different types of accommodation and to generally behave differently during their stay at a destination. Sport tourism managers who develop insights into unique desires of these niche markets will be well positioned for success.

Nostalgia tourism also represents a major opportunity for sport tourism managers. At the heart of a nostalgic experience is emotion. Visitors to sports halls of fame, high-profile sporting venues and fantasy programmes are looking for more than information. They are looking for positive emotional experiences. Sport tourism managers can learn much about how to elicit this response by studying contemporary interpretive approaches and drama. By developing interactive sports halls of fame/ museums at the actual stadia, economies of scale can be created in terms of infrastructure and suprastucture. More importantly, synergies can be developed between the hall of fame/museum and the aura of the sporting venue. In new facilities, these halls of fame/museums serve to connect the new sporting place to its sporting heritage.

Fantasy sport programmes are limited only by the imaginations of sport tourism managers. The opportunity to 'take ambrosia with the gods' (Gammon, 2002) or to live one's sporting dream is a very powerful draw. Programmes that can deliver these opportunities are likely to be popular with mid to high-end sport tourism markets. The challenge for managers will be to find a balance between fantasy and reality that is acceptable to the paying customers.

Conclusion

The long-term time horizon is characterised by the interaction of the respective life cycles found in sport and tourism. It is evident that sport can influence the nature and pace of tourism destination life cycles and that tourism can have similar impacts on sport life cycles. The conscious manipulation of these forces not only helps to avoid costly mistakes, but also offers a powerful tool for pursuing sustainable development strategies.

Sport and tourism are dynamic in the long term, just as they are in the short and medium terms. A significant manifestation of this dynamic is nostalgia sport tourism, in which tourists seek out the past by visiting places infused with sport heritage and by participating in programmes that bring the past to life. The sport tourism industry has only recently started to appreciate the breadth of products that are of interest to these tourists. Sport tourism nostalgia offers the opportunity for sport tourists to become time travellers, if only in their imaginations.

Finally, it is clear that sport tourism does not operate in a vacuum. There is a variety of trends in the economic, political, socio-demographic and technological realms that may have a direct and, in some cases, overbearing influence on sport tourism. By studying trends that exist within the external environment, sport tourism managers will be in a better position to set sustainable sport tourism development goals and objectives, and to develop effective plans of action.

Further Reading

At the heart of this chapter is the concept of the tourist area life cycle of evolution, as articulated by Butler (1980). Numerous articles on the topic have been published since 1980, with Johnston (2001a,b) providing one of the most recent overviews of the topic. Two new edited volumes on the tourist area cycle will soon be available, with one focusing on theoretical and conceptual discussions, while the other will provide a variety of applications and case studies (Butler, forthcoming a, b). Keller (2001) provides direct insight into the evolving nature of sport tourism and offers a useful framework for understanding how sport and tourism interact over the long term. The work of Gammon (2002) is especially welcomed in the neglected area of nostalgia sport tourism. He has effectively drawn on writings from outside the bounds of sport or tourism to provide much needed insight into this particular dimension of sport tourism. Finally, the major trends associated with sport tourism are drawn from a diverse range of sources. Especially useful among them are Bourdeau *et al.* (2002), who highlight specific trends in sport along with Standeven and De Knop (1999), and Turco *et al.* (2002), who focus more directly on sport tourism.

Case study 10.1

The Mecca of Golf: St Andrews, Scotland

Richard Butler, University of Surrey

Introduction and History

There are few communities as strongly related to a specific sport as St Andrews is to golf. Known worldwide as 'the home of golf', it holds a privileged and somewhat unique position in sports and tourism. The town today represents a good example of the beneficial and problematic results of being the centre of global awareness for a specific popular sporting activity and, in effect for many decades, a pilgrimage site for aficionados of that activity.

St Andrews' claim to the parentage of golf stems from two principal factors: first, it appears to be the oldest site of recorded golf and, second, it is the location of the establishment which sets the rules for the sport (except in the USA and Mexico). The St Andrews Links Trust, a body established by an Act of Parliament in 1974, records that the land on which the current courses lie was given to the townspeople as common land in 1123. The ownership of the links has remained in public hands for most of the nine centuries since then. Some 300 years later, golf was recorded as being played over this land, and in 1457, because its popularity was felt to be distracting young men from practising archery, King James II banned the sport. The ban was renewed by subsequent monarchs until James IV became an avid player himself half a century later.

Organisation and Arrangements

The body currently responsible for establishing the rules of the game came into being in 1754, first as the Society of St Andrews Golfers, and then, in 1834, as the Royal and Ancient Golf Club, its current title. The game was traditionally played on the links over what is now the Old Course, initially consisting of 22 holes. In 1764 the number of holes was reduced to 18, the number now accepted as the standard round of golf. The land was sold in 1797 by the bankrupt Town Council into private hands for operation as a rabbit farm, and subsequent conflict between farmers and golfers was only resolved when the land was purchased privately by golfing interests. Subsequently, the land reverted again to the Town Council, until the Links Trust took over the task of managing the links and preserving them as a public park. Preserving part of the tradition of public access, the Old Course is still closed to golf on Sundays to allow the citizens to walk over the links, much to the amazement of many visitors.

Current Facilities and Use

Today there are six public golf courses (99 holes in all) on the links, run by the Trust, representing the largest golfing complex in Europe, with over 200,000 rounds being played each year. There are two clubhouses, the new irrigation system which cost $US6 million and maintenance equipment which cost a further $US4 million. Up to 250 people are employed in the high season and just under 200 year-round. In addition, approximately 250 licensed caddies find employment on the links' courses. In preparation for the Millennium Open in 2000, 56 greenkeepers worked on the Old Course, compared to the normal squad of 11.

Approximately 60% of all rounds played over the links are played by 'locals', residents of the town or of the Kingdom of Fife, reflecting the commitment of residents to golf as a pastime as well as the links' role as a tourist attraction. In years in which the Open Championship is played at St Andrews (26 occasions, beginning in 1873), rounds on the courses drop. The 2000 Championship season was no exception, with the number of rounds declining from the previous peak of 1997 to just under 195,000. In 2001, despite the outbreak of foot-and-mouth disease, numbers had increased to a new record level of 215,000.

Recent Developments in Tourism

The presence of the Royal and Ancient and the relatively frequent holding of the Open at St Andrews (currently approximately every six years), serve to keep the town in the public's mind as uniquely associated with golf. In the past decade several other developments have strengthened this association and reflected the importance of golf to tourism in the town, thus marking the most recent era of golf tourism at St Andrews. The two largest hotels in the town are located adjoining the Old Course, Rusaks being built in the nineteenth century and renovated and expanded in the last decade, and the Old Course Hotel being built in the 1980s and subsequently expanded over the last decade also. This hotel, which stands beside the seventeenth fairway, has around 150 rooms and suites, with rates running from $US600 to $US1200 a night for half of the year. It remained the largest hotel in the area until 2001, when the St Andrews Bay resort, with just over 200 rooms, opened some five miles south of the town, with its own two golf courses and luxurious facilities. A similar distance to the north of the town is the Drumoig Golf Resort, which, although composed of a much smaller hotel development (only 29 rooms), is the site of both a new golf course and the National Golf Academy (the Scottish National Golf Centre). Claiming to be 'Europe's finest purpose-built coaching facility', in association with Nike, it is an added attraction with its extensive coaching and training facilities. On the edge of the town at Craigtoun, the Duke's Course, affiliated with the Old Course Hotel opened, in 1995. Finally, in St Andrews itself the British Golf Museum is located adjacent to the Royal and Ancient clubhouse and functions as a major tourist attraction in its own right. This attraction was again developed in the last decade.

Golf and Tourism

Not unexpectedly, the tourism industry in St Andrews is heavily structured towards golf. The town has several golf equipment and clothing shops, three manufacturers of clubs, and several organisations offering tours, packages and even a 'Golf Widows' range of programmes. While the main tourist season is from May to September, golf is played throughout the year and tourists visit, although in much smaller numbers, during the winter. For those tourists who do not play golf, but who come to see the historic town or the oldest university in Scotland (established in 1412, its most famous student being Prince William), or who, as traditional tourists did, come to use its beach (immortalised, if mislocated, in the film 'Chariots of Fire'), there is the added attraction of celebrity spotting. St Andrews, like other centres with specific features, attracts many well-known individuals, including presidents of the USA and other heads of state, British royalty, film stars such as Sean Connery and Samuel L. Jackson, the top players of many other sports and, of course, the elite of golf on busman's holidays.

When the Open is being held, the town becomes virtually besieged (for example, there were 230,000 visitors over the week for the Millennium Open) and access to and within the town is severely limited. Major temporary development takes place adjacent to the links, severe but necessary restrictions are placed on vehicle use, and properties are rented for close to a year's normal rental for the two weeks involved (the Open beginning in one week and ending in the next). Ironically, some merchants claim a loss of business during the main week of the tournament, particularly those who do not cater to tourists, as many people cannot or choose not to try to access the centre of the town during this period. As with many major events, a proportion of locals choose to take their holidays during this period. Overall, however, given the fact that golf has been an integral part of the life of St Andrews for almost 600, it not unnaturally has strong support from the local residents.

The Future

Tourism in St Andrews is not based entirely on golf. In the period prior to the Second World War, the tourism industry was based on the beach, with its associated swimming pools and other facilities, and on the historical heritage of the town. Access was by railway until the 1960s, when the British railway system was dramatically reduced. The University also generates a considerable amount of visitation. The economy of the town is, in fact, highly diversified, with several flourishing components: tourism (golf and heritage plus some traditional beach tourism), the education function with the University and several private schools, the RAF base at Leuchars (five miles away), limited industry and its role as rural regional centre. There is little indication that any of these functions are likely to decline in the near future at least, but of all of them, tourism based on golf seems to have the greatest potential for continued growth, given the global popularity of the game and St Andrews' unique position. While the town itself has grown from 12,000 in 1971 to 16,000 in 1991, golf rounds played on the public links have increased from 151,000 in 1979 to 215,000 in 2001. Further growth in numbers is limited by the capacity of the links' courses. These figures do not include rounds played on the recently completed private courses in St Andrews Bay, Drumming and Craigtoun. The use of these new courses is likely to rise significantly in the years ahead, as they add to the golfing attractions found in the St Andrews area.

Acknowledgement

The considerable assistance of Carolyne Nurse, St Andrews Links Trust, in providing statistics and information, is gratefully acknowledged.

Further reading

Butler, R. W. (1980) The concept of the tourist area lifecycle of evolution: Implications for the management of resources. *Canadian Geographer* 24 (1), 5–12.

Part 5: Conclusions

Chapter 11
Management Principles for Sport Tourism Development

Introduction

The study of sport tourism development provides varied and important insights into the ways in which sport tourism has changed, and continues to change, in space and time. Chapter 1 raised three basic questions: 'What makes sport unique as a focus for tourism development?', 'How is sport tourism manifested in space?' and 'How do these manifestations change over time?' In addressing these questions, the objective of this book was to build understanding and help sport tourism managers influence the nature of sport tourism development. This chapter serves to highlight these insights and to present guiding principles of sport tourism development.

Foundations for Sport Tourism Development

The study of sport tourism development requires a solid foundation that includes an underlying framework highlighting the relationship between sport and tourism, an appreciation of sport tourism markets and an understanding of fundamental development concepts and issues. The conceptual foundation of this book defines sport tourism as sport-based travel away from the home environment for a limited time, where sport is characterised by unique rule sets, competition related to physical prowess and a playful nature. Under this definition, the conceptual focus of the book is based on sport as a tourist attraction. By consciously treating sport as a unique type of tourist attraction, readers will be in a better position to understand the nature of, and influence patterns of, sport tourism development. The nature of sport tourism markets must also be appreciated. Sport tourism is not only a specialised segment of the tourism market, but it is in fact comprised of multiple niche markets. The nature of these niche markets varies in terms of intensity, types of involvement in sports (e.g. event, active, nostalgia) and types of sport. Not only do the motivations, needs and general socio-demographic characteristics differ

207

for each niche, but so, too, do travel behaviours and destination impacts. Tourism destination managers may, therefore, identify sport tourism as a development strategy at a strategic level, but operational plans designed to influence tourism development patterns need to be specific about the type of sport tourist that is being targeted.

Sport tourism development implies the progressive improvement of the quality of life in a destination and the fulfilment of the destination's potential. Manifestations of development occur in time and space. Planning offers a powerful way to intervene into the development process to obtain desired future states. However, if planning interventions are to be effective, they must be driven by an underlying goal of sustainable development.

Three key development issues that exist in the context of sport tourism development are explored in this book. The first relates to commodification and authenticity. Tourism is just one of the forces that is commodifying sport, but it is an important one. One of the primary advantages of sport as a tourist attraction is that it is authentic and it provides sport tourists with access to the 'back stage' of a destination. Sports that become indistinguishable from other types of 'staged' entertainment lose their competitive advantage as tourist attractions.

Globalisation is a second key issue in the context of sport tourism development. Sports such as football (soccer) are global phenomena, yet there remain important distinctions in the way the game is played in different parts of the world. These differences represent opportunities for sport tourism development. In such cases, sport can contribute to the unique regional character of a place, thereby providing a competitive tourism advantage.

Strategic alliances and partnerships in sport tourism address the third development issue – that of fragmentation. Attempts to overcome the problem of fragmentation through the creation of sport tourism alliances have been encouraging, but little progress has been made in other areas of sport tourism development. Continued articulation of the benefits of cooperation is required. If these benefits cannot be demonstrated, it is unlikely that the various stakeholders in sport tourism, including sports event organisers and promoters, sports associations, managers of sporting venues, destination managers and tourism marketers, will work in a cooperative fashion.

Sport Tourism Development and Space

The study of the locations and travel flows associated with sports, the way sport infuses space with meaning to create unique tourism places and the resource requirements and impacts of sport tourism are all key themes within the spatial analysis of sport tourism development. Central place theory is a particularly useful tool to explain the locational tendencies of urban sport facilities, events and professional sport teams. Sports that require the construction of major indoor facilities or that depend upon high numbers of spectators or participants will gravitate towards the larger centres. This is especially true of commercial sports. The challenge of sport tourism managers in these locations is to maximise the synergies that are inherent in existing transportation networks, accommodation, food and beverage facilities and other elements of urban infrastructure.

Sport tourism in peripheral areas is characterised by quite different spatial dynamics. Rather than development being driven by the location of the market, it tends to be driven by the location of the resource. The distinguishing feature in most cases is that the sporting activity is dependent on natural resources that are not normally found in or adjacent to urban areas. The planning and development of peripheral sports locations present the challenges of relative isolation and much lower levels of available infrastructure. Significant competitive advantages can be achieved where sport tourism developments in peripheral areas are clustered, so as to allow the concentrated development of tourism infrastructure and services.

Place may be described as space with meaning. It is especially attractive to tourism marketers who use sport to sell destinations. The spectre of homogenised sportscapes threatens tourism, as it contributes to a breakdown of distinctive regional place meaning based on sport. Sport tourism managers should, therefore, be proactive in the retention of unique regional meanings and identities associated with sporting facilities and activities. It is particularly important that tourism interests should support the efforts of sport managers who defend the 'integrity' of their sports. There should also be consistency between the images used to promote a sport tourism destination and the images that residents have of their home. Conflicting views of place may result in conflicting attitudes and behaviours.

The environment and, more particularly, regional landscapes and resources, are important elements of sport tourism development. Urban-based sport tourism is often connected to the cultural landscape, while sport tourism activity in the periphery tends to be connected to natural landscapes. Large-scale sports events are typical of the urban context, and it is usually the scale of urban sports events that determines the range and extent of the associated impacts. Sport tourism in peripheral areas often requires substantial alteration of the physical landscape and due consideration must be made to mitigate any negative impacts.

The requirement that Olympic organising committees articulate and implement an environmental protection policy represents a significant shift in the approach to planning large-scale events. With the continued pressure of environmental and social advocacy groups, it is likely that this shift will be echoed in social and cultural environments. Sport tourism managers not only have an ethical obligation to be proactive in this regard, but they also have an economic and professional interest. Tourism revenues depend on the maintenance of the resources upon which the attraction is built and upon the hospitality of the hosts.

Sport Tourism Development and Time

The temporal dimensions of sport tourism include the experience of sport tourists during their travels, seasonal variations in sport and tourism activities and the cyclical dynamics of sport tourism. The sport tourism experience takes place in several phases, including anticipation, travel to the destination, on-site experience, return travel and recollection. Generalisations about on-site experiences are difficult, as it is clear that these experiences vary substantially between specific market segments. However, the extent to which sport tourists engage in other types of touristic activities in the destination is influenced by two key factors. The first is the travel profile of the tourist, including the distance travelled, mode of transportation and length of stay. The nature of the sporting activity, including scheduling, sporting role (e.g. athlete, spectator, etc.), performance, level of competition and the outcome of the competition, is the second factor to influence the propensity of sport tourists to engage in other touristic activities. Essentially these types of characteristics determine or reflect the extent to which the sport tourist is interested and, indeed, able to partake in other types of tourism activities. Sport tourism managers should, therefore, develop detailed profiles of market segments rather than generalise about the motivations and behaviours of sport tourists as a whole.

Seasonal patterns in sport and tourism represent a distinct temporal dimension of sport tourism development. Tourism managers have typically seen seasonal variation in visitors as a problem due to underutilised capacity and decreased revenue flows during the low season. From a tourism management perspective, sport can be used as a strategy to influence seasonality with considerable success. The scheduling of sporting events during the shoulder tourism seasons is an increasingly prominent aspect of event production and planning. In terms of active sport tourism, destinations that are characterised by specialised resources available during the off-season can be particularly attractive to sport subculture groups. Similarly, nostalgia sport tourism attractions remain functional outside the main tourism seasons. If properly promoted, they too offer the opportunity to alter seasonal patterns of visitation to a destination.

Tourism destination cycles as well as sport life cycles offer valuable theoretical insight into the long-term evolution of sport and tourism. As sports progress through their life cycles, they impact the destinations where they take place. For example, evolving trends in alpine skiing have a direct impact on alpine resort developments. Fortunately for these resorts, declining participation in downhill skiing has been offset by the emergence of snowboarding and other new alpine sports. Sport life cycles are also influenced by tourism. Leisure-based activities such as windsurfing are popular tourist activities that have become serious competitive sports disseminated throughout the world.

Nostalgia sport tourism demonstrates how the evolution of sport can have a direct impact on tourism. Sport nostalgia is, in part, a reaction to a rapidly changing society. It is not only a chance for tourists to revisit their youth, but it is an opportunity to escape back into what is often considered a simpler time. These temporal journeys are facilitated by spatial journeys as tourists seek out sports halls of fame, sites of historic sporting moments and fantasy programmes that enable participants to recreate or relive history.

More generally, there is a variety of macro-level trends that will influence the future of sport tourism. Globalisation processes appear to underlie the majority of these trends. Particular challenges include the need to position sport tourism relative to the increasing influence of media in sport and to position sport tourism in a turbulent political environment. In addition to these challenges, current trends suggest a variety of opportunities for sport tourism. One of the most significant is the increasing popularity of individual sports and active sport tourism. This trend is reflected in the emergence of new 'extreme' sports for which participants are motivated to travel significant distances in pursuit of their sporting interests.

Principles of Sport Tourism Development

The chapters presented in this book may be read as a series of purposely positioned essays on related themes of sport tourism development. While this provides a coherent approach to the study of sport tourism, it tends to understate the integrated nature of the practice of sport tourism. The use of Case studies and 'Focus points' in each of these chapters demonstrates the strong links that exist between theory and practice in sport tourism. Clearly, success in this field requires effective cooperation between sport and tourism managers and stakeholders. The following principles emerge from the discussions presented in the preceding chapters. They are intended to provide direction that fosters an integrated, effective and sustainable approach to the practice of sport tourism development.

Sport tourism curriculum development

Managers in sport and tourism must have the knowledge base necessary to make appropriate decisions in the realm of sport tourism. To this point, much of this knowledge has come from trial and error, intuition and the hard-earned experience of individuals working in sport tourism and related fields. Further development of specialised academic and professional programmes designed to provide students with a detailed understanding of this phenomenon is required. In addition, students with interests in sport tourism, whose study programmes are primarily based in tourism or sports management, must develop a balanced knowledge of the respective fields of study. Specialised sport tourism courses will help to achieve this goal. The development of teaching and research links between the disciplines of sport and tourism will also foster synergies in this area. Where students may be advised or encouraged to complete their course options in the fields of sport management, tourism management and other disciplines of relevance (including leisure studies, marketing, business studies, the sociology of sport and sport geography), the same goal will be fostered. At the very least, this approach will help future professionals to develop an appreciation of the convergence and mutual interests of these fields.

Coordination and leadership through alliance and partnership

The need for coordinated efforts within and between sport and tourism agencies emerges consistently throughout the pages of this book. Weak alliances and partnerships will undermine the effectiveness of sport tourism development initiatives. The establishment and maintenance of strong alliances and partnerships is critical, although such initiatives may seem to be secondary to the core functions of sport and tourism managers. An enduring commitment requires that the purpose and benefits of such alliances be clearly articulated and demonstrated from the outset.

Policy development

While day-to-day operating decisions are the things that ultimately determine the nature of sport tourism, it is necessary to have policy direction so that these decisions are made systematically, rather than on an *ad hoc* basis. It is incumbent upon policy makers to consciously and publicly set directions for sport tourism. The logical starting point is to recognise the mutual relationship of sport and tourism within public and private organisational structures. This does not mean that existing sport and tourism ministries should necessarily combine, although there are numerous present and past examples where this has been the case. Unfortunately, the divisions within sport and tourism organisations can be just as rigid as they are between organisations. Effective sport tourism development policy requires real commitment. As in the case of alliance and partnership, the mutual benefit of cooperation must be evident. Policy initiatives must then be articulated and operationalised in a way that captures these benefits in a measurable manner. The guiding rule of such initiatives should be sustainable development, which requires a long-term rather than a short-term perspective.

Active planning interventions

Policy is implemented through planning. Planning, in turn, occurs at a variety of levels, from strategic through to operational. Various spatial levels of planning ranging from global through to local site plans need to be considered. A full array of public and private sector stakeholders must be involved as sport tourism plans require popular support if they are to be successful. As in any planning exercise, the probability of success is enhanced as a better understanding of the dynamic nature of sport tourism development emerges.

Data collection and research

Several of the preceding principles require accurate measurement of many aspects of the sport tourism phenomenon. The various costs associated with the development of partnerships, policy and planning in sport tourism should form one part of the measurement process. To a large extent, the need to demonstrate the return-on-investment explains the prevalence of economic impact studies associated with major sporting events. These impact studies should continue, albeit with rigorous and standardised methodologies that allow for accurate and comparable findings. However, research must move beyond a narrow economic focus. Just as there is a multitude of research questions being asked in a tourism and sport context, there is a multitude of useful questions that can be asked in relation to sport tourism. By addressing these questions, policy makers, planners and managers will be able to make more informed decisions.

Theory building

It is beneficial to know what has happened in the context of sport tourism development, but it is much more useful to know how it happened and why it happened. Data collection and research are not ends in themselves. Ideally, they provide insight into the world in which we live. Research in sport tourism should move beyond description to the realms of explanation and prediction as facilitated by theory. At this stage in the evolution of the study of sport tourism, theoretical insight is likely to come from more advanced fields of study. If existing theories can be used to provide additional insight into sport tourism development, then these theories should be adopted, applied and perhaps modified and further developed in their application to the study of sport tourism. As the knowledge bases relating to sport and tourism grow, they will contribute to advances in sport tourism curricula and, ultimately, to the practice of sustainable sport tourism development.

Concluding Statement

Sport provides a unique focus for the study of tourism. The significant, and in some cases overwhelming, profile of sports in a broad range of local, regional, national and global media, provides considerable advantages and opportunities in terms of the way sport is harnessed to foster tourism development interests. Perhaps more importantly, the fundamental rule structures, competitive dimensions and ludic qualities of sport present a complex array of opportunities and challenges associated with tourism development. Thus, sport is characterised by markets that are distinguishable from those associated with other forms of tourism, and by development issues that warrant dedicated research and publication.

This book explores the functions of sport as a distinctive and potentially powerful type of tourist attraction. The defining qualities of sport provide an exceptional and unique attraction nucleus that offers tourism industry interests and sport tourism researchers fertile grounds to explore. The human element of sport as a tourist attraction is notable for its diversity. Among the many dimensions or continua upon which sport tourists may be conceptualised, elite athletes and recreational participants, event competitors and sport spectators, sports teams and individual contestants, and sports junkies and casual sport tourists are just a few. The diverse forms of sport tourism that exist within these continua may be explored in terms of the diverse market niches that they represent. The profile that sports generate, through media coverage, commercial interests and live or delayed broadcasting, may contribute significantly to marking sport tourist attractions, and the destinations with which they are associated, as unique.

In treating sport as a peculiar and distinctive type of tourist attraction, this book demonstrates that sport tourism has real manifestations in space and time. Sport tourism influences travel patterns, sport and tourism locations, the meaning ascribed to tourism destinations and the impacts on the landscapes – built (e.g. stadia, arenas) and natural (e.g.

marine environments, ski areas) – that form the theatres of sport. It also influences the nature of travel experiences, seasonal visitation patterns and the evolution of sport, tourism and the host destinations where sport tourism takes place.

An appreciation of these dynamics means that sport tourism managers do not have to be passive observers or reactive players in the sport tourism development process. This book concludes by setting forth six key management principles that emerge from the discussions presented in the preceding chapters. By understanding the processes inherent in sport tourism, managers can influence the nature and pace of development. With an awareness and understanding of these processes, sport tourism managers can be proactive in striving for sustainable development in this vibrant field.

Bibliography

Abad, J. M. (2001) The growth of the Olympic city of Barcelona. *Olympic Review* 27 (38), 16–19.

Ajzen, I. and Driver, B. L. (1992) Application of the theory of planned behavior to leisure choice. *Journal of Leisure Research* 24 (3), 207–225.

Alexander, M. (2001) Sport relays billions to NZ economy. *Sunday Star Times*, 15 April, E:3.

Alexandris, K. and Carroll, B. (1999) Constraints on recreational sport participation in adults in Greece: Implications for providing and managing sport services. *Journal of Sport Management* 13 (4), 317–332.

Allcock, J. B. (1989) Seasonality. In S. F. Witt and L. Moutinho (eds) *Tourism Marketing and Management Handbook* (pp. 387–392). Englewood Cliffs, NJ: Prentice Hall.

Andueza, J. M. (1997) The role of sport in the tourism destinations chosen by tourists visiting Spain. *Journal of Sport Tourism* 4 (3), 5–12.

Anon. (1996) Business money is the champion. *Marketing*, 18 July, 3.

Anon. (2000) Shared vision? Australian leisure management considers the development of shared community and school sports facilities in country areas. *Australian Leisure Management* 19, 24–25.

Archer, B. and Cooper, C. (1994) The positive and negative impacts of tourism. In W. Theobald (ed.) *Global Tourism: The Next Decade* (pp. 73–91). Oxford: Butterworth-Heinemann.

Atkisson, A. (2000) *Believing Cassandra: An Optimist Looks at a Pessimist's World.* New York: Scribe Publishers.

Bale, J. (1982) *Sport and Place: A Geography of Sport in England, Scotland and Wales.* London: C. Hurst and Co. Ltd.

Bale, J. (1989) *Sports Geography.* London: Spon.

Bale, J. (1993a) *Sport, Space and the City.* London: Routledge.

Bale, J. (1993b) The spatial development of the modern stadium. *International Review for the Sociology of Sport* 28 (2/3), 121–134.

Bale, J. (1994) *Landscapes of Modern Sport.* Leicester: Leicester University Press.

Ball, R. M. (1988) Seasonality: A problem for workers in the tourism labour market? *The Service Industries Journal* 8 (4), 501–513.

Ball, R. M. (1989) Some aspects of tourism, seasonality, and local labour markets. *Area* 21 (1), 35–45.

Baloglu, S. and McCleary, K. W. (1999) A model of destination image formation. *Annals of Tourism Research* 26 (4), 868–897.

216

Barker, M. (2004) Crime and sport events tourism: The 1999/2000 America's Cup. In B. Ritchie and D. Adair (eds) *Sport Tourism: Interrelationships, Impacts and Issues.* Clevedon: Channel View Publications.

BarOn, R. R. V. (1975) *Seasonality in Tourism: A Guide to the Analysis of Seasonality and Trends for Policy Making.* London: Economist Intelligence Unit.

Bartoluci, M. and Čavlek, N. (2000) The economic basis of the development of golf in Croatian tourism: Prospects and misconceptions. *Acta Turistica* 12 (2), 105–138.

Basset, C. and Wilbert, C. (1999) Where you want to go today (like it or not). In D. Crouch (ed.) *Leisure/Tourism Geographies* (pp. 181–194). London: Routledge.

Baum, T. and Hagen, L. (1999) Responses to seasonality: The experiences of peripheral destinations. *International Journal of Tourism Research* 1, 299–312.

Baum, T. and Lundtorp, S. (2001) Seasonality in tourism: An introduction. In T. Baum and S. Lundtorp (eds) *Seasonality in Tourism* (pp. 1–4). London: Pergamon.

Beardsley, D. (1987) *Country on Ice.* Markham: Paperjacks Ltd.

Beezer, A. and Hebdige, D. (1992) Subculture: The meaning of style. In M. Barker and A. Beezer (eds) *Reading into Cultural Studies* (pp. 101–117). London: Routledge.

Belanger, A. (2000) Sport venues and the spectacularization of urban spaces in North America. *International Review for the Sociology of Sport* 35 (3), 378–397.

Bell, R. (2000) A modern perspective of the ancient Olympic events. *The Sport Journal* 3 (3), 1–2.

Bellan, G. L. and Bellan-Santini, D. R. (2001) A review of littoral tourism, sport and leisure activities: Consequences on marine flora and fauna. *Aquatic Conservation: Marine and Freshwater Ecosystems* 11 (4), 325–333.

Bentley, T. A., Page, S. J. and Laird, I. S. (2000) Safety in New Zealand's adventure tourism industry: The client accident experience of adventure tourism operators. *Journal of Travel Medicine* 7 (5), 239–245.

Beresford, S. (1999) The sport–tourism link in the Yorkshire region. In M. Scarrott (ed.) *Exploring Sports Tourism: Proceedings of a SPRIG Seminar Held at the University of Sheffield on 15 April 1999* (pp. 29–37). Sheffield: Sheffield Hallam University.

Bernstein, A. (2000) Things you can see from there you can't see from here: Globalization, media, and the Olympics. *Journal of Sport and Social Issues* 24 (4), 351–369.

Binns, T. (1995) Geography in development: Development in geography. *Geography* 80, 303–322.

Bloch, C. and Laursen, P. F. (1996) Play, sports and environment. *International Review for the Sociology of Sport* 31 (2), 205–217.

Boniface, B. G. and Cooper, C. (1994) *The Geography of Travel and Tourism* (2nd edn). Oxford: Butterworth-Heinemann.

Boorstin, D. J. (1975) *The Image: A Guide to Pseudo-events in America.* New York: Atheum.

Booth, D. (1993) Sydney 2000: The games people play. *Current Affairs Bulletin* (December/January), 4–11.

Booth, D. (1997) Sports history: What can be done? *Sport, Education and Society* 2 (2), 191–204.

Booth, D. (1999) Gifts of corruption? Ambiguities of obligation in the Olympic movement. *Olympika* 8, 43–68.

Booth, D. (2000) Modern sport: Emergence and experiences. In C. Collins (ed.) *Sport in New Zealand Society* (pp. 45–63). Palmerston North, New Zealand: Dunmore Press.

Booth, D. and Loy, J. W. (1999) Sport, status, and style. *Sport History Review* 30, 1–26.

Borish, L. J. and Rischler, B. L. (2001) Labour, leisure and sport in cultural perspective. *Rethinking History* 5 (1), 1–9.

Bourdeau, P., Corneloup, J. and Mao, P. (2002) Adventure sports and tourism in the French mountains: Dynamics of change and challenges for sustainable development. *Current Issues in Tourism* 5 (1), 22–32.

Boyle, R. and Haynes, R. (1996) 'The grand old game': Football, media and identity in Scotland. *Media, Culture and Society* 18 (4), 549–564.

Bramwell, B. (1999) Sport, tourism and city development. *International Journal of Tourism Research* 1 (6), 459–460.

Brayley, R. E. (1999) Using technology to enhance the recreation education classroom. *Journal of Physical Education, Recreation and Dance* 70 (9), 23–25.

British Tourist Authority (BTA) (2000) *Sporting Britain: Play it, Love it, Watch it, Live it, Visit.* London: Haymarket Magazines Ltd.

Brown, C. and Paul, D. M. (1999) Local organized interests and the 1996 Cincinnati sports stadia tax referendum. *Journal of Sport and Social Issues* 23 (2), 218–237.

Brown, G. (2000) Emerging issues in Olympic sponsorship: Implications for host cities. *Sport Management Review* 3 (1), 71–92.

Brown, G. (2001) Sydney 2000: An invitation to the world. *Olympic Review* 27 (37), 15–20.

Brown, G., Chalip, L., Jago, L. and Mules, T. (2002) The Sydney Olympics and Brand Australia. In N. Morgan, A. Pritchard and R. Pride (eds) *Destination Branding: Creating the Unique Destination Proposition* (pp. 163–185). Oxford: Butterworth-Heinemann.

Bull, C. and Weed, M. (1999) Niche markets and small island tourism: The development of sports tourism in Malta. *Managing Leisure* 4 (3), 142–155.

Burgan, B. and Mules, T. (1992) Economic impact of sporting events. *Annals of Tourism Research* 19 (4), 700–710.

Burnstyn, V. (1999) *The Rites of Men: Manhood, Politics, and the Culture of Sport.* Toronto: University of Toronto Press.

Burton, R. (1995) *Travel Geography* (2nd edn). London: Pitman Publishing.

Butler, R. W. (1980) The concept of the tourist area lifecycle of evolution: Implications for the management of resources. *Canadian Geographer* 24 (1), 5–12.

Butler, R. W. (1993) Tourism: An evolutionary perspective. In J. G. Nelson, R. W. Butler and G. Wall (eds) *Tourism and Sustainable Development: Monitoring, Planning, Managing* (pp. 27–43). Department of Geography Publication Series 37. Waterloo, Ont.: University of Waterloo

Butler, R. W. (1994) Seasonality in tourism: Issues and problems. In A. V. Seaton (ed.) *Tourism: The State of the Art* (pp. 332–339). Chichester: John Wiley and Sons.

Butler, R. W. (1996) The role of tourism in cultural transformation in developing countries. In W. Nuryanti (ed.) *Tourism and Culture: Global Civilization in Change* (pp. 91–101). Yogyakarta: Gadjah Mada University Press.

Butler, R. W. (2001) Seasonality in tourism: Issues and implications. In T. Baum and S. Lundtorp (eds) *Seasonality in Tourism* (pp. 5–23). London: Pergamon.

Butler, R. W. (forthcoming a) *The Tourist Area Life Cycle: Conceptual and Theoretical Issues.* Toronto: Channel View Publications.

Butler, R. W. (forthcoming b) *The Tourist Area Life Cycle: Applications and Modifications*. Toronto: Channel View Publications.

Butler, R. W. and Boyd, S. W. (eds) (2000) *Tourism and National Parks: Issues and Implications*. Chichester: John Wiley and Sons Ltd.

Butler, R. W. and Mao, B. (1996) Seasonality in tourism: Problems and measurement. In P. E. Murphy (ed.) *Quality Management in Urban Tourism* (pp. 9–23). Chichester: John Wiley and Sons.

Camy, J., Adamkiewics, E. and Chantelat, P. (1993) Sporting uses of the city: Urban anthropology applied to the sports practices in the agglomeration of Lyon. *International Review for the Sociology of Sport* 29 (2/3), 175–185.

Canadian Sport Tourism Alliance (2002) On WWW at http://www.canadian sporttourism.com/home.htm. Accessed December 2002.

Canadian Tourism Commission (CTC) (2002) Sport tourism impact. *Tourism: Canada's Tourism Monthly*, 6 (6) (July–August), 6.

Canadian Tourism Commission (CTC) and Coopers and Lybrand (1996) *Domestic Tourism Market Research Study*. Ottawa: Canadian Tourism Commission.

Cantelon, H. and Gruneau, R. S. (1988) The production of sport for television. In J. Harvey and H. Cantelon (eds) *Not Just a Game: Essays in Canadian Sport Sociology* (pp. 177–194). Canada: University of Ottawa Press.

Cantelon, H. and Letters, M. (2000) The making of the IOC environmental policy as the third dimension of the Olympic movement. *International Review for the Sociology of Sport* 35 (3), 294–308.

Carmichael, B. and Murphy, P. E. (1996) Tourism economic impact of a rotating sports event: The case of the British Columbia Games. *Festival Management and Event Tourism* 4, 127–138.

Carus, L. (1998) For the strategic analysis and forecasting stage within the strategic tourism management process. *Journal of Sport Tourism* 4 (4), 23–35.

Cashmore, E. (1996) *Making Sense of Sports* (2nd edn). London: Routledge.

Castells, M. (1997) *The Rise of the Network Society*. Oxford: Blackwell.

Chadwick, G. (1971) *A Systems View of Planning*. Oxford: Pergamon Press.

Chalip, L. (1992) The construction and use of polysemic structures: Olympic lessons for sport marketers. *Journal of Sport Management* 6, 87–98.

Chalip, L. (2001) Sport and tourism: Conceptualising the linkage. In D. Kluka and G. Shilling (eds) *The Business of Sport* (pp. 78–89). Oxford: Meyer and Meyer.

Chalip, L. (2004) Beyond impact: A general model for host community event leverage. In B. Ritchie and D. Adair (eds) *Sport Tourism: Interrelationships, Impacts and Issues*. Clevedon: Channel View Publications.

Chalip, L., Green, C. and Vander Velden, L. (1998) Sources of interest in travel to the Olympic Games. *Journal of Vacation Marketing* 4 (1), 7–22.

Chang, P. C. and Singh, K. K. (1990) Risk management for mega-events: The 1988 Olympic Winter Games. *Tourism Management* 11 (1), 45–52.

Chelladurai, P. and Chang, K. (2000) Targets and standards of quality in sport services. *Sport Management Review* 3 (1), 1–22.

Chen, K. C., Groves, D. and Lengfelder, J. (1999) A system model of sport tourism with implications for research. *Visions in Leisure and Business* 18 (1), 34–44.

Chernushenko, D. (1996) Sports tourism goes sustainable: The Lillehammer experience. *Visions in Leisure and Business* 15 (1), 65–73.

Chogahara, M. and Yamaguchi, Y. (1998) Resocialization and continuity of involvement in physical activity among elderly Japanese. *International Review for the Sociology of Sport* 33 (3), 277–289.

Christaller, W. (1955) Contributions to the geography of the travel trade. *Erkunde Bandix* (February), Heft 1 (Regional Science Series).

Christaller, W. (1963/1964) Some considerations of tourism location in Europe: The peripheral regions, underdeveloped countries, recreation areas. *Papers, Regional Science Association* 12: 95–105.

Clawson, M. and Knetsch, J. (1966) *The Economics of Outdoor Recreation*. Baltimore: Johns Hopkins Press.

Clay, J. (2001) Sense of place gives Derby unique allure. *Lexington Herald*, 29 April 2001, C1.

Coakley, J. L. (1990) *Sport in Society: Issues and Controversies* (4th edn). St Louis, MO: Times Mirror/Mosby College Publishing.

Coalter, F. (1999) Sport and recreation in the United Kingdom: Flow with the flow or buck with the trends? *Managing Leisure* 4 (1), 24–39.

Cohen, E. (1979) A phenomenology of tourist experiences. *Sociology* 13, 179–201.

Cohen, E. (1988) Authenticity and the commoditization of tourism. *Annals of Tourism Research* 15, 371–386.

Cohen, E. (1996) A phenomenology of tourist experiences. In Y. Apostolopoulos, S. Leivadi and A. Yiannakis (eds) *The Sociology of Tourism* (pp. 90–111). London: Routledge.

Cole, C. L. (2001) Nike goes to Broadway. *Journal of Sport and Social Issues* 25 (2), 115–117.

Collier, A. (1999) *Principles of Tourism: A New Zealand Perspective* (5th edn). Auckland: Longman.

Collins, M. F. (1991) The economics of sport and sports in the economy: Some international comparisons. In C. P. Cooper (ed.) *Progress in Tourism, Recreation and Hospitality Management* (pp. 184–214). London: Belhaven Press.

Collins, M. F. and Jackson, G. (1999) The economics of sport tourism. In J. Standeven and P. De Knop (eds) *Sport Tourism* (pp. 170–201). Champaign, IL: Human Kinetics.

Collins, M. F. and Jackson, G. (2001) Evidence for a sports tourism continuum. Paper presented at the Journeys in Leisure: Current and Future Alliances Conference, Luton, England, 17–19 July.

Commons, J. and Page, S. (2001) Managing seasonality in peripheral tourism regions: The case of Northland, New Zealand. In T. Baum and S. Lundtorp (eds) *Seasonality in Tourism* (pp. 153–172). London: Pergamon.

Commonwealth Department of Industry, Science and Resources (2000) *Towards a National Sport Tourism Strategy*. Draft report. Canberra: Commonwealth Department of Industry, Science and Resources.

Cooper, C., Fletcher, J., Gilbert, D. and Wanhill, S. (1993) *Tourism: Principles and Practice*. Harlow: Longman Group Limited.

Cottle, R. L. (1981) Economics of the Professional Golfers' Association Tour. *Social Science Quarterly* 62 (4), 721–734.

Cowell, R. (1997) Stretching the limits: Environmental compensation, habitat creation and sustainable development. *Transactions of the Institute of British Geographers* 22 (3), 292–306.

Crawford, D. W., Jackson, E. L. and Godbey, G. (1991) A hierarchical model of leisure constraints. *Leisure Sciences* 13, 309–320.

Crawford, S. A. G. (1995) Rugby and the forging of national identity. In J. Nauright (ed.) *Sport, Power and Society in New Zealand: Historical and Contemporary Perspectives* (pp. 5–19). Sydney: University of New South Wales Printery.

Crompton, J. L. (1995) Economic impact analysis of sports facilities and events: Eleven sources of misapplication. *Journal of Sport Management* 9, 14–35.

Crouch, D. (2000) Places around us: Embodied lay geographies in leisure and tourism. *Leisure Studies* 19 (2), 63–76.

Cuthbertson, B., Heine, M. and Whitson, D. (1997) Producing meaning through movement: An alternative view of sense of place. *Trumpeter* 14 (2), 72–75.

Dann, G. M. S. (1981) Tourist motivation: An appraisal. *Annals of Tourism Research* 8 (2), 187.

Dauncey, H. and Hare, G. (2000) World Cup France '98: Metaphors, meanings and values. *International Review for the Sociology of Sport* 35 (3), 331–347.

Dear, M. and Flusty, S. (1999) The postmodern urban condition. In M. Featherstone and S. Lash (eds) *Spaces of Culture: City–Nation–World* (pp. 64–85). London: Sage.

De Knop, P. (1998) Sport tourism: A state of the art. *European Journal for Sport Management* 5 (2), 5–20.

Delpy, L. (1997) An overview of sport tourism: Building towards a dimensional framework. *Journal of Vacation Marketing* 4 (1), 23–38.

Delpy, L. (1998) Editorial. *Journal of Vacation Marketing* 4 (1), 4–5.

Delpy, L. (2001) Preparing for the rise in sports tourism. Paper presented at the World Conference on Sport and Tourism, Barcelona, Spain, 22–23 February.

Delpy Neirotti, L., Bosetti, H. A. and Teed, K. C. (2001) Motivation to attend the 1996 Summer Olympic Games. *Journal of Travel Research* 39 (3), 327–331.

De Melo, V. and Mangan, J. A. (1997) A web of the wealthy: Modern sport in the nineteenth-century culture of Rio de Janeiro. *The International Journal of the History of Sport* 14 (1), 168–173.

de Villiers, D. J. (2001) Sport and tourism to stimulate development. *Olympic Review* 27 (38), 11–13.

Dietvorst, A. G. J. (1995) Tourist behaviour and the importance of time–space analysis. In G. J. Ashworth and A. G. J. Dietvorst (eds) *Tourism and Spatial Transformations: Implications for Policy and Planning* (pp. 163–182). Wallingford: CAB International.

Dietvorst, A. G. J. and Ashworth, G. J. (1995) Tourism transformations: An introduction. In G. J. Ashworth and A. G. J. Dietvorst (eds) *Tourism and Spatial Transformations: Implications for Policy and Planning* (pp. 1–13). Wallingford: CAB International.

Donnelly, P. and Young, K. M. (1985) Reproductions and transformation of cultural forms in sport: A contextual analysis of rugby. *International Journal of the History of Sport* 20, 19–37.

Donnelly, P. and Young, K. M. (1988) The construction and confirmation of identity in sport subcultures. *Sociology of Sport Journal* 5, 223–240.

Doxey, G. (1975) Visitor–resident interaction in tourist destinations: Inferences from empirical research in Barbados, West Indies and Niagara-on-the-Lake, Ontario. Paper presented at the Symposium on the Planning and Development of the Tourist Industry in the ECC Region, Dubrovnik, Yugoslavia, 8–11 September.

Duncan, M. and Brummett, B. (1989) Types and sources of spectating pleasure in televised sports. *Sociology of Sport Journal* 6 (3), 195–211.

Dunning, E. (1994) Sport in space and time: 'Civilizing processes', trajectories of state-formation and the development of modern sport. *International Review for the Sociology of Sport* 29 (4), 331–348.

Dunning, E. (1999) *Sport Matters: Sociological Studies of Sport, Violence and Civilisation*. London: Routledge.

Dunn Ross, E. L. and Iso-Ahola, S. E. (1991) Sightseeing tourists' motivation and satisfaction. *Annals of Tourism Research* 18, 226–237.

Dutch Ministry of Economic Affairs (1991) *Improving Seasonal Spread of Tourism*. Rotterdam: Markant-Adviesbureau, Dutch Ministry of Economic Affairs.

Eastman, S. T. and Riggs, K. E. (1994) Televised sports and ritual: Fan experiences. *Sociology of Sport Journal* 11 (3), 249–274.

Echtner, C. M. and Ritchie, J. B. R. (1993) The measurement of destination image: An empirical assessment. *Journal of Travel Research* (Spring), 3–13.

Edgell, D. L. (1990) *International Tourism Policy*. New York: Van Nostrand Reinhold.

Emery, P. R. (1998) Bidding to host a major sports event: Strategic investment or complete lottery. Paper presented at the Sport in the City Conference, Sheffield, 2–4 July.

Ernst and Young (1996) Economic impact analysis, America's Cup Auckland 2000. Unpublished report prepared for the Auckland Regional Services Trust. Auckland: Ernst and Young.

Ewert, A. and Shultis, J. (1999) Technology and backcountry recreation: Boon to recreation or bust for management. *Journal of Physical Education, Recreation and Dance* 70 (8), 22–31.

Faulkner, B., Tideswell, C. and Weston, A. M. (1998) Leveraging tourism benefits from the Sydney 2000 Olympics. Paper presented at the Sport Management Association of Australia and New Zealand, Gold Coast, Australia, 26–28 November.

Fejgin, N. (1994) Participation in high school competitive sports: A subversion of school mission or contribution to academic goals? *Sociology of Sport Journal* 11 (3), 211–230.

Firat, A. (1995) Consumer culture or culture consumed. In J. Costa and G. Bamossy (eds) *Marketing in a Multicultural World*. London/Thousand Oaks, CA: Sage.

Flagestad, A. and Hope, C. A. (2001) Strategic success in winter sports destinations: A sustainable value creation perspective. *Tourism Management* 22 (5), 445–461.

Fougere, G. (1989) Sport, culture and identity: The case of rugby football. In D. Novitz and B. Willmott (eds) *Cultural Identity in New Zealand* (pp. 110–122). Wellington, NZ: GP Books.

Frechtling, D. C. (1996) *Practical Tourism Forecasting*. Oxford: Butterworth-Heinemann.

Freidmann, J. (1986) The world city hypothesis. *Development and Change* 17, 69–84.

Gallarza, M. G., Saura, I. and Garcia, H. (2002) Destination image: Towards a conceptual framework. *Annals of Tourism Research* 29 (1), 56–78.

Gammon, S. (2002) Fantasy, nostalgia and the pursuit of what never was. In S. Gammon and J. Kurtzman (eds) *Sport Tourism: Principles and Practice* (pp. 61–72). Eastbourne: Leisure Studies Association.

Gammon, S. and Kurtzman, J. (eds) (2002) *Sport Tourism: Principles and Practice*. Eastbourne: Leisure Studies Association.

Gammon, S. and Robinson, T. (1997) Sport and tourism: A conceptual framework. *Journal of Sport Tourism* 4 (3), 8–24.

Gammon, S. and Robinson, T. (1999) The development and design of the sport tourism curricula with particular references to the BA (Hons) Sport Tourism degree at the University of Luton. *Journal of Sport Tourism* 5 (2), 17–26.

Gantz, W. and Wenner, L. A. (1995) Fanship and the television sports viewing experience. *Sociology of Sport Journal* 12 (1), 56–74.

Garmise, M. (1987) *Proceedings of the International Seminar and Workshop on Outdoor Education, Recreation and Sport Tourism.* Israel: Emmanuel Gill Publishing.

Getz, D. (1991) *Festivals, Special Events and Tourism.* New York: Van Nostrand Reinhold.

Getz, D. (1997) *Event Management and Event Tourism.* New York: Cognizant Communications Corporation.

Getz, D. (1998) Trends, strategies, and issues in sport-event tourism. *Sport Marketing Quarterly* 7 (2), 8–13.

Getz, D. and Cheyne, J. (1997) Special event motivations and behaviour. In C. Ryan (ed.) *The Tourist Experience: A New Introduction* (pp. 136–154). London: Cassell.

Gibson, H. J. (1998a) Sport tourism: A critical analysis of research. *Sport Management Review* 1 (1), 45–76.

Gibson, H. J. (1998b) Active sport tourism: Who participates? *Leisure Studies* 17, 155–170.

Gibson, H. J. (1998c) The wide world of sport tourism. *Parks and Recreation* 33 (9), 108–114.

Gibson, H. J. (2002) Sport tourism at a crossroad? Considerations for the future. In S. Gammon and J. Kurtzman (eds) *Sport Tourism: Principles and Practice* (Vol. 76, pp. 111–128). Eastbourne: Leisure Studies Association.

Gibson, H. J., Attle, S. and Yiannakis, A. (1998) Segmenting the sport tourist market: A lifespan perspective. *Journal of Vacation Marketing* 4, 52–64.

Gibson, H. J., Willming, C. and Holdnak, A. (2002) Small-scale event sport tourism: College sport as a tourist attraction. In S. Gammon and J. Kurtzman (eds) *Sport Tourism: Principles and Practice* (pp. 3–18). Eastbourne: Leisure Studies Association.

Gibson, H. J., Willming, C. and Holdnak, A. (2003) Small-scale event sport tourism: Fans as tourists. *Tourism Management* 24 (2), 181–190.

Gibson, H. J. and Yiannakis, A. (1992) Some characteristics of sport tourists: A life span perspective. Paper presented at the Annual Conference for the North American Society for the Sociology of Sport, Savannah, Georgia, 12 November.

Giulianotti, R. (1991) Scotland's Tartan Army in Italy: The case for the carnivalesques. *Sociological Review* 39 (3), 503–527.

Giulianotti, R. (1995a) Football and the politics of carnival: An ethnographic study of Scottish fans in Sweden. *International Review for the Sociology of Sport* 30 (2), 191–223.

Giulianotti, R. (1995b) Participant observation and research into football hooliganism: Reflections on the problems of entrée and everyday risks. *Sociology of Sport Journal* 12 (1), 1–20.

Giulianotti, R. (1996) Back to the future: An ethnography of Ireland's football fans at the 1994 World Cup finals in the USA. *International Review for the Sociology of Sport* 31 (3), 323–347.

Glyptis, S. A. (1982) *Sport and Tourism in Western Europe.* London: British Travel Education Trust.

Glyptis, S. A. (1989) Leisure and patterns of time use. Paper presented at the Leisure Studies Association Annual Conference, Bournemouth, England, 24–26 April. Eastbourne: Leisure Studies Association.

Glyptis, S. A. (1991) Sport and tourism. In C. P. Cooper (ed.) *Progress in Tourism, Recreation and Hospitality Management* (pp. 165–187). London: Belhaven Press.

Godbey, G. and Graefe, A. (1991) Repeat tourism, play and monetary spending. *Annals of Tourism Research* 18 (2), 213–225.

Goldman, R. and Papson, S. (1998) *Nike Culture: The Sign of the Swoosh*. London: Sage Publications.

Goulding, C. (1999) Heritage, nostalgia, and the 'grey' consumer. *Journal of Marketing Practice: Applied Marketing Science* 5 (6), 177–199.

Grabowski, P. (1999) Tourism and sport: Parallel tracks for developing tourism in Brunei? *Tourism Recreation Research* 24 (2), 95–98.

Graburn, N. H. H. (1989) Tourism: The sacred journey. In V. L. Smith (ed.) *Hosts and Guests: The Anthropology of Tourism* (2nd edn) (pp. 21–36). Philadelphia: University of Pennsylvania Press.

Graefe, A. R., Vaske, J. J. and Kuss, F. R. (1984) Social carrying capacity: An integration and synthesis of twenty years of research. *Leisure Sciences* 6 (4), 395–431.

Grainger, A. and Jackson, S. (1999) Resiting the swoosh in the Land of the Long White Cloud. *Peace Review* 11 (4), 511–516.

Grainger, A. and Jackson, S. (2000) Sports marketing and the challenges of globalization: A case study of cultural resistance in New Zealand. *International Journal of Sports Marketing and Sponsorship* 2 (2), 35–49.

Gratton, C., Dobson, N. and Shibli, S. (2000) The economic importance of major sports events: A case-study of six events. *Managing Leisure* 5 (1), 17–28.

Gratton, C. and Taylor, P. (2000) *Economics of Sport and Recreation*. London: Spon.

Green, B. C. (2001) Leveraging subculture and identity to promote sport events. *Sport Management Review* 4 (1), 1–19.

Green, B. C. and Chalip, L. (1998) Sport tourism as the celebration of subculture. *Annals of Tourism Research* 25 (2), 275–291.

Greenwood, D. J. (1989) Culture by the pound: An anthropological perspective on tourism as cultural commodification. In V. L. Smith (ed.) *Hosts and Guests: The Anthropology of Tourism* (pp. 17–31). Philadelphia: University of Pennsylvania Press.

Groff, D., Funderburk, J., McComb, A. and Connolly, S. (2000) Ninety minutes into the game. *Parks and Recreation* 35 (8), 70–78.

Gunn, C. (1988) *Vacationscape: Designing Tourist Regions* (2nd edn). New York: Van Nostrand Reinhold.

Guttmann, A. (1992) *The Olympics: A History of the Modern Games*. Urbana, IL: University of Illinois Press.

Halberstam, D. (1999) *Playing for Keeps: Michael Jordan and the World He Made*. New York: Random House.

Hall, C. M. (1992a) *Hallmark Tourist Events: Impacts, Management and Planning*. London: Belhaven Press.

Hall, C. M. (1992b) Review: Adventure, sport and health tourism. In B. Weiler and C. M. Hall (eds) *Special Interest Tourism* (pp. 186–210). London: Belhaven Press.

Hall, C. M. (1993) The politics of leisure: An analysis of spectacles and mega-events. In A. J. Veal, P. Johnson and G. Cushman (eds) *Leisure and Tourism: Social and Environmental Change* (pp. 620–629). Sydney: Centre for Leisure, Sport and Tourism and World Leisure and Recreation Association.

Hall, C. M. (1995) *Introduction to Tourism in Australia: Impacts, Planning and Development* (2nd edn). South Melbourne: Addison Wesley Longman Australia.

Hall, C. M. (1998) Imaging, tourism and sports event fever: The Sydney Olympics and the need for a social charter for mega-events. In C. Gratton and I. P. Henry (eds) *Sport in the City: The Role of Sport in Economic and Social Regeneration* (pp. 166–183). London: Routledge.

Hall, C. M. (2000a) *Tourism Planning: Policies, Processes and Relationships*. Harlow: Prentice Hall.

Hall, C. M. (2000b) The future of tourism: A personal speculation. *Tourism Recreation Research* 25 (1), 85–95.

Hall, C. M. (2004) Sport tourism and urban regeneration. In B. Ritchie and D. Adair (eds) *Sport Tourism: Interrelationships, Impacts and Issues*. Clevedon: Channel View Publications.

Hall, C. M., Jenkins, J. and Kearsley, G. W. (eds) (1997) *Tourism Planning and Policy in Australia and New Zealand*. Sydney: Irwin Publishers.

Hall, C. M. and Lew, A. A. (eds) (1998) *Sustainable Tourism: A Geographical Perspective*. Harlow: Addison Wesley Longman Ltd.

Hall, C. M. and Page, S. J. (1999) *Geography of Tourism and Recreation: Environment, Place, and Space*. London: Routledge.

Hall, C. M. and Weiler, B. (eds) (1992) *Special Interest Tourism*. London: Belhaven Press.

Hammitt, W. E. (1980) Outdoor recreation: Is it a multi-phase experience? *Journal of Leisure Research* 12 (2), 107–115.

Harahousou, Y. (1999) Elderly people, leisure and physical recreation in Greece. *World Leisure and Recreation* 41 (3), 20–24.

Hargreaves, J. (1990a) Changing images of the sporting female: Before the First World War. *Sport and Leisure* (July/August), 14–15.

Hargreaves, J. (1990b) Changing images of the sporting female: The inter-war years. *Sport and Leisure* (September/October), 32–34.

Hargreaves, J. (1990c) Changing images of the sporting female: After the Second World War. *Sport and Leisure* (November/December), 39–40.

Harrison, S. J., Winterbottom, W. J. and Shepard, C. (1999) The potential effects of climate change on the Scottish tourism industry. *Tourism Management* 20 (2), 25–33.

Hartmann, R. (1986) Tourism, seasonality and social change. *Leisure Studies,* 5 (1), 25–33.

Harvey, D. (1989) *The Condition of Postmodernity*. Oxford: Blackwell Publishers Inc.

Harvey, J. and Houle, F. (1994) Sport, world economy, global culture, and new social movements. *Sociology of Sport Journal* 11 (4), 337–355.

Harvey, J., Rail, G. and Thibault, I. (1996) Globalization and sport: Sketching a theoretical model for empirical analyses. *Journal of Sport and Social Issues* 23 (3), 258–277.

Hawkins, P. (1999) Sports tourism in the Peak National Park. In M. Scarrott (ed.) *Exploring Sports Tourism: Proceedings of a SPRIG Seminar held at the University of Sheffield on 15 April 1999* (pp. 38–45). Sheffield: Sheffield Hallam University.

Heino, R. (2000) What is so punk about snowboarding? *Journal of Sport and Social Issues* 24 (1), 176–191.

Heitzman, J. (1999) Sports and conflict in urban planning: The Indian National Games in Bangalore. *Journal of Sport and Social Issues* 23 (1), 5–23.

Higham, J. E. S. (1996) The Bledisloe Cup: Quantifying the direct economic benefits of event tourism, with ramifications for a city in economic transition. _Festival Management and Event Tourism_ 4, 107–116.

Higham, J. E. S. (1999) Sport as an avenue of tourism development: An analysis of the positive and negative impacts of sport tourism. _Current Issues in Tourism_ 2 (1), 82–90.

Higham, J. E. S. and Hinch, T. D. (1998) The transition to professional Rugby Union in New Zealand: An analysis of the temporal dimensions of tourism within the Otago Highlanders franchise. Paper presented at the Proceedings of the New Zealand Tourism and Hospitality Research Conference (Part I), Akaroa, New Zealand. 1–4 December.

Higham, J. E. S. and Hinch, T. D. (2000) Sport tourism and the transition to professional rugby union in New Zealand: The spatial dimension of tourism associated with the Otago Highlanders, southern New Zealand. In P. L. M. Robinson, N. Evans, R. Sharpley and J. Swarbrooke (eds) _Reflections on International Tourism: Motivations, Behaviour and Tourist Types_ (Vol. 4, pp. 145–158). Sunderland: Business Education Publishers Ltd.

Higham, J. E. S. and Hinch, T. D. (2002a) Sport, tourism and seasons: The challenges and potential of overcoming seasonality in the sport and tourism sectors. _Tourism Management_ 23, 175–185.

Higham, J. E. S. and Hinch, T. D. (2002b) Sport and tourism development: Avenues of tourism development associated with a regional sport franchise at an urban tourism destination. In S. Gammon and J. Kurtzman (eds) _Sport Tourism: Principles and Practice_ (pp. 19–34). Eastbourne: Leisure Studies Association.

Higham, J. E. S. and Hinch, T. D. (2003) Sport, space and time: Effects of the Otago Highlanders franchise on tourism. _Journal of Sports Management_ 17 (3), 235–257.

Hill, C. R. (1992) _Olympic Politics_. Manchester: Manchester University Press.

Hill, J. and McLean, D. C. (1999) Introduction: Possible, probable, or preferable future? _Journal of Physical Education, Recreation and Dance_ 70 (9), 15–17.

Hiller, H. H. (1998) Assessing the impacts of mega-events: A linkage model. _Current Issues in Tourism_ 1 (1), 47–57.

Hinch, T. D and Hickey, G. (1996) Tourism attractions and seasonality: Spatial relationships in Alberta. In K. MacKay and K. R. Boyd (eds) _Tourism for All Seasons: Using Research to Meet the Challenge of Seasonality (Conference Proceedings of the Travel and Tourism Research Association, Canada Chapter)_ (pp. 69–76). Ottawa: Travel and Tourism Research Association.

Hinch, T. D., Hickey, G. and Jackson, E. L. (2001) Seasonal visitation at Fort Edmonton Park: An empirical analysis using a leisure constraints framework. In T. Baum and S. Lundtorp (eds) _Seasonality in Tourism_ (pp. 173–186). London: Pergamon.

Hinch, T. D. and Higham, J. E. S. (2001) Sport tourism: A framework for research. _The International Journal of Tourism Research_ 3 (1), 45–58.

Hinch, T. D. and Jackson, E. L. (2000) Leisure constraints research: Its value as a framework for understanding tourism seasonality. _Current Issues in Tourism_ 3 (2), 87–106.

Hodges, J. and Hall, C. M. (1996) The housing and social impact of mega events: Lessons for the Sydney 2000 Olympics. Paper presented at the Towards a More Sustainable Tourism Conference, Dunedin, NZ, 3–6 December.

Hoffer, R. (1995) Down and out: On land, sea, air, facing questions about their sanity. _Sports Illustrated_ 83 (1), 42–49.

Holden, A. (2000) Winter tourism and the environment in conflict: The case of Cairngorm, Scotland. *International Journal of Tourism Research* 2 (4), 247–260.

Hooper, I. (1998) The value of sport in urban regeneration: A case study of Glasgow. Paper presented at the Sport in the City Conference, Sheffield, 2–4 July.

Hornby, N. (1996) *Fever Pitch*. London: Cassel Group.

Horne, J. (1996) 'Sakka' in Japan. *Media, Culture and Society* 18 (4), 527–547.

Horne, W. R. (2000) Municipal economic development via hallmark tourism events. *The Journal of Tourism Studies* 11 (1), 30–35.

Host Broadcaster Consultancy (1997) *Critical Path Analysis for the 1998 Commonwealth Games*. Kuala Lumpur: Lambang Negara Malaysia.

Hudson, S. (1999) *Snow Business: A Study of the International Ski Industry*. London: Cassell.

Hudson, S. (2002) The downhill skier in Banff National Park: An endangered species. In S. Gammon and J. Kurtzman (eds) *Sport Tourism: Principles and Practice* (pp. 89–110). Eastbourne: Leisure Studies Association.

Hudson, S. (ed.) (2003) *Sport and Adventure Tourism*. Binghampton, NY: The Haworth Press Inc.

Hudson, S. and Gilbert, D. (1998) Skiing constraints: Arresting the downhill slide. Paper presented at the Harnessing the High Latitudes Conference, University of Surrey, Guildford, 15–17 June.

Hughson, J. (1998a) Among the thugs. *International Review for the Sociology of Sport* 33 (1), 43–57.

Hughson, J. (1998b) Soccer support and social identity: Finding the 'third space'. *International Review for the Sociology of Sport* 33 (4), 403–409.

Hunter, C. (1995) Key concepts for tourism and the environment. In C. Hunter and H. Green (eds) *Tourism and the Environment: A Sustainable Relationship?* (pp. 52–92). London: Routledge.

Hunter, C. and Green, H. (eds) (1995) *Tourism and the Environment: A Sustainable Relationship?* London: Routledge.

Ingham, A. G., Howell, J. W. and Swetman, R. D. (1993) Evaluating sport 'hero/ines': Contents, forms, and social relations. *Quest* 45, 197–210.

Inskeep, E. (1991) *Tourism Planning: An Integrated and Sustainable Development Approach*. New York: Van Nostrand Reinhold.

International Olympic Committee and World Tourism Organization (IOC and WTO) (2001) *Conclusions of the World Conference on Sport and Tourism*. Barcelona: International Olympic Committee and World Tourism Organization/Lausanne: International Olympic Committee.

Irwin, R. and Sandler, M. (1998) An analysis of travel behaviour and event induced expenditures among American collegiate championship patron groups. *Journal of Vacation Marketing* 4 (1), 78–90.

Iso-Ahola, S. E. (1982) Towards a social psychological theory for tourism motivation: A rejoinder. *Annals of Tourism Research* 12, 256–262.

Iso-Ahola, S. E. and Allen, J. (1982) The dynamics of leisure motivation: The effects of outcome on leisure needs. *Research Quarterly for Exercise and Sport* 53 (2), 141–149.

Jackson, E. L. (1989) Environmental attitudes, values and recreation. In E. L. Jackson and T. L. Burton (eds) *Understanding Leisure and Recreation: Mapping the Past, Charting the Future* (pp. 357–384). State College, PA: Venture Publishing:

Jackson, E. L. (1999) Leisure and the Internet. *Journal of Physical Education, Recreation and Dance* 70 (9), 18–22.

Jackson, E. L., Crawford, D. W. and Godbey, G. (1993) Negotiation of leisure constraints. *Leisure Sciences* 15 (1), 1–11.

Jackson, G. and Reeves, M. (1997) Evidencing the sport tourism relationship. In M. F. Collins and I. S. Cooper (eds) *Leisure Management: Issues and Applications.* Wallingford: CABI.

Jackson, S. J. (1994) Gretzky, crisis, and Canadian identity in 1988: Rearticulating the Americanization of culture debate. *Sociology of Sport Journal* 11 (4), 428–450.

Jackson, S. J. (1997) Sport, violence and advertising: A case study of global/local disjuncture in New Zealand. Paper presented at the North American Society for the Sociology of Sport Conference, Toronto, 5–8 November.

Jackson, S. J. (1998) The 49th paradox: The 1988 Calgary Winter Olympic Games and Canadian identity as contested terrain. In M. Duncan, G. Chich and A. Aycock (eds) *Player Culture Studies: Exploration in the Field of Play* (pp. 191–208). Greenwich: Ablex Publishing.

Jackson, S. J. and Andrews, D. L. (1999) Between and beyond the global and local: American popular sporting culture in New Zealand. In A. Yiannakis and M. Melnik (eds) *Sport Sociology: Contemporary Themes* (5th edn) (pp. 467–474). Champaign, IL: Human Kinetics.

Jackson, S. J., Batty, R. and Scherer, J. (2001) Transnational sport marketing at the global/local nexus: The Adidasification of the New Zealand All Blacks. *International Journal of Sports Marketing and Sponsorship* 3 (2), 185–201.

Jackson, S. J. and McKenzie, A. D. (2000) Violence and sport in New Zealand. In C. Collins (ed.) *Sport in New Zealand Society* (pp. 153–170). Palmerston North, NZ: Dunmore Press.

Jamal, T. B. and Getz, D. (1994) Collaboration theory and community tourism planning. *Annals of Tourism Research* 22, 186–204.

Jefferson, A. (1986) Smoothing out the ups and downs in demand. *British Hotelier and Restaurateur* (July/August), 24–25.

Jeffrey, D. and Barden, R. D. (2001) An analysis of the nature, causes and marketing implications of seasonality in the occupancy performance of English hotels. In T. Baum and S. Lundtorp (eds) *Seasonality and Tourism* (pp. 119–140). London: Pergamon.

Jennings, A. (1996) *The New Lords of the Rings: Olympic Corruption and How to Buy Gold Medals.* London: Pocket Books.

Jhally, S. (1989) Cultural studies and the sports/media complex. In L. A. Wenner (ed.) *Media, Sports and Society* (pp. 70–93). California: Sage Publications.

Johnson, W. O. (1991) Sport in the year 2001: A fan's world. Watching sport in the 21st century. *Sports Illustrated* 75 (4), 40–48.

Johnston, C. S. (2001a) Shoring the foundations of the destination life cycle model, part 1: Ontological and epistemological considerations. *Tourism Geographies* 3 (1), 2–28.

Johnston, C. S. (2001b) Shoring the foundations of the destination life cycle model, part 2: A case study of Kona, Hawai'i Island. *Tourism Geographies* 3 (2), 135–164.

Jones, C. (2001) Mega-events and host-region impacts: Determining the true worth of the 1999 Rugby World Cup. *International Journal of Tourism Research* 3, 241–251.

Jones, I. (2000) A model of serious leisure identification: The case of football fandom. *Leisure Studies* 19 (4), 283–298.

Journal of Sport Management (2003) Special issues on sport tourism (H. Gibson guest editor). *Journal of Sport Management* 17 (2).

Journal of Vacation Marketing (1997) Special issue (L. Delphy guest editor). *Journal of Vacation Marketing* 4 (1).

Kang, Y. S. and Perdue, R. (1994) Long-term impacts of a mega-event on international tourism to the host country: A conceptual model and the case of the 1988 Seoul Olympics. *Journal of International Consumer Marketing* 6 (3/4), 205–226.

Kaspar, R. (1998) Sport, environment and culture. *Olympic Review* 20 (April/May), 1–5.

Keller, P. (2001) Sport and tourism: Introductory report. Paper presented at the World Conference on Sport and Tourism, Barcelona, 22–23 February.

Kennedy, E. and Deegan, J. (2001) Seasonality in Irish tourism, 1973–1995. In T. Baum and S. Lundtorp (eds) *Seasonality and Tourism* (pp. 119–140). London: Pergamon.

Kenyon, G. (1969) Sport involvement: A conceptual go and some consequences thereof. In G. Kenyon (ed.) *Aspects of Contemporary Sport Sociology* (pp. 77–100). Chicago: Athletic Institute.

Klemm, M. and Rawel, J. (2001) Extending the school holiday season: The case of Europcamp. In T. Baum and S. Lundtorp (eds) *Seasonality in Tourism* (pp. 141–152). London: Pergamon.

Klenosky, D., Gengler, C. and Mulvey, M. (1993) Understanding the factors influencing ski destination choice: A means–end analytic approach. *Journal of Leisure Research* 25, 362–379.

Kotler, P., Haider, D. H. and Rein, I. (1993) *Marketing Places: Attracting Investment, Industry, and Tourism to Cities, States and Nations*. New York: The Free Press.

Krawczyk, Z. (1996) Sport as symbol. *International Review for the Sociology of Sport* 31 (4), 429–438.

Kreutzwiser, R. (1989) Supply. In G. Wall (ed.) *Outdoor Recreation in Canada* (pp. 19–42). Toronto: John Wiley and Sons.

Krippendorf, J. (1986) *The Holidaymakers: Understanding the Impact of Leisure and Travel*. London: Heinemann.

Krippendorf, J. (1995) Towards new tourism policies. In S. Medlik (ed.) *Managing Tourism* (pp. 307–317). Oxford: Butterworth-Heinemann.

Kurtzman, J. (1997) The Peace Games for the new millenium. *Journal of Sport Tourism* 4 (3), 24–27.

Kurtzman, J. (2001) Sport! Tourism! Culture! *Olympic Review* 27 (38), 20–27.

Kurtzman, J. and Zauhar, J. (1995) Tourism Sport International Council. *Annals of Tourism Research* 22 (3), 707–708.

Kurtzman, J. and Zauhar, J. (1997a) Sports tourism consumer motivation. *Journal of Sport Tourism* 4 (3), 17–30.

Kurtzman, J. and Zauhar, J. (1997b) A wave in time: The sports tourism phenomenon. *Journal of Sport Tourism* 4 (2), 5–20.

Kurtzman, J. and Zauhar, J. (1998) Golf: A touristic venture. *Journal of Sport Tourism* 4 (4), 5–9.

Law, A. (2001) Surfing the safety net: 'Dole bludging', 'surfies' and governmentality in Australia. *International Review for the Sociology of Sport* 36 (1), 25–40.

Law, C. M. (2002) *Urban Tourism: The Visitor Economy and the Growth of Large Cities*. London: Continuum.

Laws, E. (1991) *Tourism Marketing: Service and Quality Management Perspectives*. Cheltenham: Stanley Thornes Publishers.

Lawson, R., Thyne, M. and Young, T. (1997) *New Zealand Holidays: A Travel Lifestyles Study*. Dunedin: The Marketing Department, University of Otago.

Lawson, R., Tidwell, P., Rainbird, S., Loudon, N. and Della Bitta, P. (1996) *Consumer Behaviour in Australia and New Zealand.* Sydney: McGraw-Hill Book Company.

Lealand, G. (1994) American popular culture and emerging nationalism in New Zealand. *The Phi Kappa Phi Journal* 74 (4), 34–37.

Leiper, N. (1981) Towards a cohesive curriculum for tourism: The case for a distinct discipline. *Annals of Tourism Research* 8 (1), 69–74.

Leiper, N. (1990) Tourist attraction systems. *Annals of Tourism Research* 17 (3), 367–384.

Leisure Time (2002) *Norway Cup.* Publication 44. Bekkelagshogda 1109 Oslo, Norway.

Lenskyj, H. J. (1998) Sport and corporate environmentalism: The case of the Sydney 2000 Olympic Games. *International Review for the Sociology of Sport* 33 (4), 341–354.

Leonard, W. M. (1996) The odds of transiting from one level of sports participation to another. *Sociology of Sport Journal* 13 (3), 288–299.

Lesjø, J. H. (2000) Lillehammer 1994: Planning, figurations and the 'green' Winter Games. *International Review for the Sociology of Sport* 35 (3), 282–293.

Lew, A. A. (1987) A framework of tourist attraction research. *Annals of Tourism Research* 14 (3), 553–575.

Lew, A. A. (2001) Tourism and geography space. *Tourism Geographies* 3 (1), 1.

Lewis, G. and Redmond, G. (1974) *Sporting Heritage: A Guide to Halls of Fame, Special Collections and Museums in the United States and Canada.* Cranbury, NJ: A. S. Barnes and Co. Inc.

Liverpool FC Supporters' Club Scandinavia (2002) *Liverpool.* On WWW at http://www.liverpool.no/. Accessed 25 September 2002.

Lockwood, A. and Guerrier, Y. (1990) Labour shortages in the international hotel industry. *Travel and Tourism Analyst* 6, 17–35.

Loverseed, H. (2000) Winter sports in North America. *Travel and Tourism Analyst* 6, 45–62.

Loverseed, H. (2001) Sports tourism in North America. *Travel and Tourism Analyst* 3, 25–41.

Loy, J. W., McPherson, B. D. and Kenyon, G. (1978) Sport as a social phenomenon. In J. W. Loy, B. D. McPherson and G. Kenyon (eds) *Sport and Social Systems: A Guide to the Analysis of Problems and Literature* (pp. 3–26). Reading, MA: Addison Wesley.

MacCannell, D. (1973) Staged authenticity: Arrangements of social space in tourist settings. *American Journal of Sociology* 79 (3), 589–603.

MacCannell, D. (1976) *The Tourists: New Theory of the Leisure Class.* New York: Schoken.

Magdalinski, T. (2000) The reinvention of Australia for the Sydney 2000 Olympic Games. *International Journal of the History of Sport* 17 (2/3), 304–322.

Maguire, J. (1994) Sport, identity politics, and globalization: Diminishing contrasts and increasing varieties. *Sociology of Sport Journal* 11 (4), 398–427.

Maguire, J. (1999) *Global Sport: Identities, Societies and Civilisations.* Cambridge: Polity Press.

Maguire, J. and Stead, D. (1996) Far pavilions? Cricket migrants, foreign sojourns and contested identities. *International Review for the Sociology of Sport* 31 (1), 1–24.

Maguire, J. and Stead, D. (1998) Border crossings: Soccer labour migration and the European Union. *International Review for the Sociology of Sport* 33 (1), 59–73.

Maier, J. and Weber, W. (1993) Sport tourism in local and regional planning. *Tourism Recreation Research* 18 (2), 33–43.

Manfredo, M. J. and Driver, B. L. (1983) A test of concepts inherent in experience-based setting management for outdoor recreation areas. *Journal of Leisure Research* 15 (3), 263–283.

Mason, P. and Leberman, S. (2000) Local planning for recreation and tourism: A case study of mountain biking from New Zealand's Manawatu region. *Journal of Sustainable Tourism* 8 (2), 97–115.

Matheusik, M. (2001) When in doubt, shop. *Ski Area Management* 40 (1), 66–67, 83.

Mathieson, D. and Wall, G. (1987) *Tourism: Economic, Physical and Social Impacts*. London: Longman.

Matsumura, K. (1993) Sport and social change in the Japanese rural community. *International Review for the Sociology of Sport* 28 (2/3), 135–144.

May, V. (1995) Environmental implications of the 1992 Winter Olympic Games. *Tourism Management* 16 (4), 269–275.

McConnell, R. and Edwards, M. (2000) Sport and identity in New Zealand. In C. Collins (ed.) *Sport and Society in New Zealand* (pp. 115–129). Palmerston North, NZ: Dunmore Press.

McEnnif, J. (1992) Seasonality of tourism demand in the European community. *Travel and Tourism Analyst* 3, 67–88.

McGuire, F. A. (1984) A factor analytic study of leisure constraints in advanced adulthood. *Leisure Sciences* 6, 313–326.

McGuirk, P. M. and Rowe, D. (2001) 'Defining moments' and refining myths in the making of place identity: The Newcastle Knights and the Australian Rugby League Grand Final. *Australian Geographical Studies* 39 (1), 52–66.

McIntosh, A. J. and Prentice, R. C. (1999) Affirming authenticity: Consuming cultural heritage. *Annals of Tourism Research* 26, 589–612.

McKay, J. and Kirk, D. (1992) Ronald McDonald meets Baron De Coubertin: Prime time sport and commodification. *Sport and the Media* (Winter), 10–13.

McKay, M. and Plumb, C. (2001) *Reaching Beyond the Gold: The Impact of the Olympic Games on Real Estate Markets (1)*. Chicago: Jones Lang LaSalle.

McKercher, B. (1993) Some fundamental truths about tourism: Understanding tourism's social and environmental impacts. *Journal of Sustainable Tourism* 1 (1), 6–16.

McMurran, A. (1999) More than 7000 expected for 2000 Games. *Otago Daily Times*, 22 January, 18.

McPherson, B. D., Curtis, J. E. and Loy, J. W. (1989) *The Social Significance of Sport: An Introduction to the Sociology of Sport*. Champaign, IL: Human Kinetics Books.

Meinig, D. (1979) The beholding eye. In D. Meinig (ed.) *The Interpretation of Ordinary Landscapes* (pp. 33–48). New York: Oxford University Press.

Melbourne Sports and Aquatic Centre (MSAC) (2002) *Facilities*. On WWW at http://www.msac.com.au/sports.html. Accessed 24 May 2002.

Melnick, M. J. and Loy, J. W. (1996) The effects of formal structure on leadership recruitment: An analysis of team captaincy among New Zealand provincial rugby teams. *International Review for the Sociology of Sport* 31 (1), 91–107.

Melnick, M. J. and Thomson, R. W. (1996) Segregation in New Zealand rugby football: A test of the anglocentric hypothesis. *International Journal of the History of Sport* 31 (2), 139–154.

Merkel, U., Lines, G. and McDonald, I. (1998) The production and consumption of sport cultures: Introduction. In U. Merkel, G. Lines and I. McDonald (eds)

The Production and Consumption of Sport Cultures: Leisure, Culture and Commerce (pp. v–xvi). Eastbourne: Leisure Studies Association.

Metcalfe, A. (1993) The development of sporting facilities: A case study of east Northumberland, England, 1850–1914. *International Review for the Sociology of Sport* 28 (2/3), 107–119.

Mihalik, B. J. and Simonetta, L. (1999) A midterm assessment of the host population's perceptions of the 1996 Summer Olympics: Support, attendance, benefits, and liabilities. *Journal of Travel Research* 37 (3), 244–248.

Millington, K., Locke, T. and Locke, A. (2001) Adventure travel. *Travel and Tourism Analyst* 4, 65–97.

Miossec, J. M. (1977) L'image touristique comme introduction y la géographie du tourisme. *Annales de géographie* 86, 473.

Miranda-Juan Andueza, J. (1997) The role of sport in the tourism destinations chosen by tourists visiting Spain. *Journal of Sport Tourism* 4 (3), 5–25.

Mitchell, L. S. and Murphy, P. E. (1991) Geography and tourism. *Annals of Tourism Research* 18 (1), 57–70.

Moore, N. S. R. (1995) National Mutual Masters Games, economic impact assessment, Dunedin, February 5th–13th. Unpublished thesis, University of Otago, Dunedin, NZ.

Moragas Spa, M., Rivenburg, N. K. and Larson, J. F. (1995) *Television in the Olympics.* London: J. Libbey.

Morley, D. and Robins, K. (1995) *Spaces of Identity: Global Media, Electronic Landscapes and Cultural Boundaries.* London: Routledge.

Morse, J. (2001) The Sydney 2000 Olympic Games: How the Australian Tourist Commission leveraged the Games for tourism. *Journal of Vacation Marketing* 7 (2), 101–107.

Moscardo, G. (2000) Cultural and heritage tourism: The great debates. In B. Faulkner, G. Moscardo and E. Laws (eds) *Tourism in the 21st Century: Lessons from Experience* (pp. 3–17). London: Continuum.

Mounet, J. and Chifflet, P. (1996) Commercial supply for river water sports. *International Review for the Sociology of Sport* 31 (3), 233–256.

Mourdoukoutas, P. G. (1998) Seasonal employment, seasonal unemployment and unemployment compensation. *American Journal of Economics and Sociology* 47 (3), 315–329.

Mowforth, M. (2002) *Tourism and Sustainability.* London: Routledge.

Mowforth, M. and Munt, I. (1998) *Tourism and Sustainability: New Tourism in the Third World.* London: Routledge.

Mules, T. (1998) Taxpayer subsidies for major sporting events. *Sport Management Review* 1 (1), 25–43.

Murphy, P. E. (1985) *Tourism: A Community Approach.* New York: Methuen.

Murray, D. and Dixon, L. (2000) Investigating the growth of 'instant' sports: Practical implications for community leisure service providers. *The ACHPER Healthy Lifestyles Journal* 47 (3/4), 27–31.

Murray, J. (1996) How seasonality affects the economic viability of Canadian tourism businesses. In K. MacKay and K. R. Boyd (eds) *Tourism for All Seasons: Using Research to Meet the Challenge of Seasonality (Conference Proceedings of the Travel and Tourism Research Association, Canada Chapter)* (pp. 135–146). Ottawa: Travel and Tourism Research Association.

Mykletun, R. J. and Vedø, K. (2002) BASE jumping in Lysefjord, Norway: A sustainable but controversial type of coastal tourism. Paper presented at the Tourism Research Conference 2002, Cardiff, 4–7 September.

Nash, R. and Johnston, S. (1998) The case of Euro96: Where did the party go? Paper presented at the Sport in the City Conference, Sheffield, 2–4 July.

Nauright, J. (1995) Introduction. In J. Nauright (ed.) *Sport, Power and Society in New Zealand: Historical and Contemporary Perspectives* (pp. 1–4). Sydney: University of New South Wales Printery.

Nauright, J. (1996) 'A besieged tribe'? Nostalgia, white cultural identity and the role of rugby in a changing South Africa. *International Review for the Sociology of Sport* 31 (1), 69–89.

Nauright, J. (1997a) *Sport, Culture and Identities in South Africa*. London: Leicester University Press.

Nauright, J. (1997b) Masculinity, muscular Islam and popular vulture: 'Coloured' rugby's cultural symbolism in working-class Cape Town c.1930–70. *The International Journal of the History of Sport* 14 (1), 184–190.

Nevo, I. (2000) Sport institutions and ideology in Israel. *Journal of Sport and Social Issues* 24 (4), 334–343.

New Zealand Tourism Board (1998) All Blacks join forces with McCully, NZTB in South Africa. *Tourism News* (August), 2.

Nogawa, H., Yamaguchi, Y. and Hagi, Y. (1996) An empirical research study on Japanese sport tourism in sport-for-all events: Case studies of a single-night event and a multiple-night event. *Journal of Travel Research* 35 (2), 46–54.

Olds, K. (1998.) Urban mega-events, evictions and housing rights: The Canadian case. *Current Issues in Tourism* 1 (1), 2–46.

Olympic Co-ordination Authority (OCA) (1997a) *Environment: Committed to Conservation*. Sydney: Olympic Co-ordination Authority, New South Wales Government.

Olympic Co-ordination Authority (OCA) (1997b) *Environment: Protecting Nature's Gift*. Sydney: Olympic Co-ordination Authority, New South Wales Government.

Olympic Co-ordination Authority (OCA) (1997c) *State of Play: A Report on Sydney 2000 Olympics Planning and Construction*. Sydney: Olympic Co-ordination Authority, New South Wales Government.

Onkvisit, S. and Shaw, J. J. (1989) *Product Life Cycles and Product Management*. New York: Quorum Books.

Orams, M. (1999) *Marine Tourism: Development, Impacts and Management*. London: Routledge.

Orams, M. and Brons, A. (1999) Potential impacts of a major sport/tourism event: The America's Cup 2000. *Visions in Leisure and Business* 18 (1), 14–28.

Orsman, B. and Bingham, E. (2000) America's Cup $640m boost to NZ economy. *New Zealand Herald*, 27 October, 1.

Osborn, G. (2000) Football's legal legacy: Recreation, protest and disorder. In S. Greenfield and G. Osborn (eds) *Law and Sport in Contemporary Society* (pp. 51–68). London: F. Cass Publishers.

Page, S. J., Brunt, P., Busby, G. and Connell, J. (2001) *Tourism: A Modern Synthesis*. London: Thomson Learning.

Page, S. J. and Hall, C. M. (2003) *Managing Urban Tourism*. Harlow: Pearson Education Ltd.

Pealo, W. and Redmond, G. (1999) Sport tourism: Moving into the new millennium. *Recreation and Parks BC* (Spring), 22–24.

Pearce, D. G. (1987) *Tourism Today: A Geographical Analysis*. Harlow: Longman Scientific and Technical.

Pearce, D. G. (1989) *Tourism Development* (2nd edn). Harlow: Longman Scientific and Technical.

Pearce, D. G. and Butler, R. W. (eds) (1999) *Contemporary Issues in Tourism Development*. London: Routledge.

Pearce, P. (1982) *The Social Psychology of Tourist Behaviour*. Oxford: Pergamon Press.

Pearce, P. (1988) *The Ulysses Factor: Evaluating Visitors in Tourist Settings*. New York: Springer-Verlag.

Persson, C. (2002) The Olympic Games site decision. *Tourism Management* 23 (1), 27–36.

Pett, R. (2000) The end of the golden weather. *Auckland Today* (September), 7.

Pickmere, A. (2000) A lot more than just a yacht race. *New Zealand Herald*, 27 October, 13.

Pigeassou, C. (1997) Sport and tourism: The emergence of sport into the offer of tourism. Between passion and reason: An overview of the French situation and perspectives. *Journal of Sport Tourism* 4 (2), 20–38.

Pigeassou, C. (2002) Sport tourism as a growth sector: The French perspective. In S. Gammon and J. Kurtzman (eds) *Sport Tourism: Principles and Practice* (Vol. 76, pp. 129–140). Eastbourne: Leisure Studies Association.

Pigram, J. J. and Wahab, S. (1997) Sustainable tourism in a changing world. In S. Wahab and J. J. Pigram (eds) *Tourism, Development and Growth* (pp. 17–32). London: Routledge.

Pitts, B. G. (1997) Sports tourism and niche markets: Identification and analysis of the growing lesbian and gay sports tourism industry. *Journal of Vacation Marketing* 5 (1), 31–50.

Plog, S. (1972) Why destination areas rise and fall in popularity. Paper presented at the Southern California Chapter of the Travel Research Bureau, San Diego, 10 October.

Poon, A. (1993) All-inclusive resorts. *Travel and Tourism Analyst* 2, 54–68.

Pope, S. W. (1997) Introduction. American sport history: Toward a new paradigm. In S. W. Pope (ed.) *The New American Sport History: Recent Approaches and Perspectives* (pp. 1–30). Urbana, IL: University of Chicago.

Porteous, B. (2000) Sports development: Glasgow. *Leisure Manager* 18 (11), 18–21.

Priestley, G. K. (1995) Sports tourism: The case of golf. In G. J. Ashworth and A. G. J. Dietvorst (eds) *Tourism and Spatial Transformations: Implications for Policy and Planning* (pp. 205–223). Wallingford: CAB International.

Pujik, R. (2000) A global media event? Coverage of the 1994 Lillehammer Olympic Games. *International Review for the Sociology of Sport* 35 (3), 309–330.

Pyo, S., Cook, R. and Howell, R. L. (1991) Summer Olympic tourist market. In S. Medlik (ed.) *Managing Tourism* (pp. 191–198). Oxford: Butterworth-Heinemann.

Pyo, S., Uysal, M. and Howell, R. (1988) Seoul Olympics visitor preferences. *Tourism Management* 9 (1), 68–72.

Redmond, G. (1990) Points of increasing contact: Sport and tourism in the modern world. In A. Tomlinson (ed.) *Sport in Society: Policy, Politics and Culture* (pp. 158–167). Eastbourne: Leisure Studies Association.

Redmond, G. (1991) Changing styles of sports tourism: Industry/consumer interactions in Canada, the USA and Europe. In M. T. Sinclair and M. J. Stabler (eds) *The Tourism Industry: An International Analysis* (pp. 107–120). Wallingford: CAB International.

Reeves, M. R. (2000) Evidencing the sport–tourism relationship: A case study approach. Unpublished Ph.D. thesis, Loughborough University.

Relph, E. (1976) *Place and Placelessness*. London: Pion Limited.

Relph, E. (1985) Geographical experiences and being-in-the-world: The phenomenological origins of geography. In D. Seamon and R. Mugerauer (eds) *Dwelling, Place and Environment* (pp. 15–38). Dordrecht: Nijhoff.

Richards, G. (1996) Skilled consumption and UK ski holidays. *Tourism Management* 17, 25–34.

Ritchie, J. B. R. (1984) Assessing the impact of hallmark events: Conceptual and research issues. *Journal of Travel Research* 13 (1), 2–11.

Ritchie, J. B. R. and Lyons, M. (1990) Olympulse VI: A post event assessment of resident reaction to the XV Olympic Winter Games. *Journal of Travel Research* (Winter), 14–23.

Roberts, R. and Olson, J. (1989) *Winning is the Only Thing: Sports in America since 1945*. Baltimore, MD: The Johns Hopkins University Press.

Robins, K. (1991) Tradition and transition: National culture in its global context. In J. Corner and S. Harvey (eds) *Enterprise and Heritage* (pp. 21–44). London: Routledge.

Robins, K. (1997) What in the world is going on? In P. Du Gay (ed.) *Production of Culture/Cultures of Production* (pp. 11–67). London: Sage Publications.

Robinson, H. (1979) *A Geography of Tourism*. London: MacDonald and Evans.

Roche, M. (1994) Mega-events and urban policy. *Annals of Tourism Research* 21, 1–19.

Roehl, W., Ditton, R., Holland, S. and Perdue, R. (1993) Developing new tourism products: Sport fishing in the south-east United States. *Tourism Management* 14, 279–288.

Rooney, J. F. (1988) Mega sports events as tourist attractions: A geographical analysis. Paper presented at Tourism Research: Expanding the Boundaries, 19th Annual Conference of the Travel and Tourism Research Association, Montreal.

Rooney, J. F. (1992) *Atlas of American Sport*. New York: Macmillan Publishing Co.

Rooney, J. F. and Pillsbury, R. (1992) Sports regions of America. *American Demographics* 14 (10), 1–10.

Ross, C. M. and Sharpless, D. R. (1999) Innovative information technology and its impact on recreation and sport programming. *Journal of Physical Education, Recreation and Dance* 70 (9), 26–30.

Ross, G. F. (1998) *The Psychology of Tourism*. Melbourne: Hospitality Press.

Rowe, D. (1996) The global love-match: Sport and television. *Media, Culture and Society* 18, 565–582.

Rowe, D. and Lawrence, G. (1996) Beyond national sport: Sociology, history and postmodernity. *Sporting Traditions* 12 (2), 3–16.

Rowe, D., Lawrence, G., Miller, T. and McKay, J. (1994) Global sport? Core concern and peripheral vision. *Media, Culture and Society* 16, 661–675.

Rowe, D., McKay, J. and Miller, T. (1998) Come together: Sport, nationalism, and the media image. In L. Wenner (ed.) *Mediasport* (pp. 119–133). London: Routledge.

Ruskin, H. (1987) Selected views of socio-economic aspects of outdoor recreation, outdoor education and sport tourism. In M. Garmise (ed.) *Proceedings of the International Seminar and Workshop on Outdoor Education, Recreation and Sport Tourism* (pp. 18–37). Israel: Emmanuel Gill Publishing.

Ryan, C. (1995) *Researching Tourist Satisfaction: Issues, Concepts, Problems*. London: Routledge.

Ryan, C., Smee, A. and Murphy, S. (1996) Creating a database of events in New Zealand: Early results. *Festival Management and Event Tourism* 4 (3/4), 151–156.

Santana, G. (1998) Sports tourism and crisis management. *Journal of Sport Tourism* 4 (4), 9–22.

Schaffer, W. and Davidson, L. (1985) *Economic Impact of the Falcons on Atlanta: 1984.* Suwannee, GA: The Atlanta Falcons.

Schlossberg, H. (1996) *Sports Marketing.* Oxford: Blakewell.

Schollmann, A., Perkins, H. C. and Moore, K. (2001) Rhetoric, claims making and conflict in touristic place promotion: The case of central Christchurch, New Zealand. *Tourism Geographies* 3 (3), 300–325.

Schreyer, R. and Lime, D. W. (1984) A novice isn't necessarily a novice: The influence of experience use history on subjective perceptions of recreation participation. *Leisure Sciences* 6 (2), 131–149.

Schreyer, R., Lime, D. W. and Williams, D. R. (1984) Characterizing the influence of past experience on recreation behaviour. *Journal of Leisure Research* 16 (1), 34–50.

Scott, D., Jones, B., Lemieux, C., McBoyle, G., Mills, B., Stevenson, S. and Wall, G. (2002) *The Vulnerability of Winter Recreation to Climatic Change in Ontario's Lakelands Tourism Region.* Occasional Paper 18. Waterloo, Ont.: Department of Geography Publication Series, University of Waterloo.

Selin, S. and Chavez, D. (1995) Developing an evolutionary tourism partnership model. *Annals of Tourism Research* 22 (4), 844–856.

Sell, B. (2000) Sport in sport-mad New Zealand under severe strain. *New Zealand Herald,* 4 April, A:3.

Sennet, R. (1999) Growth and failure: The new political economy and its culture. In M. Featherstone and S. Lash (eds) *Spaces of Culture: City–Nation–World* (pp. 14–26). London: Sage Publications.

Shapcott, M. (1998) Commentary on 'Urban mega-events, evictions and housing rights: The Canadian case' by Chris Olds. *Current Issues in Tourism* 1 (2), 195–196.

Sheard, K. (1999) A twitch in time saves nine: Birdwatching, sport, and civilising processes. *Sociology of Sport Journal* 16 (3), 181–205.

Sherlock, K. (2001) Revisiting the concept of hosts and guests. *Tourist Studies* 1 (3), 271–295.

Shibli, S. (1998) The economic impact of two major sporting events in two of the United Kingdom's 'national cities of sport'. Paper presented at the Sport in the City Conference, Sheffield, 2–4 July.

Shore, B. (1994) Marginal play: Sport at the borderlands of time and space. *International Review for the Sociology of Sport* 29 (4), 349–374.

Silk, M. (2002) 'Bangsa Malaysia': Global sport, the city and the mediated refurbishment of local identities. *Media, Culture and Society* 25 (6), 775–794.

Silk, M. and Andrews, D. L. (2001) Beyond a boundary? Sport, transnational advertising, and the reimaging of national culture. *Journal of Sport and Social Issues* 25 (2), 180–201.

Silk, M. and Jackson, S. J. (2000) Globalisation and sport in New Zealand. In C. Collins (ed.) *Sport in New Zealand Society* (pp. 99–113). Palmerston North, NZ: Dunmore Press.

Simmons, D. and Urquhart, L. (1994) Measuring economic events: An example of endurance sports events. *Festival Management and Event Tourism* 2 (1), 25–32.

Simpson, J. A. and Weiner, E. S. C. (eds) (1989) *The Oxford English Dictionary, Vol. XVII* (2nd edn). Oxford: Clarendon Press.

Slowikowski, S. S. and Loy, J. W. (1993) Ancient athletic motifs and the modern Olympic Games: An analysis of rituals and representations. In A. G. Ingham and J. W. Loy (eds) *Sport in Social Development* (pp. 21–49). Champaign, IL: Human Kinetics.

Smith, A. (2000) Civil war in England: The clubs, the RFU, and the impact of professionalism on rugby union, 1995–99. In A. Smith and D. Porter (eds) *Amateurs and Professionals in Post-war British Sport* (pp. 146–188). London: Frank Cass Publishers.

Smith, S. L. J. (1983) *Recreation Geography*. London: Longman.

Snepenger, D., Houser, B. and Snepenger, M. (1990) Seasonality of demand. *Annals of Tourism Research* 17, 628–630.

Snyder, E. (1991) Sociology of nostalgia: Halls of fame and museums in America. *Sociology of Sport Journal* 8, 228–238.

Sonmez, S. F., Apolstolopoulos, Y. and Talow, P. (1999) Tourism in crisis: Managing the effects of terrorism. *Journal of Travel Research* 38, 13–18.

Spivack, S. E. (1998) Health spa development in the US: A burgeoning component of sport tourism. *Journal of Vacation Marketing* 4, 65–77.

Sport Tourism International Council (1995) Sport tourism categories revisited. *Journal of Sport Tourism* 2 (3), 1–4.

Sport Tourism International Council (1998) Case study of a sports tourism destination: Lake Placid and region. *Journal of Sport Tourism* 4 (4), 36–38.

Standeven, J. and De Knop, P. (1999) *Sport Tourism*. Champaign, IL: Human Kinetics.

Stanley, D. and Moore, S. (1997) Counting the leaves: The dimensions of seasonality in Canadian tourism. Paper presented at the Proceedings of the Travel and Tourism Research Association, Canada Chapter, University of Manitoba, Winnipeg.

Stansfield, C. J. (1978) The development of modern seaside resorts. *Parks and Recreation* 5 (10), 14–46.

Stevens, T. (1998) Capitalising on sport: Cardiff's future strategy. Paper presented at the Sport in the City Conference, Sheffield, 2–4 July.

Stevens, T. (2001) Stadia and tourism related facilities. *Travel and Tourism Analyst* (2), 59–73.

Stevens, T. and van den Broek, M. (1997) Sport and tourism: Natural partners in strategies for tourism development. *Tourism Recreation Research* 22 (2), 1–3.

Stevens, T. and Wootton, G. (1997) Sports stadia and arenas: Realising their full potential. *Tourism Recreation Research* 22 (2), 49–56.

Stevenson, D. (1997) Olympic arts: Sydney 2000 and the Cultural Olympiad. *International Review for the Sociology of Sport* 32 (3), 227–238.

Stewart, B. (2001) Fab club. *Australian Leisure Management* (October/November), 16–19.

Stewart, B. and Smith, A. (2000) Australian sport in a postmodern age. *International Journal of the History of Sport* 17 (2/3), 278–304.

Stewart, J. J. (1987) The commodification of sport. *International Review for the Sociology of Sport* 22, 170–190.

Sugden, J. and Tomlinson, A. (1996) What's left when the circus leaves town? An evaluation of World Cup USA 1994. *Sociology of Sport Journal* 13 (3), 238–258.

SUKOM (1996) *'Let's Make it Great'*. Report to the General Assembly of the Commonwealth Games Federation (Issue 3, restricted circulation), April, Kuala Lumpur: SUKOM 98 Berhad.

SUKOM (1998) *Walkabout: Special Edition for Kuala Lumpur 98.* Kuala Lumpur: Malaysia-On-Call Sdn. Bhd./SUKOM 98 Berhad.

Swarbrooke, J. and Horner, S. (1999) *Consumer Behaviour in Tourism.* Oxford: Butterworth-Heinemann.

Swart, K. (2000) An assessment of sport tourism curricular offerings at academic institutions. *Journal of Sport Tourism* 6 (1), 11–18.

Sylvester, C. (1999) The western idea of work and leisure: Traditions, transformations, and the future. In E. L. Jackson and T. L. Burton (eds) *Leisure Studies: Prospects for the Twenty-First Century* (pp. 17–33). State College, PA: Venture Publishing, Inc.

Tabata, R. (1992) Scuba diving holidays. In B. Weiler and C. M. Hall (eds) *Special Interest Tourism* (pp. 171–184). London: Belhaven Press.

Tam, A. (1998) Critical success factors in sports tourism development: Their applicability to Singapore. *Journal of Sport Tourism* 5 (1), 16–26.

Teigland, J. (1999) Mega-events and impacts on tourism: The predictions and realities of the Lillehammer Olympics. *Impact Assessment and Project Appraisal* 17 (4), 305–317.

Thamnopoulos, Y. and Gargalianos, D. (2002) Ticketing the large scale events: The case of Sydney 2000 Olympic Games. *Facilities* 20 (1/2), 22–33.

Thompson, S. (1985) Women in sport: Some participation patterns in New Zealand. *Leisure Studies* 4 (3), 321–331.

Thompson, S. (1988) Challenging the hegemony: New Zealand women's opposition to rugby and the reproduction of a capitalist patriarchy. *International Review for the Sociology of Sport* 23, 205–211.

Thompson, S. (1990) Thank the ladies for the plates: The incorporation of women into sport. *Leisure Studies* 9, 135–143.

Thomson, R. (2000) Physical activity through sport and leisure: Traditional versus non-competitive activities. *Journal of Physical Education New Zealand* 33 (1), 34–39.

Timothy, D. and Boyd, S. W. (2002) *Heritage Tourism.* London: Prentice Hall.

Tokarski, W. (1993) Leisure, sports and tourism: The role of sports in and outside holiday clubs. In A. J. Veal, P. Jonson and G. Cushman (eds) *Leisure and Tourism: Social and Environmental Change* (pp. 684–686). Sydney: University of Technology, World Leisure and Recreation Association.

Tomlinson, A. (1996) Olympic spectacle: Opening ceremonies and some paradoxes of globalization. *Media, Culture and Society* 18 (4), 583–602.

Tomlinson, A. (1999) *The Game's Up: Essays in the Cultural Analysis of Sport, Leisure and Popular Culture.* Aldershot: Ashgate Publishing Ltd.

Tourist Authorities of Göteborg (2002) *Gothia Cup.* On WWW at http://www. gothiacup.se. Accessed 24 October 2002.

Tow, S. (1994) Sports tourism: The benefits. *Journal of Sport Tourism* 2 (1), 1–7.

Traer, R. (2002) CEO: Canadian Sport Tourism Alliance. Personal communication, 1 November 2002.

Tuan, Y. (1974) *Topophilia: A Study of Environmental Perception, Attitudes, and Values.* Englewood Cliffs, NJ: Prentice Hall.

Tuppen, J. (2000) The restructuring of winter sports resorts in the French Alps: Problems, processes and policies. *International Journal of Tourism Research* 2 (5), 227–344.

Turco, D. (1999) Travelling and turnovers: Measuring the economic impacts of a street basketball tournament. *Journal of Sport Tourism* 5 (1), 6–11.

Turco, D., Riley, R. and Swart, K. (2002) *Sport Tourism*. Morgantown, WV: Fitness Information Technology.

University Athletic Association (2000) Personal communication with staff in the University of Florida Athletic Association Office, Gainsville, Florida, September.

Upneja, A., Schafer, E. L., Seo, W. and Yoon, J. (2001) Economic benefit of sport fishing and angler wildlife watching in Pennysylvania. *Journal of Travel Research* 40 (1), 68–78.

Urry, J. (1990) *The Tourist Gaze*. London: Sage Publications.

Van Wynsberghe, R. and Ritchie, I. (1998) (*Ir)Relevant Ring: The Symbolic Consumption of the Olympic Logo in Postmodern Media Culture*. Albany, NY: State University of New York Press.

Voumard, S. (1995) Jonah's big date. *The Sydney Morning Herald*, 25 November, 14.

Wahab, S. and Cooper, C. (2001) *Tourism in the Age of Globalisation*. London: Routledge.

Wahab, S. and Pigram, J. J. (eds) (1997) *Tourism Development and Growth: The Challenge of Sustainability*. London: Routledge.

Walker, S. (2001) Sport mad nation? *Australian Leisure Management* (October/November), 32–35.

Wall, G. (1997) Sustainable tourism/unsustainable development. In S. Wahab and J. J. Pigram (eds) *Tourism, Development and Growth* (pp. 33–49). London: Routledge.

Wang, N. (1999) Rethinking authenticity in tourism experience. *Annals of Tourism Research* 26 (2), 349–370.

Washington, R. E. and Karen, D. (2001) Sport and society. *Annual Review of Sociology* 27, 187–212.

Watson, A. E. and Roggenbuck, J. W. (1991) The influence of past experience on wilderness choice. *Journal of Leisure Research* 23 (1), 21–36.

Webb, S. and Magnussen, B. (2002) Evaluating major sports events as cultural icons and economic drivers: A case study of Rugby World Cup 1999. Paper presented at the Tourism Research Conference 2002, Cardiff.

Wedemeyer, B. (1999) Sport and terrorism. In J. Riordan and A. Kruger (eds) *The International Politics of Sport in the 20th Century* (pp. 217–233). London: Spon.

Weed, M. (1999) 'More than sports holidays': An overview of the sport–tourism link. In M. Scarrott (ed.) *Exploring Sports Tourism: Proceedings of a SPRIG Seminar held at the University of Sheffield on 15 April 1999* (pp. 6–28). Sheffield: Sheffield Hallam University.

Weed, M. (2002) Football hooligans as undesirable sports tourists: Some meta-analytical speculations. In S. Gammon and J. Kurtzman (eds) *Sport Tourism: Principles and Practice* (pp. 35–52). Eastbourne: Leisure Studies Association.

Weed, M. and Bull, C. (1997a) Integrating sport and tourism: A review of regional policies in England. *Progress in Tourism and Hospitality Research* 3 (2), 129–148.

Weed, M. and Bull, C. (1997b) Influences on sport tourism relations in Britain: The effects of government policy. *Tourism Recreation Research* 22 (2), 5–12.

Weed, M. and Bull, C. (1998) The search for a sport tourism policy network. In I. Cooper and M. F. Collins (eds) *Leisure Management: Issues and Applications*. Wallingford: CAB International.

Weed, M. and Bull, C. (2003) *Sports Tourism: Participants, Policy and Providers*. Oxford: Butterworth-Heinemann.

Weighill, A. J. (2002) Canadian domestic sport travel in 2001. Report prepared for Statistics Canada and the Canadian Tourism Commission, Ottawa.

Weiss, O., Norden, G., Hilscher, P. and Vanreusel, B. (1998) Ski tourism and environmental problems: Ecological awareness among different groups. *International Review for the Sociology of Sport* 33 (4), 367–380.

Wheaton, B. (2000) 'Just do it?': Consumption, commitment, and identity in the windsurfing subculture. *Sociology of Sport Journal* 17 (3), 254–274.

Wheeler, B. (1991) Tourism's troubled times: Responsible tourism is not the answer. *Tourism Management* (June), 91–96.

White, P. and Wilson, B. (1999) Distinctions in the stands: An investigation of Bourdieu's 'habitus', socioeconomic status and sport spectatorship in Canada. *International Review for the Sociology of Sport* 34 (3), 245–264.

Whitson, D. and Macintosh, D. (1993) Becoming a world-class city: Hallmark events and sport franchises in the growth strategies of western Canadian cities. *Sociology of Sport Journal* 12, 21–40.

Whitson, D. and Macintosh, D. (1996) The global circus: International sport, tourism and the marketing of cities. *Journal of Sport and Social Issues* 23, 278–295.

Wiley, C. E., Shaw, S. M. and Havitz, M. E. (2000) Men's and women's involvement in sports: An examination of the gendered aspects of leisure involvement. *Leisure Sciences* 22 (1), 19–31.

Williams, A. M. and Shaw, G. (eds) (1988) *Tourism and Economic Development: Western European Experiences*. London: Belhaven Press.

Williams, D., Patterson, M., Roggenbuck, J. and Watson, A. (1992) Beyond the commodity metaphor: Examining emotional and symbolic attachment to place. *Leisure Sciences* 14, 29–46.

Williams, J. (1994) The local and the global in English soccer and the rise of satellite television. *Sociology of Sport Journal* 11 (4), 376–397.

Wilson, H. (1996) What is an Olympic city? Visions of Sydney 2000. *Media, Culture and Society* 18 (4), 603–618.

Wilson, H. (1998) Television's *tour de force*: The nation watches the Olympic Games. In D. Rowe and G. Lawrence (eds) *Tourism, Leisure and Sport: Critical Perspectives* (pp. 135–145). Sydney: Hodder Headline.

Wood, I. (1998) Hong Kong: The event capital of Asia. Case studies on the International Dragon Boat Championships and Hong Kong Rugby Sevens. Paper presented at the Sport in the City Conference, Sheffield, 2–4 July.

Woolley-Fisher, P. and Chambers, E. J. (1990) The Edmonton Eskimos: An economic impact study. Unpublished report. Edmonton, Canada: Western Centre for Economic Research.

World Commission on Environment and Development (WCED) (1987) *Our Common Future (The Brundtland Report)*. London: Oxford University Press.

World Tourism Organization (WTO) (1981) *Technical Handbook on the Collection and Presentation of Domestic and International Tourism Statistics*. Madrid: World Tourism Organization.

World Tourism Organization (WTO) (1994) *National and Regional Tourism Planning: Methodologies and Case Studies*. London: Routledge.

World Tourism Organization (WTO) (2001) *Tourism After 11 September 2001: Analysis, Remedial Actions and Prospects*. Special Report 18, Market Intelligence and Promotion Section. Madrid: World Tourism Organization.

World Tourism Organization (WTO) (2002) *Tourism Recovery Already Underway*. Madrid: World Tourism Organization.

World Tourism Organization and International Olympic Committee (WTO and IOC) (2001) *Sport and Tourism: Sport Activities During the Outbound Holidays of the Germans, the Dutch and the French.* Madrid, Spain: World Tourism Organization and International Olympic Committee.

Yiannakis, A. (1975) A theory of sport stratification. *Sport Sociology Bulletin* 4, 22–32.

Young, K. and Smith, M. D. (1988) Mass media treatment of violence in sport and its effects. *Current Psychology: Research and Reviews* 7 (4), 298–311.

Yusof, A. and Douvis, J. (2001) An examination of sport tourist profiles. *Journal of Sport Tourism* 6 (3), 1–10.

Index

Aboriginal 103
Accessibility 90, 94, 98, 148, 154, 164
Accommodation 35, 46, 51, 53, 88, 93, 123, 135, 148, 149, 154, 157, 161, 162, 164, 177, 178, 198, 209
Active sport tourism 9, 24, 39, 40, 42, 43, 47, 49, 51, 69, 71, 72, 79, 92, 134, 151, 155, 175, 195, 198, 207, 211
Activity participants 34, 64
Adelaide (Australia) 65
Adventure 18, 21, 22, 192, 195, 196
– Adventure activities 38
– Adventure tourism 18, 43
– Soft adventure 195
Aesthetics 101, 121, 134, 187
Ajzen, I. 155
Alaska (USA) 105
– Alaskan high kick 105
Alberta (Canada) 97
Albertville (France) 133
All Blacks (*see also* Rugby Union) 111
Allcock, J.B. 165, 168
Alliances (*see also* Strategic alliances) 71
Alpine skiers 91, 187, 211
Alsace (France) 75
Alternative tourism 128
America's Cup 44, 136, 137, 138
American Football (*see also* Superbowl) 22, 67, 149, 155
Ancillary activities and entertainment 159
Andorra 96, 98
Andrews, D.L. 66, 67, 114, 117
Angling 89
Annals of Tourism Research (Journal) 22
Anthropology 30
Anticipation phase 141, 144
Archer, B. 127, 132
Arctic Winter Games (AWG) 105
Argentina 95, 96, 97
Arsenal FC 48, 85
Ashworth, G.J 17
Asia 95, 156
Asia Pacific Economic Council (APEC) 114
Association of Surfing Professionals (ASP) World Tour 186
Association of Tennis Professionals Tour (ATP) 85
Aston Villa FC 48

Astrodome (Houston) 87
Athens (Greece) 49, 110
Athletics 124
Atkisson, A. 56
Atlanta (USA) 128, 146, 149
– Atlanta Falcons 149
Attraction (*see also* Attractions) 8, 19, 20, 24, 25, 26, 29, 50, 69, 70, 111, 118, 123, 129, 134, 138, 143, 144, 149, 154, 155, 159, 162, 163, 164, 171, 172, 173, 177, 179, 180, 182, 185, 189, 190, 191, 194, 207, 208, 210, 214
– Attraction hierarchy 25
– Attraction markers 24, 26, 29, 129, 130, 143
– Attraction system 25, 26
Attractions 8, 25, 48, 51, 80, 81, 82, 87, 88, 89, 110
Auckland (New Zealand) 136, 137, 138
Australia 7, 30, 65, 67, 68, 69, 93, 95, 96, 103, 104, 110, 113, 125, 134, 136, 146, 152, 156, 180, 181
– Australian Rugby Union 125
– Australian Rules Football 7, 67
– Australian Tourist Commission 110
Austria 92, 96, 97, 98
Authentic (*see also* Authenticity) 8, 55, 71, 101
Authenticity 7, 17, 28, 60, 61, 62, 63, 64, 69, 70, 72, 73, 100, 149, 194, 208
– Absolute authenticity 62
– Constructive authenticity 62
– Emergent authenticity 62
– Existential authenticity 63, 64
– Experiential authenticity 71
– Objective authenticity 63
– Interpersonal authenticity 64
– Intrapersonal authenticity 64
– Real authenticity 61
– Relative authenticity 63, 72
– Staged authenticity 61, 62
– Tourism authenticity 17
Aversion effects (*see also* Diversion effects) 126, 157

Babe Ruth Museum 149
Back stage 70, 208
Badminton 83, 126, 151, 152, 174
Baja Beach Club 149
Bale, J. 6, 16, 26, 40, 47, 49, 67, 79, 80, 81, 82, 83, 84, 85, 87, 94, 95, 101, 102, 106, 111,

119, 125, 126, 127, 129, 130, 133, 134, 136, 149, 154, 155, 157, 167, 191
Ball, R.M. 165
Balls Sports Bar 149
Baloglu, S. 109
Baltimore 86, 149
– Baltimore Orioles 86, 149
Barcelona (Spain) 3, 68, 98, 128, 191
– FC Barcelona Football Stadium 191
Barden, R.D. 164
Barker, M. 160
Barmy Army 65
BarOn, R.R.V. 163, 164, 167
Bartoluci, M. 144, 187
BASE jumping 21, 26, 131
Baseball 7, 41, 86, 89, 121, 149, 152, 155, 160
Basketball 41, 66, 67, 80, 83, 155, 160, 170, 174
– National Basketball League (NBL) 66
– National Basketball Hall of Fame 190
– Street basketball 41, 43, 126, 186
Basset, C. 197
Baum, T. 164, 165, 173, 174, 175, 176, 179, 180
Bavaria (Germany) 88
Beach volleyball 43, 125, 173, 187
Beardsley, D. 106
Beckham, David 8
Bedouin 106
Beezer, A. 107
Behaviour (*see also* Visitor behaviour) 19, 42, 44, 45, 50, 79, 101, 141, 147, 157, 161, 172, 181, 208, 209, 210
Beijing (China) 98
Belanger, A. 87, 110, 191
Belgian Grand Prix 62
Bellan, G.L. 131
Bellan-Santini, D.R. 131
Benelux 98
Berlin (Germany) 49
Bernstein, A. 4, 67
Boarder X 188
Bolton 48
Boniface, B.G. 80, 81, 95, 118, 122, 127
Boorstin, D.J. 63
Booth, D. 4, 41, 49, 51
Boston (USA) 97
Boston Marathon 44
Botham, Ian 8
Bourdeau, P. 90, 91, 95, 184, 192, 194, 200
Bowling 41
Boxing 152
Boyd, S.W. 63
Blake, Sir Peter 137
Brand 52, 110, 196
– Brand image 111
Branding 109
Brazil 7, 97, 153
Brittany (France) 75, 88

British Bodyboard Club 186
British Columbia (Canada) 97
British Golf Museum 48, 202
British Olympic team 53
British Tourist Authority 7, 8
Brons, A. 138
Brown, C. 110
Built environment 40, 95, 135
– Built facilities 80
– Built resources 79
Bukit Jalil (Kuala Lumpur) 116
Bulgaria 96
Bull, C. 4, 19, 24, 28, 29, 33, 49, 50, 51, 68, 69, 73, 94
Bullfighting 38
Bungee jumping 38, 131
Burgan, B. 127
Burton, R. 118
Butler, R.W. 10, 58, 63, 82, 163, 164, 165, 166, 168, 169, 170, 171, 179, 180, 184, 185, 200, 203

Caldetas (Spain) 41
Calgary (Canada) 124
California (USA) 89, 93, 136
Camden Yards 86
Canada 20, 30, 70, 95, 96, 97, 105, 106, 110, 124, 164, 166, 172, 174, 175, 180, 191, 197
Canadian Football League 84
Canadian Rockies 97
Canadian Sport Tourism Alliance 69, 70
Canadian Tourism Commission 20, 164
Canoeing 23, 43, 132
Cantelon, H. 131, 133
Canterbury Crusaders (*see also* Rugby Super 12) 181
Car rallies 126
Cardiff (Wales) 11, 167
Caribbean 65, 93
Carisbrook (Dunedin) 182
Carmichael, B. 44, 48, 147, 157
Carry capacity 127
Casino 87, 123
Castells, M. 114
Casual sport spectators 27, 84, 86, 172
Caving 43
Cavlek, N. 144, 187
Celebrity 67
Centerparcs 174
Central place theory 80, 209
Central place model 84
Central places 89
Central locations 84, 88, 90, 91, 118, 122, 127
Chadwick, G. 59
Chalip, L. 4, 15, 24, 26, 29, 33, 39, 42, 43, 46, 50, 51, 52, 54, 107, 108, 113, 147, 154, 160
Champs Elysées (Paris) 129, 153
Chariots of Fire 202
Chelsea F.C. 48

Chernushenko, D. 9, 133, 134
Cheyne, J. 143, 155
Chile 95, 96
China 7, 85, 96, 98
Chogahara, M. 47
Christaller, W. 89, 135, 184
Christchurch (New Zealand) 47, 181
Clawson, M. 10, 141, 157, 159
Climate 81, 89, 91, 97, 118, 131, 135, 164, 166, 167, 168, 169, 170, 171, 177, 187
– Climate change 165, 166
Climbing 43, 91, 108, 113, 124, 197
Club Méditerranée 38
Clustered nuclei 154
Coalter, F. 195
Cohen, E. 60, 62, 73, 100, 101
Collier, A. 144, 147
Collins, M.F. 5, 21, 33, 193
Colonial Stadium 11
Colorado 97
Commercialisation 60, 61
Commodification (*see also* Commoditisation) 7, 9, 11, 55, 60, 62, 66, 69, 72, 109, 112, 185, 187, 193, 208
Commoditisation 60, 61, 73
Commonwealth Department of Industry, Science and Resources 33, 68, 69
Commonwealth Games 99, 104, 114
Compatibility 128, 131, 132
Competition 6, 16, 20, 26, 28, 35, 37, 39, 42, 64, 69, 81, 82, 103, 105, 124, 127, 128, 129, 133, 134, 142, 143, 144, 146, 148, 151, 153, 158, 166, 178, 180, 187, 189, 194, 195, 207, 210, 211, 214
Competitions 7, 61, 105, 128, 158
Competitive hierarchy 106
Conference travel 38
Connery, Sean 202
Connoisseur observer 38, 142
Conservation 133
Conspicuous commitment 107
Constraints 176, 177, 188
– Interpersonal constraints 177
– Intrapersonal constraints 177
– Structural constraints 177
Consumer behaviour 11
Content analysis 74
Cooper, C. 5, 73, 80, 81, 92, 95, 118, 122, 127, 132, 144
Coopers and Lybrand 164
Corfu 41
Cornwall (England) 186
Côte-d'Azur (France) 75, 88
Cowell, R. 134
Crawford, D.W. 176
Cricket 7, 8, 65, 121, 152, 155, 156, 174
– Cricket World Cup 85
– Indoor cricket 124
– One-day cricket 27

– World Series Cricket 27
Crompton, J.L. 21
Cross country skiing 39, 124, 132, 175, 195
Crouch, D. 99, 113
Cruise ships 38, 49, 137, 191
– Sport cruises 37
Cuba 41
Cultural capital 107
Cultural landscapes 119, 209
Culture (*see also* Subculture) 4, 7, 8, 35, 56, 57, 58, 59, 62, 65, 66, 74, 75, 81, 94, 99, 100, 102, 105, 110, 111, 112, 113, 130, 131, 133, 138, 147, 170, 186, 210
– American culture 62
– Counter-culture 107
– Consumer culture 4
– Cultural imperialism 64
– Cultural performance 62
Current Issues in Tourism (Journal) 22
Curriculum development 30
Cuthbertson, B. 100
Cyberspace 197
Cycle races 126, 129
Cycling 38, 43, 111, 174
Czech Republic 92, 96

Dann, G.M.S. 144
Dauncey, H., 104, 106, 153
Davidson, L. 87, 149
De Knop, P. 4, 5, 12, 19, 20, 24, 25, 38, 51, 88, 99, 100, 101, 118, 122, 123, 126, 130, 135, 142, 192, 200
de Villers, D.J. 55, 186, 187, 193
Decision making 141, 142, 143, 144
Deegan, J. 165
Definition 15, 16, 18
Delpy Neirotti, L. 146, 160
Delpy, L. (*see also* Delpy Neirotti) 3, 4, 33, 39, 51, 189, 192, 195
Demand groups 34
Democratisation 4
Dene (*see also* Indigenous) 105
Denmark 92
Destination 8, 10, 25, 33, 34, 39, 40, 43, 46, 47, 49, 50, 53, 54, 56, 60, 63, 66, 71, 72, 74, 82, 83, 84, 85, 88, 91, 92, 100, 101, 103, 108, 109, 111, 116, 122, 126, 127, 128, 130, 135, 143, 144, 146, 147, 151, 152, 154, 155, 157, 158, 159, 163, 165, 170, 171, 172, 173, 174, 177, 178, 179, 184, 185, 186, 187, 189, 193, 194, 198, 208, 209, 210, 211, 214, 215
– Destination image 7, 71, 111, 116, 123, 135, 144
Dietvorst, A.G.J. 17, 87, 88
Disneyland 62
– Disney Corporation 66
– Disneyfied landscapes 100, 113
– Disney movies 66

Displacement 125, 127

Distance decay 80, 81, 83, 147

Diversion effects (*see also* Aversion effects) 45, 46

Diving 40, 41, 124, 132

Dixon, L. 186, 196

Dog sled racing 105

Donnelly, P. 43, 107, 108, 156, 160

Douvis, J. 39

Downhill skiing 39, 122, 132, 166, 176, 195, 211

Doxey, G. 184

Dragon Boat Racing 38

Driver, B.L. 141, 155, 159

Dunedin (New Zealand) 47, 180, 181, 182

Dunning, E. 156, 160

Dutch 92

Dutch Ministry of Economic Affairs 164

Eastern Europe 97

Echtner, C.M. 144

Ecological restoration 133

Economic geography 8, 12

Economic 5, 82, 84, 90, 106, 110, 115, 131, 135, 137, 160, 165, 170, 187, 189, 193, 199, 210

Economic impact 87, 136, 137, 151, 152, 157

Ecotourism 18

Edmonton (Canada) 111

– City of Champions 111

Edwards, M 104

Elite 45, 48, 50, 127, 128, 142, 143, 145, 146, 166, 168, 214

– Elite competitors 20, 44, 63

– Elite sport 26

– Elite sports events 3

Emergent authenticity (*see* Authenticity)

Emotional involvement 155

Engadin (Switzerland) 98

England 65, 68, 85, 89, 121, 152, 156, 186

English Premier Football League 84

Entertainment 27, 63, 66, 69, 103, 122, 123, 149, 154, 164, 188, 193, 194

Environment 4, 11, 19, 56, 58, 59, 60, 68, 74, 79, 100, 102, 118, 119, 131, 134, 165, 188, 189, 192, 193, 197, 198, 209, 210

Equestrian 124

Ernst and Young 138

ESPN (*see also* Television) 187, 188

Ethnic intruder 63, 72

Eurocamp 176

Europe (*see also* Eastern Europe) 30, 68, 88, 95, 97, 98, 126, 135, 136, 148, 156, 164, 174, 176, 186

European Alps (*see also* French Alps) 97

European Football Championship 154, 167

Event (*see also* Elite sports events) 3, 19, 23, 26, 33, 43, 44, 46, 47, 64, 69, 71, 80, 83, 102, 103, 105, 111, 113, 114, 116, 120, 121, 127, 129, 133, 136, 137, 138, 147, 148, 149, 157, 158, 159, 161, 162, 164, 173, 174, 175, 184, 185, 190, 191, 195, 198, 207, 208, 209, 210, 212, 213, 214

– Event sport tourism 9, 24, 39, 43, 44, 45, 48, 49, 50, 51, 69, 71, 81, 91, 92, 93, 122, 127, 134, 151, 153, 154, 157, 195

– Event production 10

– *Event Management* (Journal) 22

– Hallmark events 22, 23, 109, 110

– Mega-events 22, 35, 127, 128

– Sports event 3, 5, 6, 22, 54, 70

Everton FC 89

Evolutionary 10, 186

Ewert, A. 132

Excursionists 17, 86, 101, 148, 161

Existential authenticity (*see* Authenticity)

Experience (*see also* Visitor experience) 4, 10, 25, 34, 37, 49, 63, 94, 100, 124, 126, 127, 132, 134, 141, 144, 146, 147, 149, 154, 158, 190, 210

Experiences 6, 33, 34, 38, 45, 46, 49, 50, 55, 65, 72, 90, 99, 101, 148, 151, 160, 198, 215

Extreme sports 21, 71, 108, 131, 173, 187, 198, 211

Facilities 9, 10, 19, 35, 46, 47, 50, 52, 53, 71, 80, 81, 82, 87, 88, 93, 94, 109, 110, 111, 118, 122, 125, 128, 130, 133, 142, 143, 144, 149, 154, 158, 164, 167, 171, 173, 175, 176, 179, 182, 191, 197, 199, 201, 209

– Facility sharing 83

Fandom 64, 146, 156

Fans 65, 84, 86, 101, 146, 149, 151, 155, 156, 157, 158, 161, 162, 182, 193, 196

– Fan club 86

Faulkner, B. 5, 45, 46, 54, 126, 127, 157, 160, 161

Federation Internationale de Football Association (FIFA) 85, 112, 134, 153

Festival 85, 105, 126, 129, 173, 186

Field archery 128

Finland 96, 168

Firat, A. 116

Fishing 41, 44, 127, 132, 186

Flagestad, A. 126, 131

Florida (USA) 89, 93, 101, 108, 114, 160, 162

Football (*see also* Soccer) 8, 26, 65, 80, 87, 101, 108, 114, 134, 167, 208

Formula One Grand Prix 44, 46, 62, 85, 129

Fougere, G. 106

Fragmentation 69, 71, 72, 73, 208

– Industry fragmentation 7

France 40, 55, 74, 75, 76, 88, 91, 92, 93, 96, 98, 112, 133, 134, 138, 153, 167, 172, 184

Franche-Comté (France) 75

Franchise 87, 89

Frechtling, D.C. 167

Freidmann, J. 56

French 92
French Alps 68
Fuerteventura (Spain) 41

Gaelic football 7
Gainesville (Florida) 101, 160, 161, 162
Gallarza, M.G. 109
Game 16
– Game occurrence approach 16
– Game strategy 17
Gammon, S. 4, 19, 20, 24, 25, 30, 31, 32, 35,
   37, 38, 48, 49, 51, 76, 92, 102, 143, 146,
   158, 160, 189, 190, 191, 199, 200
Gargalianos, D. 46
Garmise, M. 23
Gastronomy 75
Gateway city 154
Gay and lesbian sport tourism 42
Gayageum (Korean zither) 112
General dabbler 34
German 41, 92
Germany 40, 93, 96, 98, 172, 195
Getz, D. 5, 23, 44, 68, 73, 110, 127, 143, 155,
   192
Gibson, H.J. 4, 5, 17, 19, 20, 24, 30, 39, 42, 48,
   49, 50, 51, 84, 87, 101, 102, 143, 153, 157,
   158, 160, 162
Gilbert, D. 176
Giulianotti, R. 65, 155, 156, 160
Glasgow (Scotland) 111, 152
Global
– Global culture 64
– Global markets 66
– Global standardisation 66
– Global village 64
– Global warming 166
Globalisation 4, 7, 11, 55, 60, 64, 65, 66, 67,
   69, 71, 72, 73, 102, 109, 165, 166, 193, 195,
   208, 211
Glyptis, S.A. 4, 5, 20, 28, 34, 51, 68, 94, 142,
   145, 158
Godbey, G. 149, 150, 152
Gold Coast (Australia) 52, 53, 54
Golden Oldies Rugby Festival 47
Golf 7, 10, 41, 67, 75, 93, 93, 143, 144, 145,
   152, 155, 170, 174, 175, 184, 187, 197, 200,
   201, 202, 203
– Masters Golf 38
– Mini golf 37
Göteborg, Sweden 6
Gothia Cup 6
Gothia Heden Centre 6
Goulding, C. 189
Graburn, N.H.H. 101
Graefe, A.R. 149, 150, 152
Grand Slam Opens (*see also* Golf) 93, 145
Gratton, C. 151, 152, 160
Gravity model 81
Great Britain 88, 89, 92, 93, 151, 165, 176, 202

Greece 96
Green Bay Packers 84
Green sports 124
Green, C. 4, 15, 24, 26, 29, 39, 42, 43, 50, 51,
   107, 108, 113, 147
Green, H. 131
Greenland 105
Green-White Games 133
Greenwood, D.J. 63
Gretzky, Wayne 106
Guerrier, Y. 165
Gymnasia 53, 118, 123, 126
Gymnastics 83

Hagen, L. 164, 165, 173, 174, 175, 176, 179
Halberstam, D. 5
Hall, C.M. 5, 19, 20, 22, 23, 34, 50, 51, 57, 58,
   59, 73, 95, 109, 110, 127, 128, 130, 175,
   193, 194, 197
Hallmark events (*see* Event)
Hallmark teams 85
Halls of Fame (*see* Sport Halls of Fame)
Hang gliding 118
Hapjukseon (Korean traditional fan) 112
Harahousou, Y. 42, 105
Harbin (China) 98
Hare, G. 104, 106, 153
Harrison, S.J. 166
Hartmann, R. 165, 167
Harvey, D. 116
Harvey, J. 64, 66
Hauraki Gulf (*see also* America's Cup) 136
Hawai'i (USA) 93, 185
Health and fitness 5, 22, 23, 35, 37, 42, 195,
   198
Hebdige, D. 107
Heilongjiang (China) 98
Heino, R. 43, 107, 108, 113, 188
Helsinki (Finland) 168
Heritage 7, 8, 44, 48, 49, 63, 75, 86, 102, 106,
   122, 129, 189, 191, 199, 203
– Heritage centre 62
Heterogenisation 66
Hickey, G. 170, 176
Hierarchy 93, 118, 134, 171, 176, 177
– Hierarchy of sport locations 84, 94, 122
Higham, J.E.S. 15, 20, 24, 29, 47, 50, 73, 84,
   85, 124, 127, 128, 141, 157, 163, 167, 168,
   170, 180, 183
Hiking 37, 40
Hiller, H.H. 127
Hinch, T.D. 15, 20, 24, 29, 50, 73, 84, 85, 124,
   141, 163, 167, 168, 170, 172, 173, 176, 180,
   183
Hockey 53, 105, 174
Hodges, J. 127
Hoffer, R. 187
Hokkaido 11
Holden, A. 131

Holdnak, A. 162
Holmenkollen ski jump 49, 124
Home team 101
Homogenisation 66, 67, 130
Hong Kong 38, 85, 155
– Hong Kong Sevens 85, 155
Honolulu (Hawai'i) 185
Hooliganism 156, 160
Hooper, I. 111
Hope, C.A. 126, 131
Hornby, N. 198
Horner, S. 39, 41, 42, 43, 44
Horse riding 43
Hospitality 71, 137, 210
Houston (USA) 87
Hub and spoke 88, 197
Hudson, S. 73, 89, 92, 108, 119, 136, 143, 176
Hunter, C. 131
Hunting 132, 170
Hurling 7, 38
Hwaseong Fortress (Korea) 112

Ice fishing 166
Ice hockey 89, 110, 124, 155, 191
Ice-skating 37, 124
Identity 102, 103, 104, 116, 146, 156, 165
– Cultural identity 108
– National identity 104
Image 99, 109, 111, 112, 113, 114, 182, 209
Impacts 46, 56, 57, 58, 62, 99, 118, 119, 120,
    126, 128, 131, 132, 134, 135, 138, 151, 154,
    155, 214
Incheon (Korea) 112
Indoor bowls 37
India 156
Indian Ocean 93
Indigenous (*see also* Aboriginal) 103, 105
Information services 88
Infrastructure 35, 45, 47, 83, 88, 91, 93, 98,
    118, 122, 123, 127, 133, 136, 137, 141, 148,
    149, 165, 168, 199, 209
Inline skating 186
Innovation 9, 11, 27, 94, 125, 131, 133, 150,
    166, 167, 171, 187, 188, 189, 196
Inskeep, E. 60
Internet 66, 123, 194, 197
Institutional factors (*see also* Seasonality)
    167, 170, 171, 176, 181
International Amateur Athletics Federation
    (IAAF) 85, 152
International Cricket Council (ICC) 85
International Olympic Committee (IOC) 3,
    5, 9, 34, 39, 40, 92, 103, 110, 160, 172
International Rugby Board (IRB) 85, 155
International Sevens 85
Inuit (*see also* Indigenous) 105
Iran 96
Ireland 38, 156
Irwin, R. 50, 160, 162

Isle of Man (England) 173, 174
Israel 194
Italy 92, 96, 98, 138, 153

Jackson, E.L. 43, 173, 176, 180, 197
Jackson, G. 21, 33, 142
Jackson, S.J. 5, 64, 66, 67, 104
Jacksonville (USA) 160
Jamaica 7, 165
Japan 7, 47, 93, 95, 96, 112, 133, 134, 136, 138
Jefferson, A. 165
Jeffrey, D. 164
Jeju (Korea) 112
Jeonju World Cup Stadium 112
Jet boat racing 132
Jet skiing 21, 131, 132
Jilin Province (China) 98
Johnson, W.O. 194
Johnston, C.S. 185, 200
Johnston, S. 154
Jones, C. 151, 159
Jones, I. 146, 156
Journal of Sports Management 12, 24, 54, 183
Journal of Sport Tourism 12, 24, 32, 76
Journal of Vacation Marketing 24, 51, 98, 162

Kang, Y.S. 46
Kaspar, R. 133
Kayaking 37, 43, 127, 132, 173
– White water kayaking 43
Keller, P. 3, 185, 186, 188, 189, 193, 197, 200
Kennedy, E. 165
Kentucky Derby 38
Kirk, D. 61, 193
Kite surfing 131
Klemm, M. 176, 180
Klenosky, D. 43
Knetsch, J. 10, 141, 157, 159
Knuckle hop 105
Kona (Hawai'i) 185
Korea 7, 96, 97, 111, 112, 134
Kotler, P. 109
Kreutzwiser, R. 168
Krippendorf, J. 118, 128
Kuala Lumpur (Malaysia) 99, 104, 114, 115,
    116, 117
Kurtzman, J. 5, 24, 29, 30, 76, 183

Landscape (*see also* Cultural landscape) 9,
    73, 99, 101, 102, 118, 119, 120, 121, 122,
    126, 128, 130, 132, 134, 135, 136, 138, 144,
    168, 197, 209, 214
Langkawi Island (Malaysia) 116
Law, A. 16, 107
Law, C.M. 84, 149
Lawrence, G. 67
Laws, E. 165
Lawson, R. 40
Lebanon 96

Leeds (England) 154
Leiper, N. 17, 24, 25, 29, 87, 154
Leisure (*see also* Serious leisure) 19, 24, 25,
    30, 32, 37, 42, 75, 83, 85, 105, 108, 110,
    111, 145, 147, 151, 152, 158, 164, 167, 176,
    177, 185, 189, 193, 197, 211, 212
– Leisure activities 7, 10
– Leisure centres 123
– Leisure constraints 10, 176, 177, 179, 180
– Leisure management 30
Leisure Studies Association 21
Leisure Time (Newsletter) 7
Lesjø, J.H. 133
Less sport orientated holidays 34, 92, 93
Letters, M. 131, 133
Leveraging 46, 50, 53, 154, 160, 162, 178
– Leveraging strategies 45
Lew, A.A. 25, 57, 73, 79, 95
Lifecycles 184, 189, 198, 199, 203, 211
Lillehammer (Norway) 9, 68, 91, 133, 134,
    154
Limousin (France) 75, 88
Liverpool (England) 48, 154
– Liverpool FC 48, 85, 89
Location hierarchy 80, 82, 91, 97
Locational flux 89
Lockwood, A. 165
London (England) 37, 129
– London marathon 37, 44, 129
Lorraine (France) 75
Lords (London) 7
Loverseed, H. 41, 51, 151, 152, 195
Loy, J.W. 4, 16, 41, 49, 51
Ludic (*ludus*) 16, 17, 214
Lundtorp, S. 179, 180
Lysefjord (Norway) 21

MacCannell, D. 60, 61, 100, 101
Macintosh, D. 65, 114, 116, 117
Magnussen, B. 157
Maguire, J. 66, 73
Maier, J. 33, 34, 35, 51, 88, 93, 95, 142, 143,
    158
Malaysia 99, 114, 115, 116, 117
Manchester 8, 86
– Manchester City FC 89
– Manchester United FC 48, 85
Mandela Trophy 125
Manfredo, M.J. 141, 159
Manx TT road race (*see also* Isle of Man) 174
Mao, B. 164
Marathon 80, 84, 126, 129
Market (*see also* Marketing) 4, 6, 7, 8, 9, 23,
    28, 33, 38, 40, 43, 45, 61, 81, 89, 100, 102,
    109, 113, 124, 125, 143, 152, 171, 173,
    175, 179, 188, 194, 195, 196, 199, 207,
    209, 214
– Market access 9, 125, 134
– Market analysis 33, 44

– Market catchment 93, 129
– Market diversification 173, 175, 176
– Market information 49
– Market range 85, 94, 97
– Market segments 6, 23, 25, 33, 34, 35, 39,
    44, 46, 50, 51, 52, 143, 147, 158, 173, 210
Market segmentation 6, 33, 40, 41, 44, 51
– Behaviouristic market segmentation 43, 51
– Demographic market segmentation 39, 41,
    51
– Geographic market segmentation 39, 40,
    50, 176
– Psychographic market segmentation 39,
    42, 51
– Socio economic market segmentation 39,
    41, 50
Marketing (*see also* Market) 8, 35, 67, 94, 97,
    109, 111, 113, 114, 116, 123, 143, 212
– Marketing plan 8
– Marketing strategy 8
Martial arts 7
Maryland Science Centre 149
Mass tourism 97, 128
Mathieson, D. 127, 131, 135
May, V. 131, 133
McCleary, K.W. 109
McConnell, R. 104
McEnnif, J. 165, 170
McGuirk, P.M. 104, 106, 113
McIntosh, A.J. 63
McKay, J. 61, 193
McKercher, B. 131
McPherson, B.D. 16, 17, 26, 29, 166, 170
Mechanized sports 21
Media 8, 17, 35, 46, 52, 53, 54, 61, 62, 65, 67,
    68, 69, 85, 102, 105, 110, 111, 114, 116,
    117, 129, 137, 166, 187, 188, 189, 190, 193,
    194, 198, 214
– Media conglomerates 66
– Media markets 83
Mediterranean 23, 186
Meinig, D. 119
Melbourne (Australia) 11
– Melbourne Sports and Aquatic Centre 82
Merkel, U. 67, 195
Mexico 7, 97, 200
– Mexican wave 39
Millennium Stadium (Cardiff) 11, 167
Millington, K. 43
Miossec, J.M. 81
Mitchell, L.S. 79, 81, 95, 126, 130
Mobility 91
Molson Centre 110, 191
Monaco 129
Montreal (Canada) 110, 128, 191
– Montreal Canadians 110
– Montreal Forum 191
Moore, N.S.R. 47
Moore, S. 164

Moragas Spa, M. 103
Morley, D. 116
Moscardo, G. 63
Motivation 6, 19, 25, 33, 34, 35, 36, 38, 40, 43,
    44, 46, 48, 50, 51, 71, 90, 92, 101, 108, 132,
    132, 141, 144, 145, 146, 155, 158, 160, 161,
    162, 172, 175, 191, 198, 207, 210
Mountain biking 42, 43, 131, 173
Mountaineering 89, 184
Mourdoukoutas, P.G. 165
Mowforth, M. 57, 64, 66
Mules, T. 127
Munhak Stadium 112
Munich (Germany) 195
Munt, I. 57, 64, 66
Murphy, P.E. 17, 18, 44, 48, 59, 79, 81, 95,
    126, 130, 147, 157, 160, 164
Murray, D. 186, 196
Murray, J. 164
Museums 38, 48, 62, 72, 89, 123, 154, 178,
    189, 190, 191, 199
Mykletun, R.J. 21, 131

Nash, R. 154
National Football League 84
National Sports Festival for the Elderly 47
Natural factors (*see also* Seasonality) 171,
    177
Nauright, J. 5, 103, 104, 105, 106
Netball 80, 83, 124, 174
Netherlands 40, 92, 172, 197
New Orleans (USA) 87
New York (USA) 97, 118, 129, 190
New York Marathon 44, 129
New Zealand 30, 40, 47, 65, 67, 95, 96, 106,
    111, 136, 137, 138, 156, 163, 167, 168, 180
– New Zealand Masters Games 47
– New Zealand Rugby Football Union
    (NZRFU) 168
– New Zealand Tourism Board (NZTB) 111
Newcastle (Australia) 113
Newcastle United FC 84
Newmarket Horse Racing Museum 48
Newquay (England) 186
Niche markets 33, 34, 42, 48, 49, 50, 52, 72,
    90, 155, 160, 175, 178, 195, 196, 198, 207,
    214
Nigeria 7
Nike 66, 202
Nogano (Japan) 133
Nogawa, H. 16, 19, 42, 43, 51, 86, 101, 148,
    161
Non-elite events sport tourism 47, 128
Non-transportable sports 79, 84, 124
Nordic skiing 166, 168
Normandy (France) 75
North America 41, 48, 87, 88, 89, 95, 98, 126,
    152, 174, 195
Northern Russia 105

Norway 6, 7, 9, 21, 84, 91, 96, 124, 133, 134, 167
Norway Cup 6
Norwegian Football League 167
Nostalgia 113, 143, 145, 190, 191, 199, 207
Nostalgia sport tourism 10, 24, 39, 48, 49, 51,
    63, 69, 72, 86, 89, 102, 143, 145, 178, 184,
    189, 191, 195, 200, 211
Nuisance activities 21

Objective authenticity (*see* Authenticity)
Old Trafford (*see also* Manchester United
    FC) 86
Olds, K. 127
Olympic Games (*see also* Winter Olympic
    Games) 3, 22, 26, 33, 37, 38, 44, 45, 46, 49,
    52, 53, 54, 67, 68, 68, 85, 102, 103, 110,
    114, 124, 128, 129, 146, 154, 160, 187, 190,
    195, 209
– Olympic Charter 62
– Olympic cultural programme 103
– Olympic Environmental Charter 133
– Olympic rings 62
– Olympic teams 52
Ontario (Canada) 97, 166
Orams, M. 89, 136, 138
Orienteering 124, 132
Oriole Park 86, 149
Orlando (USA) 160
Oslo (Norway) 7, 49, 124
– Oslo Transportation System 7
Otago Highlanders (*see also* Rugby Super
    12) 181, 182, 183
Outdoor recreation 22
– Outdoor pursuits 16

Packer, Kerry 27
Page, S.J. 95, 109, 130, 142, 148
Pakistan 156
Pamplona (Spain) 129
Paraguay 153
Parapenting 124
Paris (France) 129, 153
Participants 5, 45, 101, 102, 155, 177, 198,
    209, 211, 214
– Participation 4, 42, 49, 50, 95, 130, 132, 134,
    147, 148, 151, 188, 192
Partnerships 60, 68, 69, 71, 208, 212, 212
Pearce, D.G. 57, 73, 79, 81, 95
Pearce, P. 143
Perdue, R. 46
Performance 64, 143, 148
Periodic marketing 85, 94
Periphery (*see also* Peripheral) 132
Peripheral 79, 80, 81, 130, 133, 135, 164, 180,
    192, 198, 209
– Peripheral locations 89, 90, 91, 92, 93, 94
Petronas Twin Towers (Kuala Lumpur) 115,
    116
Philadelphia (USA) 97

Philosophy 30, 55
Physical activity
– Physical prowess 16, 17, 26
Pigeassou, C. 74, 88
Pigram, J.J. 56, 57, 73
Pilgrimage 101, 145, 200
Pillsbury, R. 40, 88, 95
Pitts, B.G. 42, 51
Place (*see also* Placelessness) 4, 7, 8, 9, 11, 16,
      99, 100, 101, 102, 103, 104, 107, 110, 112,
      113, 114, 121, 134, 198, 199, 208, 209
– Place identity 104, 105, 106, 107, 108, 109,
      111
– Place marketing 103, 109
– Place promotion 8, 85, 123, 134
– Place wars 109, 114
Placelessness 102
Planning 7, 59, 60, 69, 72, 122, 123, 133, 135,
      141, 143, 148, 151, 159, 191, 208, 209, 213
Play 16, 17, 20, 79, 144, 207, 210
– Playful 26
– Playfulness 28
Plog, S. 184
Poland 92, 96
Policy 24, 29, 57, 68, 74, 98, 131, 212, 213
Policy development 212
Political 5, 56, 57, 64, 110, 115, 187, 189, 193,
      194, 199
Poon, A. 165
Porteous, B. 111
Prentice, R.C. 63
Preston 48
Priestley, G.K. 5, 93, 118, 119, 136, 143, 187
Prince Edward Island (Canada) 174, 175
Product diversification 173, 174, 175
Product mix 173
Professional 145, 151, 185, 196, 209
– Professional Golf Association Tour (PGA)
      85, 93
– Professionalisation 185, 193
– Professionalism 62
– Professional sport 17, 42, 82
Project Environmental Friendly Olympics
      (PEFO) 133
Psychographic profile 43
Psychology 30
Pulsate Wanaka Big Air 125
Pyo, S. 146

Quebec (Canada) 97, 110
Queenstown (New Zealand) 181

Racket ball 124
Rafting 38, 43, 89
Rawel, J. 176, 180
Recollection 10, 141, 157, 158
Recreation 20, 32, 37, 42, 43, 49, 69, 79, 122,
      127, 128, 132, 137, 151, 187, 188, 189, 214
– Recreational activities 23

– Recreational running 130
– Recreational sport 5, 6, 16, 17, 37, 47
Redmond, G. 4, 5, 23, 39, 48, 49, 95, 102, 190
Reeves, M.R. 34, 36, 142, 143, 151
Region 88, 106, 109, 125, 130, 143, 145, 148,
      156, 164, 165, 166, 178, 181, 188, 208, 209
– Regional analysis 88, 95
Re-imaging places 110
Relph, E. 100, 102, 113, 116, 119
Repeat visitation 10, 148, 149
Resort 81, 90, 97, 98, 113, 122, 131, 174, 175,
      186, 202
– Integrated golf resorts 93, 118, 145
– Ski resort 40, 90, 93, 96, 97, 108, 166, 174,
      211
Resources 34, 40, 71, 74, 80, 84, 89, 93, 95,
      118, 119, 126, 130, 134, 135, 138, 178, 185,
      209
– Resource analysis 122
Richards, G. 43, 44, 50
Rip Curl Newquay Boardmasters 186
Ritchie, I. 62
Ritchie, J.B.R. 22, 144
Robins, K. 114, 116
Robinson, H. 165
Robinson, T. 4, 19, 20, 25, 31, 32, 35, 37, 38,
      51, 92, 146, 158, 160
Rock climbing 64, 122, 124
Roche, M. 127
Roehl, W. 44
Roggenbuck, J.W. 143
Rooney, J.F. 24, 40, 80, 88, 89, 95
Rowe, D. 67, 104, 106, 113, 193
Royal and Ancient Golf Club (*see also* St.
      Andrews) 200
Royal Ascot 7
Royal New Zealand Yacht Squadron (*see
      also* America's Cup) 136
Rugby league 67, 113, 156
Rugby Super 12 (RS12) 168, 180, 181, 182
Rugby Union 7, 106, 112, 156, 163, 167, 174,
      180
– Rugby World Cup (RWC) 44, 103, 151,
      157, 168
Rules 7, 16, 20, 26, 27, 28, 50, 62, 80, 130, 144,
      185, 187, 188, 193, 196, 200, 207, 214
Running of the Bulls (*see also* Spain) 129
Russia (*see also* Northern Russia) 96
Ryan, C. 23, 157

Sacred 101, 108, 196
Safety (*see also* Security) 102, 129, 144
Saibei (China) 98
Sailing 41, 53, 89, 111, 124, 167, 172
Samual L. Jackson 202
San Diego (USA) 136
Sandler, M. 160, 162
Sapporo (Japan) 11
– Sapporo Dome 11

Saskatchewan (Canada) 84
Saskatchewan Roughriders 84
Satisfaction (*see* Visitor satisfaction)
Scandinavia (*see also* Norway, Sweden,
    Finland, Denmark) 98, 167
Schaffer, W. 87, 149
Schlossberg, H. 191
Schollmann, A. 113
Schreyer, R. 143
Scotland 65, 102, 184, 200, 201, 202, 203
Scott, D. 166
Scuba diving 44, 89, 118, 131, 143, 167
Season 7, 10, 41, 47, 85, 91, 152, 161, 163,
    164, 165, 166, 167, 170, 171, 173, 174, 175,
    176, 177, 178, 179, 180, 183, 210, 215
– Tourist shoulder season 10, 173, 178
Seasonality 4, 10, 11, 163, 164, 165, 166, 167,
    170, 171, 173, 174, 175, 176, 177, 178, 179,
    180, 183, 210
Security 46, 129, 148, 157
Self identity 64, 71
Senegal 112
Sennet, R. 116
Sense of place 100, 121
Seoul (Korea) 112, 128
Serbia 96
Serious leisure 156
Services 38, 87, 88, 122, 123, 135, 141, 143,
    148, 149, 154, 162, 168
Shapcott, M. 127
Shangri-La 63
Sharajah 65
Shaw, G. 130
Sherlock, K. 113
Shopping 123, 149, 150, 164
– Shopping centre 54
Show jumping 41
Shultis, J. 132
Silk, M. 64, 66, 104, 114, 117
Skateboarding 43, 64, 126, 197
Skidooing 21
Skiing (*see also* Downhill skiing, Cross
    country skiing, Water skiing, Jet skiing)
    9, 23, 26, 37, 38, 40, 41, 43, 44, 89, 91, 95,
    95, 97, 98, 108, 113, 119, 120, 122, 124,
    130, 133, 143, 169, 170, 172, 184, 187, 215
Ski industry 95
Skydome (Toronto) 197
Sledge jump 105
Slovakia 96
Slovenia 96
Smith, A. 195, 196
Snorkeling 40
Snowboarding 39, 42, 43, 95, 105, 108, 113,
    125, 131, 170, 175, 186, 187, 188, 211
– Acrobatic snowboarding 125
Snow making 91, 119, 125, 166, 175
Snowmobiling 166, 170
Snowshoeing 175, 195

– Snowshoe biathlon 105
Snyder, E. 189, 190
Soccer 41, 152, 155, 156, 174, 208
– Soccer World Cup 44, 67, 106, 112, 156
– Masters Soccer World Cup 47
Socio-demographic trends 195
Sonmez, S.F. 194
Sotdae (Korean bird image) 112
South Africa 7, 65, 103, 125, 168, 180, 181
South Pacific Ocean 93
South-east Asia 97
Space (*see also* Spatial) 3, 4, 8, 11, 12, 16, 20,
    56, 57, 64, 86, 99, 100, 113, 132, 183, 197,
    207, 208, 214
Spain 3, 38, 92, 96, 98, 118
Spatial (*see also* Space) 26, 41, 79, 80, 129,
    130, 134, 151, 154, 188, 212, 213
– Spatial analysis 80, 84, 92, 93, 95, 208
– Spatial demand curve 83, 84
– Spatial dimension 17
– Spatial patterns 10
– Spatial reorganisation 57
– Spatial travel patterns 93, 148
Special interest tourism 23, 175
Specialist 34
Spectacularisation of space 87
Spectator 20, 27, 38, 39, 44, 45, 64, 80, 82, 86,
    102, 105, 125, 126, 129, 134, 142, 149, 152,
    155, 156, 157, 178, 179, 181, 182, 188, 196,
    197, 198, 209, 210, 214
– Spectator catchment 82, 129
– Spectatorship 26, 50, 65, 83, 112, 125, 149,
    156, 195, 198
Sport (*see also* Sports)
– Sport centre 87, 88, 94, 148
– Sport camps 38
– Sport culture 60, 66, 67, 72
– Sport devotees 40
– Sport experiences 15, 82
– Sport fishing 44
– Sport halls of fame 38, 39, 48, 89, 123, 149,
    154, 162, 178, 184, 189, 190, 191, 199, 211
– Sport junkies 46, 127, 157, 214
– Sport locations 82, 83, 93, 94
– Sport management 11, 15
– Sport museums 38, 39, 189, 191
– Sport places 99, 102
– Sport sociology 11, 16, 30, 170, 212
– Sport tourism centre 88, 94, 154
– Sport tourist 19
– Sport vacations 39
Sport and culture 8, 103, 113
Sport as culture 8, 104, 113
Sport-for-all 16, 42
Sport orientated holidays (*see also* Less sport
    orientated holidays) 34, 92
Sportification of society 5
Sportlover 39
Sport subcultures 8, 42

Sport tourism markets 28, 38
Sports
– Sports bars 154
– Sports resort 88
– Sports marketing 11, 50, 82
– *Sports Travel* (newsletter) 24
– Sports venues 7
Sportscapes 67, 102, 119, 124, 130, 209
Sports geography 8, 12, 79, 80, 95, 119, 212
Springboks (*see also* Rugby Union) 125
Squash 37, 83, 124, 126
St. Andrews (Scotland) 7, 48, 102, 184, 200, 201, 202, 203
St. Andrews Links Trust 200
St. Moritz (Switzerland) 98
Stadia 39, 40, 53, 62, 66, 67, 87, 88, 89, 112, 118, 122, 123, 129, 199, 214
Stadium (*see also* Stadia) 11, 84, 86, 87, 102, 112, 124, 126, 130, 137, 149, 155, 162, 178, 182, 191
– Stadium Tours 38, 162, 178
Staged authenticity (*see* Authenticity)
Standeven, J. 4, 12, 19, 20, 24, 25, 38, 51, 88, 99, 100, 101, 118, 122, 123, 126, 130, 135, 142, 192, 200
Stanley, D. 164
Stansfield, C.J. 184
Stern, David 66
Stevens, T. 48, 83, 85, 86, 87, 89, 149, 154, 159, 178, 191
Stevenson, D. 104
Stewart, B. 46, 144, 146, 195, 196
Stewart, J.J. 61
Strategic alliances 60, 68, 208
Strategic plan 70
Student Festival of Sport 174
Subculture 43, 51, 147, 155, 175, 178, 187, 194
– Subcultural tribes 64, 194
– Subcultures 42, 102, 107, 108, 111, 113
Sugden, J. 67
SUKOM 114, 115, 116
Sumo Wrestling 7
Sunningdale (England) 152
Super League 167
Superbowl (*see also* American Football) 22, 44, 151
Superdome (New Orleans) 87
Surfing 16, 23, 40, 41, 107, 108, 118, 124, 127, 130, 132, 155, 170, 186
– Surfers 64, 132
Surf skiing 132
Sustainable 11, 28, 58, 60, 72, 119, 126, 128, 131
– Sustainability 7, 55, 58, 69, 159, 179, 211
– Sustainable development 57, 199, 208
– Sustainable sport tourism 59, 155, 199, 214
– Sustainable tourism 58, 128, 131
Suwon (Korea) 112

Swarbrooke, J. 39, 41, 42, 43, 44
Sweden 6, 96
Swimming 7, 41, 83, 124, 132, 132, 152, 160, 174
– Swimming pool 53, 123, 126
Switzerland 92, 96, 97, 98
Sydney (Australia) 45, 52, 103, 104, 110, 118, 129, 133, 134, 15
– Sydney 2000 Olympic Games 133, 134, 154
– Sydney Opera House 129
– Sydney Cultural Olympiad 103, 104

Tabata, R. 44
Tae Kwon Do 7
Tartan Army 65
Taylor, P. 160
Team New Zealand (*see also* America's Cup, Yachting) 136, 137
Technological trends 196, 199
Technology 66, 102, 109, 130, 132, 135, 166, 170, 171, 187, 193, 196, 197, 198
Teigland, J. 91, 154, 155
Television 27, 104, 110, 114, 119, 153, 157, 161, 181, 182, 187, 190, 193, 194, 196
– Television broadcasting 5
– Television broadcasts 26
Tennis 41, 85, 124, 126, 155, 160
Terrorism 194
– Thailand 7, 38
– Thai Boxing 7, 38
– Thakraw 7
Thamnopoulos, Y. 46
Theme park 54, 66, 122, 149, 197
Theory 4, 10, 15, 24, 81, 82, 90, 134, 155, 176, 180, 209, 211, 213, 214
Thompson, S. 147
Thomson, R.W. 41, 43, 186
Time/cost/distance 79, 86, 147, 148
Timothy, D. 63
Tokarski, W. 41, 42
Tomlinson, A. 67
Toronto (Canada) 197
Touch rugby 43
Tour de France 120, 129, 134
Tourism
– Tourism attraction hierarchy 28
– Tourism sport 19, 20, 37, 92
– Tourism systems 10, 147, 154, 159
– *Tourism Management* (Journal) 22, 162, 183
Tourist (*see also* Visitor)
– Tourist area lifecycle theory 10, 82, 185, 199, 200, 203
– Tourist attraction (*see also* Attractions) 3, 5, 15, 24, 26, 28, 29, 37
– Tourist attraction framework 15
– Tourist attraction system 25
– Tourist attraction theory 24
– Tourist authenticity (*see* Authenticity)
– Tourist Authorities of Göteborg 6

– Tourist experience 25, 28, 148
– Tourist precincts 87, 93, 148, 154, 159
Tower Bridge (London) 129
Traer, R. 69
Trail biking 21
Train 88
Training 45, 143, 168
– Fantasy camps 72, 162, 178, 184, 191, 199, 211
– Training camps 53
– Training venues 52
Transport 51, 81, 88, 93, 98, 122, 123, 135, 148, 149, 154, 158, 165, 209
– Transport networks 88
Transportability 95, 122, 125, 134, 135
Transportation 53, 91, 124, 148, 150, 162, 163, 166, 170, 197, 198, 210
Travel 80, 87, 89, 148
– Travel experience 20
– Travel flows 25, 80, 81, 94, 111, 208
– Travel motivations 37
– Travel nodes 83
Triathlon 126, 129, 131, 174
Trip purpose 164
Trollveggen (Norway) 21
Tuan, Y. 119
Tuppen, J. 68, 166, 174
Turco, D. 4, 12, 24, 192, 200
Turin (Italy) 98
Turkey 96
Twickenham 7
Tyrol (Italy) 98

Uncertain outcome 17, 64, 144, 149
United Kingdom (UK) (*see also* Great Britain) 7, 15, 20, 21, 31, 32, 48, 53, 93, 97, 98, 167, 173, 197
United States of America (USA) 7, 30, 41, 52, 67, 84, 93, 95, 96, 97, 108, 114, 121, 136, 138, 149, 156, 160, 161, 190, 200
University Athletic Association 160, 162
University of Florida Gators 160
University of Luton 15, 24, 30, 31, 32
– Department of Tourism and Leisure 30
Upper Franconia (Germany) 88
Urban 21, 33, 41, 84, 85, 87, 88, 109, 118, 125, 126, 127, 129, 136, 151, 160, 164, 182, 183, 192, 197, 209
– Urban geography 12
– Urban imagery 5
– Urban regeneration 87, 95
– Urban renewal 5
Urry, J. 60, 63

Vail (Colorado) 97
Van Wynsberghe, R. 62
Vander Velden, L. 54
Vedø, K. 21, 131
Velodrome 53

Virtual reality 197
Visitor 55
– Visitor behaviour 25, 43, 155, 156
– Visitor expectations 141, 143, 158
– Visitor expenditure patterns 148
– Visitor expenditures 10, 34, 48, 87, 148, 149, 150, 151, 155, 159, 162
– Visitor experience 10, 43, 44, 50, 86, 150, 152, 153, 154, 155, 158, 159, 162
– Visitor satisfaction 9, 10, 148, 157
Volvo Round the World Ocean Race 134
Voumard, S. 104
Vuokatti (Finland) 168
– Vuokatti Ski Tunnel 168

Wahab, S. 56, 57, 73
Wales (Principality of) 151, 157, 167, 168
Walking 37, 40, 41
Wall, G. 56, 57, 58, 73, 127, 131, 135
Wallabies (*see also* Rugby Union) 125
Wanaka (New Zealand) 125
– Wanaka Snowfest 125
Wang, N. 62, 64, 73
Water skiing 41
Watson, A.E. 143
Webb, S. 157
Weber, W. 33, 34, 35, 51, 88, 93, 95, 142, 143, 158
Wedemeyer, B. 194, 195
Weed, M. 4, 19, 20, 21, 24, 28, 29, 33, 49, 50, 51, 68, 69, 73, 94, 130, 155, 156, 157, 160
Weighill, A.J. 164, 172
Weiler, B. 175
Wembley Stadium 49
Wheaton, B. 42, 107, 113, 132
Wheeler, B. 128
Whistler (Canada) 97, 175
White water rafting 173
Whitson, D. 65, 114, 116, 117
Wilbert, C. 197
Wiley, C.E. 42
Williams, A. M. 130
Williams, D. 100
Willming, C. 162
Wimbledon 7, 37, 44, 49
– Wimbledon Lawn Tennis Championship 38
– Wimbledon Tennis Museum 48
Windsurfing 42, 107, 108, 113, 124, 131, 132
Winter Olympic Games 9, 68, 91, 133, 154, 187
Winter resorts 68
Winter sports 91, 125, 195
Winter X (extreme) Games 188
Women's British Open Golf Championship 152
Wootton, G. 154, 159, 160
World Badmonton Championship 151
World Commission on Environment and Development (WCED) 57

World Heli Challenge (*see also* Wanaka) 125
World Tourism Organization (WTO) 3, 5,
   17, 18, 34, 39, 40, 60, 92, 160, 172, 195

Yachting 132, 170
Yamaguchi, Y. 47
Yiannakis, A. 39, 41, 51

Yorkshire (England) 8
Young, K.M. 43, 107, 108, 156, 160
Yusof, A. 3

Zauhar, J. 5, 29
Zermatt (Switzerland) 97
Zimbabwe 65